Time Bites

By the same author

DORIS LESSING

Time Bites

Views and Reviews

Fourth Estate • *London* and *New York*

First published in Great Britain in 2004 by
Fourth Estate
A Division of HarperCollins*Publishers*
77–85 Fulham Palace Road
London W6 8JB
www.4thestate.com

A catalogue record for this book is available from the British Library

ISBN 0-00-717985-5

Typeset in Sabon by
Rowland Phototypesetting Ltd,
Bury St Edmunds, Suffolk

Printed in Great Britain by
Clays Ltd, St Ives plc

CONTENTS

CONTENTS

Jane Austen

If there is one generally popular novel in the English language, it is *Pride and Prejudice* and this was true before a recent successful television version. It has always been taken seriously by the eminent in society and in literature: Jane Austen was celebrated from her first book, *Sense and Sensibility*. It is a very English novel, and foreigners have been known to question our admiration. Class and money! – and where are the great themes of Life and Death? So come the criticisms, still, and the reply often is that class and money defined the lives of the novel's characters, not to mention the life of the woman who wrote it. So let us deal with these issues first, leaving aside for the moment the real themes of the book.

Jane Austen was a member of a network of middle-class families that merged upwards into the aristocracy, but her own family was poor. Her father, with six children – two girls and four boys – to feed and clothe and find careers for, had to take in pupils, so the home was for part of the year a school, noisy and full of rambunctious boys. Jane and her sister Cassandra felt themselves to be, and were often treated as, poor relations, dependent on presents, little trips and handouts from better-off and generous relatives. Not until – late – Jane earned some money writing, did she enjoy any kind of independence. Her situation was a common one then for poor unmarried women anywhere in Europe.

She has often been portrayed as a conventional spinster, partly because of Mary Mitford's unfriendly description of her as 'a poker' – upright and judging. She was malicious – this time the critic is Virginia Woolf quoting not very attractive *bon mots* at others' expense. She wrote her immortal novels in corners, always ready to set them aside to take part in tea and gossip. What do we have here? A woman of the kind I remember from when I was a girl, the unmarried maiden aunt, ready to be useful to others, without any life of her own, a pitiable figure. Austen was supposed, so we have often read, to be a sheltered woman, her experience limited to village life and a narrow middle-class circle.

Here is a quote from an article by a once influential critic, Demetrius Capetanakis, in the very influential periodical *New Writing and Daylight* for winter 1943–4 – that is, in the middle of the war. 'Round every page of Jane Austen's novels one feels the hedge of an eighteenth-century English home. It is the hedge of "sense", of logic, or rather the logic of a person leading a secure life in the midst of a secure society. Jane Austen was protected by a hedge of unquestionable values . . .' Nothing could be further from the truth. First of all, her situation among the genteel poor exposed her: there can be few worse positions in society, even if often useful for the creation of literature. She had a close woman friend in the fashionable world, a cousin, probably Warren Hastings' illegitimate child, married to a French count who lost his head to the guillotine. The whole course of the French Revolution and its aftermath must have seemed as close to her as news from her own family. Her four brothers were often off fighting in the Navy against Napoleon, in danger, and afflicting their family with anxiety. Above all,

Jane was enmeshed in the lives of female relatives and friends, who were always pregnant, nursing, giving birth to innumerable children who died then so easily and often. And, more potent as an influence than anything, Jane was sent as a tiny child to boarding school, and there was as miserable and neglected as Jane Eyre was at her school.

The triumph of Jane Austen's art was that the little piece of ivory she claimed as her artistic territory was carved out of such an abundance of experience and material. She excluded and refined. That means for people now who know even a little about that time, her stages seem confined brightly lit places where all around loom and mass shadows, dangers, tragedy. Nowhere in an Austen novel does an aristocrat lose his head, a woman die from milk fever or puerperal fever, or give birth to a mentally sick child, like her cousin Eliza. Pain and grief are cured by love, kindness and presumably kisses, though I cannot imagine more than a chaste kiss in an Austen novel: more and the delicate fabric, the tone, would be destroyed.

Jane Austen loved well and lost, young. He was Irish and he loved her too, and now it seems this marriage would have been made in heaven, but he was poor, had a mother and sisters to support, and so he must marry for money. This abnegation was understood by both sides. But she did love him, and he her, and the pain of it is, so it is generally thought, in *Persuasion*.

Later, when her single state was at its most circumscribing and difficult, she was asked in marriage by a neighbouring estate owner, who was rich, with a big house. The temptation was such that she accepted him, and the prospect of running an estate, being wife to a man of considerable standing, having children, leaving behind for ever her status as poor relation. But next day she changed her mind and refused him. This seems to me as sharp a glimpse into her mind as any we have. It is suggested that the memory of her love for Tom Lefroy made it impossible for her to marry anyone else. But it is useful to remember here that Cassandra reported Jane's moments of exultation at being free and unmarried. Free from what? Surely, childbearing. Again and again one reads how some cousin, or friend, has died in childbed with her eighth or ninth child, having been pregnant or breastfeeding for all those years. Matrimony at the level it was being observed by Jane and Cassandra cannot have appeared salubrious. Looking back now it is hard not to conclude that perhaps those despised spinsters had the best of it. Cassandra was always off attending sickbeds and deathbeds, and Jane did her share. Those two sisters' confidential talk in their shared bedroom – what we wouldn't give to have a recording of it. Perhaps there are hints in Elizabeth Bennet's bedtime chats with sister Jane.

In *Pride and Prejudice* is a painful moment which it is easy to overlook, as it is presented as comedy. Elizabeth has been invited to marry one of the unpleasantest men in literature, Mr Collins. Had she agreed, she would have ensured her family's safe future in a house which would belong to him on the death of her father. But she refused. Jesting about it with her friend and sister Jane she says there is no future for her unless another Mr Collins turns up, and proposes. The point is, there is a horrid truth there. The novel does not paint a picture where eligible and sensible (not the same thing) men abound. On the contrary, the young women are all on the lookout for a husband – no husband, no future – and the young men are spoiled for choice. Elizabeth earns the fury of her mother, who is all cunning and worldly wisdom, and the commendation of her father, a man of discrimination, who reminds his daughter, indicating his silly wife, what may happen if one marries indiscreetly. But the fact remains, one's blood does suffer a chill, even if a brief one, even now, looking back at the fate of women, their choices. Elizabeth turned down appalling

Mr Collins but could have remained insecure all her life. Incidentally it is interesting that teachers inviting students to read *Pride and Prejudice* report that many of today's young women have so little sense of history, or of the history of women, or of their own good fortune, that they say things like 'Why didn't Elizabeth and Jane get jobs? Why were they always going on about getting husbands?'

Elizabeth said No to Mr Collins and flouted the conventions of the time. A young woman must look out for a young man with prospects and marry him. Love shouldn't – and for centuries didn't – come into it.

To say 'I don't love him' was a recent right.

Which brings us to the core of this novel. A poor young woman, literary, of discrimination, proud of it, saying she will not marry except for love was a direct heiress of the Enlightenment and particularly of Jean Jacques Rousseau and most particularly of *La Nouvelle Héloïse*. This writer, this novel, had realigned women's expectations and their self-definition. It was not only in the field of romantic love and marriage that Rousseau had changed manners and morals, for aristocratic women were already in Austen's time breastfeeding their infants and aspired to educate their children rationally.

This novel, *Pride and Prejudice*, breaks new ground because of the new morality flourishing everywhere – for instance, in Fielding's *Tom Jones*. When Elizabeth refuses Darcy's first proposal, she tells him he is not gentlemanly. It could be argued that he was being honest when he frankly confessed the reasons why he had been reluctant to propose: surely the new morality must mean that he should be admired by Elizabeth, because he was being honest. Openness was a great good. To be open with your lover was to be in credit for the future.

Darcy was articulating the values of his class. Elizabeth was a misalliance, not because of her looks and education, both as good as his, but because of her vulgar relations – an uncle in trade, her unfortunate mother and sisters. Yet one has to notice that his aunt Lady Catherine de Bourgh has nothing to learn of vulgarity: she is a crude, stupid woman. And Darcy does not criticise the behaviour of his friend Bingley's sister, who is setting her cap at him, not at all better than that of Elizabeth's silly sisters. If this novel were published now, the reviewers would surely note these inconsistencies. Did they then? Were they in such awe of Darcy's wealth and position they did not criticise him? Perhaps to be wealthy and noble was enough: he was a gentleman.

But Elizabeth told him he was not being gentlemanly.

Elizabeth refuses Darcy out of a new morality, superior to his, and while obeying the stultifying eyes-lowered maidenly correctness demanded by the situation, she clearly does not feel inferior to him, even while he is telling her she is.

Elizabeth is using a definition of a gentleman that we have lost: it was once powerful and even now we hear echoes of an old excellence. The ideal came from chivalry. Honour was the key, and while Falstaff mocked, nevertheless he was a knight and honour defined his position socially if not on the battlefield. Honour: one kept one's word, was always honest, a man's word is his bond – now that's a laugh, these days. One succoured the weak and defended them against the wicked. Respect must be paid where it was earned. Respect was due to women that came from the Courts of Love and from the Troubadours. All these nuances were in Elizabeth's passionate and scornful refusal of Darcy – a middle-class girl, speaking to an aristocrat.

There was a novel I remember from when I was a girl, *John Halifax, Gentleman* by Mrs Craik; it was about a lower-class person earning the right to the appellation because of his honourable behaviour and his aspirations. It was a popular novel: once, the title gentleman was something to be aimed for.

Here we have this uppity young woman Elizabeth, first refusing to marry a disagreeable man, though she could secure her family's future by doing it, and then saying no to a very rich nobleman because of his arrogant behaviour. This was, indeed, a new thing in the novel. This was why *Pride and Prejudice* was so immediately popular: it defined, in the person of Elizabeth Bennet, how young women were thinking about themselves, as violent a change as happened later, in the twenties and then the sixties.

Certainly her mother and three of her sisters could not understand Elizabeth. Her mother, Mrs Bennet, a figure of fun throughout, is at the same time dangerous, because her silliness exposes her daughters to risk and obloquy. She belongs to a different world from Elizabeth, and Jane, and her own husband. This family is split. Elizabeth, Jane, Mr Bennet – a gentleman – judge people and situations from a fine and sensitive discrimination. Lydia, the youngest daughter, who elopes with an attractive young officer, talks only of having fun. So does her sister Kitty. They have their counterparts today: their descendants are in multitudes. A good time – that's the thing. Lydia and Kitty could not understand Elizabeth's and Jane's idea of a good time. But wait – here we have to remember that the severe Mary Mitford described Jane Austen as a 'silly husband-hunting butterfly'. So it took time to stiffen her into 'a perpendicular precise taciturn piece of single blessedness' and she wrote about the silliness of Lydia and Kitty from her own experience and memories. She had not always been the quiet observer. There is another sister, Mary, who aspires to be more than a husband-hunting butterfly, but she is a silly would-be bluestocking, quoting aphorisms like a Chinese cracker. Quite a gallery of women here: Elizabeth who knows how to love well and wisely; beautiful Jane, with none of Elizabeth's cleverness, but with a more patient and forgiving heart; Lydia who will grow up to be as tiresome as her mother; Kitty who longs for fun; Mary, a bookish fool. There is Darcy's sister, scarcely delineated, except perhaps to prove that the sisters of aristocrats may also run away with handsome officers, and Bingley's stupid sister, and Lady Catherine, the crass tyrant. Charlotte, Elizabeth's friend, marries Mr Collins because he is a good catch, and she hasn't the backbone to be a single woman.

And the men? Mr Bennet, from whom Elizabeth has got her sagacity and good sense, is a weak man, one of those whose ironical judgements on their own behaviour must compensate for their deficiencies. Bingley is rich, handsome and weak. The villain Wickham is unscrupulous and conceited. Elizabeth's uncle is a serious, intelligent man. The officers in the regiment in their scarlet coats are like a chorus to the action.

So, when you look at it, Elizabeth is the only female with anything like the moral size and weight to take on Darcy, and he is the only man equal to her.

And now here comes my personal caveat, but I am not the only one to think Darcy would not marry Elizabeth. Aristocrats do not marry poor middle-class girls much encumbered with disagreeable relatives. Yes, you believe it for the space and time of the tale, and that is all that is needed. Lords marry chorus girls and models, as we have seen so often in this country, enlivening the annals of the doings of high society. 'New Blood' they have been heard to cry, justifying misalliances. Some of these marriages have had a fairy-tale quality. Very beautiful girls, from nowhere, marrying lords in their castles? It all appeals to our nursery memories.

We may wonder – and I've read critics who do just that – whether *Pride and Prejudice* may fairly be classed among the novels now described as 'Chick-lit', girls hunting for husbands, a sophisticated and witty version. Barbara Cartland, the grande dame of the genre, when asked why her stories always had the same plot replied, 'There is only one plot. You need a girl who knows she is underestimated, in love with a difficult, problematical or wicked hero who recognises her worth. She will cure him, she is sure, but the story must end with the wedding, before she discovers that no, she will not change him.' That fits.

We may acknowledge that the marriage market in Austen's England, while far from what girls in Europe would recognise, is similar to what goes on now, for instance, in India, in many Islamic countries, and in parts of Africa.

We may entertain ourselves with imagining a meeting between Jane Austen and Jean Jacques Rousseau. Would he recognise that in this apparently prim maidenly lady were united the two strands of the Enlightenment, Romance and Reason? Would she see the debt her heroines owed to him even if they had never read a word of him or even heard of him?

One thing has changed utterly. Jane Austen's landscape is more alien than the mountains and deserts that television invites us to travel in. We move about, country to country, continent to continent, and think nothing of it. Then, to visit a family a few miles off was a big thing. I can understand this, because when I was a girl in Africa, the early rattling cars, the poor roads, some of them not more than wheelmarks through grass, meant that to go to supper with a neighbour was the same as us going to Paris or even New York. We used to be invited to 'spend the day' since the effort of travelling meant you had to make the most of it. You could go on a visit to another part of the country for days or weeks. 'You must come for a whole week, otherwise it won't be worth it.' Elizabeth Bennet stays six weeks when she visits her friend Charlotte after her marriage to Mr Collins.

If you didn't keep your own carriage and horses then well-off neighbours could be applied to. Or the horses might be in better employment than used for jaunting about. Mr Bennet is reluctant to take his horses away from farm work.

My mother would say, 'Can we send the wagon in to get the . . .' whatever it was, spare parts for the harrow, sacks of meal. 'No, we are ploughing the big field this afternoon.'

The five Bennet sisters walk into the little town to shop and sightsee, and to hope for a glimpse of the officers. In bad weather they do not walk on the muddy roads, they stay cooped up.

When Jane falls ill at Darcy's house, Elizabeth refuses to wait for the carriage and horses to become available, and she walks the three miles by herself, across country, getting her skirts muddy in the process. The females at Darcy's, jealous of her brilliant colour and her health, whisper and condemn, saying it is unladylike behaviour, walking by herself, without a chaperone. These are the genteel classes, not the robust, much freer farm women of Hardy's novels. This action of the spirited heroine must have surprised and impressed the readers then. Ladies simply did not go about alone. If a young woman visited somewhere far off, even a few miles, she had to wait to come home until a male relative or a trusted servant came to fetch her. The watchful care of young women, as much as the bad roads and the slowness of horse travel, slowed everybody's movements. Yet here was Elizabeth Bennet venturing independent and alone. Not all Austen heroines are robust: Fanny in *Mansfield Park* becomes faint after a few minutes' stroll, and you have to wonder about corsets. We know now that the fainting and vapours and the paraphernalia of women's ill health was due to tight-lacing. But the French Revolution (and Rousseau) had enabled women in England as well as in France to throw away corsets. For the time being, for they were soon to return, even worse. So if Fanny didn't faint and languish because of corsets, what was it? Was she anaemic?

There is a dark under-stratum in Austen's novels where the ill health, mostly of women, is hinted at. Not only childbirth killed women: people died then as they do not now. Jane's feverish cold that kept her at Darcy's might easily have become something worse, with no antibiotics to come to the rescue. In *Emma* the father, a skilled valetudinarian, is permitted his hypochondria as he wouldn't be now. Jane does laugh, a little, at the father, but the truth was they brought out the horse and carriage for a half mile's visit in the damp evening air.

Not easy for us now to imagine those lives where illness lurked so near, and most of it as mysterious to them as some new horror like Ebola is to us. Those brothers of Jane's, always off to foreign parts – malaria has to come to mind, and they had no idea what caused it, talked of miasmas and bad air. Perhaps if there is one thing that distinguishes our world from that one, it is how we live in a clear light of knowledge, information, while they were as much threatened by the unknown as savages.

When Jane's cousin Eliza's mother got a lump in her breast there was nothing to be done but take painkillers – not very effective – and pray. She could have had an operation – without anaesthetic.

What threats and dangers and illnesses did lie in wait for those women – and that is why Elizabeth Bennet's impulsive walk across country, jumping over stiles and over puddles, alone, must have been to the young female readers of *Pride and Prejudice* as good as a trumpet call.

I imagine fearful mammas and alarmed papas putting down the novel to lecture their daughters on the dangers of Elizabeth's behaviour.

For others, the lively but virtuous Elizabeth must have been a reassurance. The French Revolution had unleashed in England not only terrors of revolt and the guillotine, but of the unfettered females who yelled for more blood as the heads fell, who rampaged about streets in screaming mobs, giving the world a glimpse of just what manic rebellions were being kept in check by chaperones and corsets.

Elizabeth Bennet was both more alarming and reassuring than we can possibly imagine. Her bold and unladylike dash across country presaged young women climbing the Eiger, shooting rapids, sailing boats by themselves across the Atlantic. Her sense of humour and fastidiousness told novel readers that a young woman could claim freedoms unthought of by her mother and grandmothers, but remain in command of herself, and in balance.

This tale is set firmly in its place and time, detail by certain detail, fact by verifiable fact. The magic of Jane Austen's skill means that it is only at the end of the story you realise its kinship with 'girl gets her man', and begin to suspect that it is older even than that. The Cinderella tale is in every culture in the world. At least four hundred versions are known to exist, but however much it changes according to time and culture, there is a core. A heroine superior in insight and goodness is bullied by a sometimes cruel mother who prefers stupid and frivolous sisters. It is the poor girl who in the end charms the Prince's – or spirit's, or noble being's – heart, and she lives happy ever after while her ignoble relatives repine.

Here we have a superior girl, in Elizabeth Bennet, but she does have a good sister, so she is not alone. She has not two but three awful sisters who are the favourites of their mother. Her fairy godmother is her aunt, a kind and sensible woman. Elizabeth Bennet achieves her noble lover through force of her own character and against the will of the awful Lady Catherine de Bourgh, surely the wicked witch.

Pride and Prejudice is recognisably from the same level of human experience, a tale that merges back into the unconscious depths of humanity everywhere. Surely its ancient origins are why it enthrals generation after generation of readers?

D. H. Lawrence's 'The Fox'

Lawrence the man and D. H. Lawrence the writer: both provoked strong reactions in his lifetime, and it all still goes on.
He had the defects of his qualities; he had no defects, he was
a genius; he is at the heart of English literature; he is secure in
his place in world literature; he was a misogynist and a scumbag.
But pick up a Lawrence tale and the old magic begins working.
I read him as a young woman in the old Rhodesia, and not in
the proper order: in wartime one grabs what one can get. It
was *Aaron's Rod*, my first one: and nearly sixty years later in
my mind are scenes as bright as they were then. The sounds of
water as a man washes, listening while his wife bad-mouths him,
for he is leaving her for ever. Nascently fascist Italy, plagued by
gangs of unemployed youths; mountains streaked with snow
like tigers; the vividness of it all: I was seduced while resisting
the man's message, which seemed to be a recommendation to
find a strong personality to submit oneself to. And so with
Kangaroo and the Australian bush which I can see now as he
described it, dreamlike and spectral, different from the bush I
actually saw later. Quite forgotten is the nonsense about the
strong Leader and his followers, suspiciously like storm
troopers. All his books have it, he spellbinds, he knocks you

over the head with the power of his identification with what he sees. It is generally agreed, even by antagonists, that *Sons and Lovers* and *The Rainbow* remain unassailable, but that is about it. Then things go from bad to worse, they say, and as for the swooning Mexican rhapsodies – better forget them. No writer has been easier to parody. I myself have shrieked as loudly with laughter as anyone, even while mentally hearing Lawrence's '*Canaille, canaille*' and his intemperate ranting, for like many who have a talent for abusing others, he could not stand so much as a whisper of criticism. Amid all this noise it is often forgotten that he wrote fine poems, and that some of his short stories are as good as any in the language.

The story 'The Fox' is quintessential Lawrence, on the cusp, as it were, of the light and the dark. Its atmosphere is so strong one may easily forget how firmly it is set in its time and place. The war is just over, and the soldiers are coming home. It must be 1919 because the great flu epidemic has victims in the near village. We have had another postwar grimness since then: poor food, cold, bare sufficiency, endurance. This one preceded what some of us remember by 30 years. Food is short. So is fuel. The winter is coming. A little farm where two young women are trying for independence is shadowed by the war. They are failing, they don't know how to farm. Emotionally they aren't doing too well either: there is bleakness and fear for the future. Despondency finds an easy entry, and they have a visible enemy, a fox that steals their precious chickens. It is decided this thief must be shot, but he is too clever for them.

This animal obsesses March, the stronger of the two women. From the first, this beast is more than itself. 'For he had lifted his eyes upon her and his knowing look entered her brain. She did not so much think of him: she was possessed by him.' The biblical echoes here are part of the spell: the fox again and again 'came over her like a spell'.

14

Strongly set as this tale is in its social place, we have left realism behind. So it always is with Lawrence's animals. His feeling for them, or with them, is much more than anthropomorphism or the sentimentality these islands are sometimes accused of. The fox is representative of some force or power, alien, inhuman, other, part of an old world, inaccessible to humans. Except of course through intermediaries, like Lawrence, whom it is easy to see in a line of descent from the old shamans, whose knowledge of animals was a reaching out to other dimensions. This fox is demonic. 'She felt him invisibly master her spirit.'

We are not unfamiliar with special relationships in our mundane world, human with animal – cats, dogs, horses, birds, even pigs. They are so common we scarcely think about them. But it is odd how the animal world is tamed and domesticated in our homes and often in our hearts. We may imagine that useful space alien reporting that here is a world where humans are surrounded by animals, even submerged in them, often hard to distinguish one from the other. Some scientists say man's friendship with dogs goes back to the dawn of our history: they even suggest that those first human groups who domesticated wolves that later became dogs prospered, and dominated groups who did not, eventually conquering them. There, in the dawn of humankind, it is not only humans we see outlined against the flames of those cave fires, but the dogs. And surely, just outside the circle of firelight, the first foxes. Animals shade off into the wild and the wilderness, in tales and in legends, and the first men probably did not know where their thoughts ended and the consciousness of beasts began.

Reading Lawrence, such ideas have to present themselves. Who, what is this impudent fox?

Perhaps it is that – coming nearer by thousands of years – we modern people, who have killed the wild animals that lurked once at the edges of human life, miss them and want them back, and have replaced them with dogs and cats and innumerable tales about wild beasts. I once owned a cottage on the edge of Dartmoor, and the deed that gave me possession said I might keep four sheep on the moor in return for killing wolves and bears that threatened the safety of Queen Elizabeth. The First. Quite close, that was, only a little run of the centuries. So recently was the howling of wolves in people's ears at night; and travellers might have to run from a bear. In Africa now, where humans have not completely triumphed, you feel the presence of animals always, watching you as you move about, aware of you, wary of you. In the English countryside, Reynard, of all the wild animals, must know every movement we make. His eyes are on us, and now in our towns as well. The busy marauders visit our gardens. The fox of this tale knows the ways of the two young women.

Wolves and bears have gone, both of them animals powerful in magic and in folklore, and once their pelts and paws dangled from the shamans' shoulders and headgear, as did the fox's. Lawrence was brought up in a mining town but really he was a country boy: the fields and woods were all around him, and are in what he wrote. No writer has ever identified so strongly with the wild, and with beasts. The old shamans did, the storytellers. For them and for Lawrence an animal was never what it seemed. A white peacock is the spirit of a screeching woman. Who could forget St Mawr, the horse who comes out of some primeval world? Even the pheasants' chicks being raised in the dim and dusky wood are like emanations of the forces of fecundity. And here is the fox in this tale. Into the sylvan scene where two young women are struggling for economic survival, a young man comes, impudent, and daring, like the fox. In fact he is a soldier, from the fighting in Salonika. Soldiers come home from wars to the women who have been holding the fort. Nothing much is made of him, as a fighter, though he does remark that they had had enough of rifles. What we do feel, though, is his restlessness, his homelessness.

March sees him as the fox. She dreams of singing outside the house, which she cannot understand and made her want to weep. She knew it was the fox singing, but when she went to touch he bit her wrist, and whisked his brush across her face, and it seemed this fiery brush was on fire because it burnt her mouth. Any old magical man or woman would have recognised this dream's fear, and power, and warnings, and its deep attraction for the forbidden.

What is forbidden is man, is men, the masculine. The tale is full of the feminism of the time, strong in Lawrence's work, and what a simple and naive feminism it seems now, after getting on for nearly a century. The relationship between March and Banford excludes men. Whether or not this is a sexual relationship is not spelt out. Lawrence is hardly bashful about describing explicit sex and this is significant. Or perhaps, as writers often do, he avoids a direct statement so that readers will not focus on something irrelevant. What is important is the emotional relationship. And, too, we should not put our assumptions back into such a different time. They shared a bed, but women often did then. They were solicitous and careful of each other. Don't forget, it was wartime and men were in short supply. Many a female couple kissed and cuddled because of that great absence. And this kind of speculation is probably precisely what Lawrence wanted to avoid.

When the youth announces that March is to marry him, Banford says it isn't possible. 'She can never be such a fool.' She says March will 'lose her self-respect'. It is independence she is talking about. Sex, lovemaking, is 'tomfoolery'. Men's tomfoolery.

But March is drawn to the young soldier, and Banford, who

will be left out if March marries, weeps and complains, and the boy hears the weeping and the commotion and learns how much he is seen as an interloper, a thief. He goes off into the dark and shoots the fox.

March dreams again. Her Banford dies and there is nothing to bury her in but the fox's skin. She lays the dead girl's head on the brush of the fox, and the skin makes a fiery coverlet. Awake she stands by the dead fox that is hanging up waiting to be skinned, and she strokes and caresses the beautiful flowing tail. The soldier watches and waits.

So, one thieving fox is dead, but the human fox is alive and determined to have March. He began by coveting the little farm, but now it is the woman he wants. He is in a contest with Banford, and for a while this battle dominates the tale, and March, the contested one, is almost an onlooker. The young man detests Banford. This is a power struggle, naked and cold, like the one between the human world and the fox, ending in its death. There has to be a victim. Banford is a frail thing, dependent on March, and it is clear she will do badly without her.

The tale progresses through scenes where every detail has significance, reminding us of how much we miss in life, how much we don't see. March has been wearing farm clothes, breeches and boots, looking 'almost like some graceful loose-balanced young man'. Now she puts on a dress and for the first time the young man sees her as dangerously feminine, and beautiful. Bludgeoned and shouted at as we are by fashion, and often by nakedness, I cannot imagine a scene in a modern novel where the putting on of a dress, the revelation of the power of a woman's body, could have such an impact. And March, in a dress, is undermined and made defenceless.

Against all Banford's entreaties and guiles, he draws March out into the night 'to say what we have to say', and makes her put her hand on his heart. She feels the heavy, powerful stroke of the heart, 'terrible, like something beyond'. As for him, now he is seeing her in a dress, he is afraid to make love to her, for 'it is a kind of darkness he knew he would enter finally'.

Perhaps what annoys some feminists about Lawrence is that he insists lovemaking, sex, is serious, a life-and-death thing. Well, it used to be that children resulted from the terrible gamble of the genes, and often enough, death, and disease, as we now have Aids. And death ends the conflict in this tale: the rejected woman, Banford, is killed by a falling tree; the young man, the soldier, engineers this death.

And so now there is nothing to prevent the banns and the wedding bells and happiness, but this is Lawrence. March is not happy. We are at once in the old Lawrentian situation. The man wants the woman to be passive: like the seaweed she peers down on from a boat, she must be utterly sensitive and receptive. He wants her to submit to him, 'blindly passing away from her strenuous consciousness'. He wants to take away that consciousness so that she becomes, simply, his woman.

Well, yes, it is easy to laugh. But women do not seem to be particularly happy having their own way – as Lawrence and the Wife of Bath would put it.

And men are certainly not happy.

I wonder what his prescription would be now?

'The awful mistake of happiness,' mourns Lawrence, claiming that things go wrong, if you insist on talking about happiness.

But what do we care about his pronouncements on the sex war? What stays in my mind is the entranced woman, wandering about her little farm in the darkness watching for her enemy the fox, for the white tip on his fiery brush, the ruddy shadow of him in the deep grass, then the struggle to the death between the two women and the young soldier, in the long cold evenings of that winter after the war where they watch each other in the firelight. 'A subtle and profound battle of wills taking place in the invisible,' he says.

In his later life unpleasant tales were told about Lawrence in New Mexico; his treatment of animals could be cruel. Yet he often writes about them as if he was one. Probably he was punishing himself. He was very ill then. I have read theses and tracts, and analyses about Lawrence, which never mention the consumption that was eating him up. Young, it was surely this illness that gave him his supernormal sensitivity, his quickness, his fine instincts. He was fiery and flamy and lambent, he was flickering and white-hot and glowing – all words he liked to use. Consumption is a disease that oversensitises, unbalances, heightens sexuality, then makes impotent; it brings death and the fear of death close. 'The defects of his qualities', yes, but what qualities.

Carlyle's House:
Newly discovered pieces by Virginia Woolf

These pieces are like five-finger exercises for future excellence.
Not that they are negligible, being lively, and with the direct and
sometimes brutal observation, the discrimination, the fastidious
judgement one expects from her . . . but wait: that word *judgement*, it will not do. Virginia Woolf cared very much about
refinement of taste, her own and her subjects'. 'I imagine that
her taste and insight are not fine; when she described people
she ran into stock phrases and took rather a cheap view' ('Miss
Reeves'). This note is struck often throughout her work, and
because of her insistence one has to remember that this woman,
aged 28, took part in a silly jape, pretending to be one of the
Emperor of Ethiopia's party on a visit to a British battleship;
that she and her friends went in for the naughty words you
would expect from schoolchildren who have just discovered
smut; that she was sometimes anti-Semitic, capable of referring
to her admirable and loving husband as 'the Jew'. This was
rather more than the anti-Semitism of her time and class. The
sketch here, 'Jews and Divorce Courts', is an unpleasant piece
of writing. But then you have to remember a similarly noisy and
colourful Jewess in *Between the Acts*, described affectionately:

Woolf likes her. So, this writing here is often unregenerate Woolf, early work pieces, and some people might argue they would have been better left undiscovered. Not I: it is always instructive to see what early crudities a writer has refined into balance – into maturity.

None of that lot, the Bloomsbury artists, can be understood without remembering that they were the very heart and essence of Bohemia, whose attitudes have been so generally absorbed it is hard to see how sharply Bohemia stood out against its time. They are sensitive and art-loving, unlike their enemies and opposites, the crude business class. E. M. Forster, Virginia Woolf's good friend, wrote *Howards End*, where the battle between Art and the Wilcoxes is set out. On the one hand the upholders of civilisation, on the other, Philistines, 'the Wilcoxes'. To be sensitive and fine was to fight for the survival of real and good values, against mockery, misunderstanding and, often, real persecution. Many a genuine or aspiring Bohemian was cut off by outraged parents.

But it was not only 'the Wilcoxes', crass middle-class vulgarians, but the working people, who were enemies. The snobbery of Woolf and her friends now seems not merely laughable, but damaging, a narrowing ignorance. In Forster's *Howards End* two upper-class young women, seeing a working person suffer, remark that 'they don't feel it as we do'. As I used to hear white people, when they did notice the misery of the blacks, say, 'They aren't like us, they have thick skins.'

With Woolf we are up against a knot, a tangle, of unlikeable prejudices, some of her time, some personal, and this must lead us to look again at her literary criticism, which was often as fine as anything written before or since, and yet she was capable of thumping prejudice, like the fanatic who can see only his own truth. Delicacy and sensitivity in writing was everything and that meant Arnold Bennett and writers like him were not

merely old hat, the despised older generation, but deserved
obloquy and oblivion. Virginia Woolf was not one for half
measures. The idea that one may like Arnold Bennett *and*
Virginia Woolf, Woolf *and* James Joyce was not possible for
her. These polarisations, unfortunately endemic in the literary
world, always do damage: Woolf did damage. For decades the
arbitrary ukase dominated the higher reaches of literary
criticism. (Perhaps we should ask why literature is so easily
influenced by immoderate opinion?) A fine writer, Arnold
Bennett, had to be rejected, apologised for, and then – later –
passionately defended, in exactly her own way of doing
things: attack, or passionate defence. Bennett: good; Woolf:
bad. But I think the acid has leaked out and away from the
confrontation.

A recent film, *The Hours*, presents Woolf in a way surely her
contemporaries would have marvelled at? She is the very image
of a sensitive suffering lady novelist. Where is the malicious
spiteful witty woman she in fact was? And dirty-mouthed, too,
though with an upper-class accent. Posterity it seems has to
soften and make respectable, smooth and polish, unable to see
that the rough, the raw, the discordant, may be the source and
nurse of creativity. It was inevitable that Woolf would end up
as a genteel lady of letters, though I don't think any of us
could have believed she would be played by a young, beautiful,
fashionable girl who never smiles, whose permanent frown
shows how many deep and difficult thoughts she is having.
Good God, the woman enjoyed life when she wasn't ill; liked
parties, her friends, picnics, excursions, jaunts. How we do love
female victims, oh how we do love them.

What Virginia Woolf did for literature was to experiment all
her life, trying to make her novels nets to catch what she saw
as a subtler truth about life. Her 'styles' were attempts to use
her sensibility to make of living the 'luminous envelope' she

insists our consciousness is, not the linear plod which is how she saw writing like Bennett's.

Some people like one book, others another. There are those who admire *The Waves*, her most extreme experiment, which to me is a failure, but a brave one. *Night and Day* was her most conventional novel, recognisable by the common reader, but she attempted to widen and deepen the form. From her first novel, *The Voyage Out*, to the last, the unfinished *Between the Acts* – which has for me the stamp of truth: I remember whole passages, and incidents of a few words or lines seem to hold the essence of let's say, old age, or marriage, or how you experience a much-loved picture – her writing life was a progression of daring experiments. And if we do not always think well of her progeny – some attempts to emulate her have been unfortunate – then without her, without James Joyce (and they have more in common than either would have cared to acknowledge) our literature would have been poorer.

She is a writer some people love to hate. It is painful when someone whose judgement you respect comes out with a hymn of dislike, or even hate, for Virginia Woolf. I always want to argue with them: but how can you not see how wonderful she is . . . For me, her two great achievements are *Orlando*, which always makes me laugh, it is such a witty little book, perfect, a gem; and *To the Lighthouse*, which I think is one of the finest novels in English. Yet people of the tenderest discrimination cannot find a good word to say. I want to protest that surely it should not be 'the dreadful novels of Virginia Woolf', 'silly *Orlando*' but rather 'I don't like *Orlando*, I don't like *To the Lighthouse*, I don't like Virginia Woolf.' After all, when people of equal discrimination to oneself adore, or hate, the same book, the smallest act of modesty, the minimum act of respect for the great profession of literary critic should be 'I don't like Woolf, but that is just my bias.'

Another problem with her is that when it is not a question of one of her achieved works, she is often on an edge where the sort of questions that lurk in the unfinished shadier areas of life are unresolved. In this collection is a little sketch called 'A Modern Salon', about Lady Ottoline Morrell, who played such a role in the lives and work of many artists and writers of the time, from D. H. Lawrence to Bertrand Russell. We are glad to read what Woolf thinks, when so many others have had their say. Woolf describes her as a great lady who has become discontented with her own class and found what she wanted in artists, writers. 'They see her as a disembodied spirit escaping from her world into purer air.' And, 'She comes from a distance with strange colours on her.' That aristocrats had, and in some places still have, glamour, we have to acknowledge, and here Woolf is trying to analyse it and its effects on 'humbler creatures', but there is something uncomfortably sticky here; she labours on, sentence after sentence, until it seems she is trying to stick a pin through a butterfly's head. There were few aristocrats in the Bohemian world of that time: it is a pity Ottoline Morrell was such a bizarre representative. A pitiful woman, she seems now, so generous with money and hospitality to so many protégés, and betrayed and caricatured by many of them. They don't come out very well, the high-minded citizens of Bohemia, in their collision with money and aristocracy.

It is hard for a writer to be objective about another who has had such an influence – on me, on other women writers. Not her styles, her experiments, her sometimes intemperate pronouncements, but simply her existence, her bravery, her wit, her ability to look at the situation of women without bitterness. And yet she could hit back. There were not so many female writers then, when she began to write, or even when I did. A hint of hostilities confronted is in her sketch here of a visit to James Strachey and his Cambridge friends. 'I was conscious that not only my remarks but my presence was criticised. They wished for the truth, and doubted whether a woman could speak or be it.' And then the wasp's swift sting: 'I had to remember that one is not fully grown at 21.'

I think a good deal of her waspishness was simply that: women writers did not, and occasionally even now do not, have an easy time of it.

We all wish our idols and exemplars were perfect; a pity she was such a wasp, such a snob – and all the rest of it, but love has to be warts and all. At her best she was a very great artist, I think, and part of the reason was that she was suffused with the spirit of 'They wished for the truth' – like her friends, and, indeed, all of Bohemia.

On Tolstoy

Tolstoy was always in trouble with the censor and the Czar's police. He was expected by the common people and the liberal opposition to take a stand – and he did – on every kind of humanitarian issue, from famines mishandled by the government, to persecutions by an arbitrary and often cruel regime. He was known as much as a social critic and moralist as an author. 'There are two czars in Russia,' pronounced one liberal spokesman, 'and the other is Tolstoy.' He was described as the conscience of the world. *The Kreutzer Sonata*, published in 1889 when Tolstoy was 61, caused instant scandal. The censor was going to ban it but a compromise was reached by allowing an edition too expensive for ordinary people. Not that banning Tolstoy did much good: his works were copied out by disciples and distributed in hundreds of copies. Samizdat was not invented by the Soviets. (Samizdat was the illegal distribution of works banned by the Communist Party.) Because of Tolstoy's moral authority it was not possible to ignore it or pretend that these unappetising views were of no importance. In the United States the US Postal Service banned the mailing of newspapers serialising *The Kreutzer Sonata*. Theodore Roosevelt said that Tolstoy was a sexual moral pervert. The nascent women's movements were furious: this was the time of the New Woman. Chekhov, who revered Tolstoy, defended the book because of its aesthetic virtues and because, he said, the whole subject needed discussion. The emotional reactions to the novel have always been inordinate, but something written at white heat must provoke incandescent reactions. Reading it now I think people will feel first of all, curiosity – what was all that fuss about? – and then almost certainly, disquiet, dismay, and incredulity that anything so wrongheaded could be written by a favourite author: *War and Peace*, *Anna Karenina*, *Resurrection*.

Reading it now something has to strike you. The tale originated in a true story, which was in all the newspapers, and used by Tolstoy for polemic purposes. A husband did kill his wife from jealousy, but the tale as told by Tolstoy makes you ask, 'Wait a minute, but what, in fact, did this erring wife do?' Nothing much, even according to the stricter modes and morals of that time. A furore of suspicion and rage is built on atmosphere, glances, possibilities by a husband's jealous imagination. We may imagine her defending herself. 'But, Your Honour, nothing happened! I have the misfortune to be married to a jealous maniac who has made my life a misery. He himself introduced this man who is supposed to be my lover into our house and encouraged his visits to play music – we are both keen amateur musicians. The evening my husband returned unexpectedly and found me having supper with this supposed lover I had thought that for once I could invite him around without being made to feel a criminal. Sir, nothing could have been more innocent. How could I possibly have done anything wrong? The servants were up, serving supper, and the children were awake and watching everything, the way children do. Nothing happened. Nothing could have happened.' She never did get the chance to defend herself because her husband killed her dead, in a jealous fury.

The novel could be read as a brilliant account of unjustified male jealousy. There could not be a better description of a man working himself up into jealous madness. It could be analysed, and almost certainly has been, by psychiatrists presenting it as a case history of latent homosexuality, textbook stuff, really.

It is useful to contrast the fevered voice of Tolstoy in *The Kreutzer Sonata* with *Anna Karenina*, a panoramic account of sexual and marital relations. In it, a newly married couple, Kitty and Levin, are just settling into their life together in the country. Levin is modelled on the young Tolstoy. He is described as eccentric in his social views, awkward in company and immoderately in love with his wife. It is summer, the house is full of visitors, and one of them is a young man from the fashionable life that Levin (and Tolstoy) despises. He is a comic character, stout, wearing a ridiculous Scottish bonnet and streamers, is greedy, and he has a crush on Kitty. Flirting with her is normal behaviour for the Moscow and St Petersburg salons, but Levin suffers and throws him out of the house. His worldly male relatives mock him and call him 'a turk'. Wonderfully observed are the absurd quarrels of the young couple, instigated always by the husband, who is ashamed of himself and cannot stop watching his imagined rival and putting the worst possible interpretation on everything he sees. Levin is seen as an oddball by family and neighbours – all those ridiculous ideas about the peasants and agriculture – and as foolishly jealous, but held in the sweep and power of that novel, when Levin throws the society peacock out of the house Tolstoy's affectionate portrait tells us that he thinks Levin is no more than rather touchingly absurd. But the same author wrote *The Kreutzer Sonata*. The same author wrote *War and Peace*, whose great quality is balance, the command of a panoramic sweep of events and people. That dispassionate eagle eye is nowhere here. What we have in *The Kreutzer Sonata* is the power and the energy, but not the sanity of judgement. His position could not be more extreme, and in case anyone might imagine that he regretted *The Kreutzer Sonata* he wrote an apologia, *Sequel to The Kreutzer Sonata*, some time later, where he reiterated it all, like hammering nails into a coffin, burying any possibility of joy, enjoyment, even the mildest fun in sex, love, lovemaking. Yet the author of the two great novels describes all kinds of passion, enjoyment, the emotions that we sinful lesser mortals might associate with sex.

In the grip of his fanaticism, Tolstoy advocated chastity for the entire human race, and when it was objected that this would end the human race, his reply was the equivalent of 'And so what!' Or, rather *tant pis*, as this member of a francophile caste would have put it.

But he could not have believed in the possibility of chastity, for his own life taught him otherwise. His struggles with his sexuality are documented, and by himself, sometimes confusingly, not because he tried to conceal them, but because his behaviour and his principles did not match.

Before marriage he was corrupt and debased – so he said. He slept around with peasant women and there was at least one illegitimate child. There were always the gypsies, too, rather, THE GYPSIES! always charming young men from the paths of virtue, and Tolstoy went off to the gypsies, like so many of the characters from the novels of that time. After marriage no gypsies, and he tried hard to be a faithful husband. He was strongly sexed, going at it well into his seventies.

Late in his life Tolstoy became what we would call a born-again Christian. He had a religious experience which changed him. A type of religious conversion is described in *Anna Karenina*. Levin is in despair because he has no faith. Hard for us now to understand this, unless it is transposed into political terms, but people in the nineteenth century went through torments over losing faith, lacking faith, longing for faith. I myself met, when a girl, survivors of that struggle, much battered by the experience. Now, looking back, we may hear, louder than any other voice, Matthew Arnold's 'melancholy, long with-drawing roar' – the loss of faith in God.

Levin was suicidal. In a beautifully moving chapter Tolstoy describes him at last achieving faith: now we would say that the psychological conflict and tension was so great it would have to be resolved one way or the other.

Christianity's great contribution to human happiness has been a hatred of the body, and of the flesh; distrust of women, dislike of sex. In this it is unlike the two other Middle Eastern religions. Judaism, far from denouncing sex, prescribes love-making for the faithful on their Sabbath, thus sanctifying and celebrating sex. Islam is not a puritan religion. Not in Judaism and Islam do we find celibate priests who use nuns or their housekeepers as their mistresses, or are driven to sex with little boys. But Christianity might have been tailored to fit Tolstoy's needs and nature.

He became what he always had the potential for – a fanatic. There are descriptions of him, after his conversion, his fevered fervid face, his bullying manner, telling people of their duty to become like him, because being a fanatic, there was only one truth, his. There is such a thing as the logic of the fanatic, who begins with a proposition or a set of them, and from there develop inexorably all the rest.

It was wrong, it was wicked, to have sex with a pregnant woman or a lactating one. His wife Sonya protested at his inconsistencies, but Tolstoy was never afraid of contradicting himself. Thus he is driven – by logic – at least for the period of the argument, to support polygamy, for the sensible Tolstoy knows that celibacy is impossible. He is rather like those poli-ticians, their fiery years forgotten, who tell teenagers that it is easy to 'just to say No'. Say No – that's all there is to it!

Anyone with an ounce of common sense, or even with a working memory of their young selves, must know it is absurd: but we are in the grip of fanatic logic.

My favourite is the Inquisition which, having burned a heretic alive, used to send their police around to collect from the relatives money to pay for the wood used for the bonfire. Who else? The relatives might not have wanted their loved one incinerated, but obviously it was they who were responsible for the monster and therefore they must pay. It makes an entertaining, if painful, pastime, watching the logic-chopping of extremists, unfortunately so numerous in our sad times, and Tolstoy's recommendation for celibacy for the entire human race is an excellent example.

What women might think about these prohibitions (and his wife had many loudly-voiced ideas of her own) did not interest Tolstoy. He insists that women are 'pure'. Even 'as pure as doves'. The sane Tolstoy knows this is rubbish, but he has to insist that women all hate sex, which is vile, shameful and even unnatural – these are only some of his epithets. A pure maiden will always hate sex.

Chekhov, who stood by him in the fuss over the book, told him that he talked nonsense about female sexuality. At some point one does have to ask if perhaps the trouble was really a simple one: Tolstoy was no good in bed. There must be some explanation for his insistence that women dislike sex. His Sonya did not like it but saw sex as a way of keeping him at heel. When he did ask to sleep alone, she refused. She welcomed sex with him because he became friendly, simple, affectionate: if his disciples knew, she mocked, the reason for his saintliness, that his good moods were the result of sex with his wife, then they too would mock this apostle for total celibacy.

If Tolstoy was bad at sex, there is a parallel, D. H. Lawrence, who clearly knew little about sex: at least, the author of his earlier books did not. Yet he also wrote wonderfully about love, sexual power struggles, the higher and lower reaches of passion. Very odd, that. Later, the earthy Frieda would have taught him better, but poor Sonya Tolstoy slept with only one man in her life, whose embraces were described as bear-like.

When he is writing his great novels there is no suggestion that his characters hate sex, but as a polemicist he says that women hate sex and after sex are cold and hostile, and that this hostility is the real relationship between men and women, concealed by the recurring cycles of sexual attraction and indifference.

When Tolstoy was very old, sex ceased, and Sonya Tolstoy complained that what she had always feared had happened: without the sexual bond all ties were cut between them. Yet, very old, they were writing loving notes saying they could not live without each other.

This cycle of sex and quarrelling has always fascinated me. Anybody who has enjoyed passionate sex will recall as passionate quarrels, but surely it is not surprising, when sex is such a promoter of strong emotions of all kinds that antagonism should sometimes be one of them. It is not unknown, either, for people to report enjoying the crazy quarrels that may spice and heighten sex. *Enjoy* – out with the word. Woman is an unwilling victim and man the guilt-ridden and driven aggressor.

Thirteen children did his countess and Tolstoy get between them. Sonya Tolstoy had eight children in eight years. Yes, there were nannies and nursemaids, but the implications of the simple physical fact are surely enough to explain a lot of that rioting emotion.

They lost three children, in three years, to illnesses that these days would not amount to more than a few days' indisposition. Of the thirteen children they lost four. Sonya Tolstoy must always have been pregnant, nursing, and a good part of the time in mourning. Tolstoy was as affected by these deaths as his wife. After a particularly poignant death of a much loved child – the thirteenth, he said: 'Yes, he was a delightful wonderful little boy. But what does it mean to say he is dead? There is no death; he is not dead because we love him, because he is giving us life.' This apparently monstrous egotism was not what it looks like, for we have an account of Tolstoy, crazed with grief, running across the fields to escape from his emotion, repeating 'in a jerky savage voice' 'There is no death! There is no death!'

The Kreutzer Sonata was written after hearing the music played, which affected him strongly: he was white and suffering, and arranged to have it played again. As a result of the first hearing he made love to Sonya – if that is the word for it – and as a result of that she got pregnant with the little boy Ivan, who died seven years later and caused Tolstoy to insist: There is no death.

By this time he was claiming that there was no justification for art that is not polemical. In 1865 he wrote 'The aims of art are incommensurable with the aims of socialism. An artist's mission must not be to produce an irrefutable solution to a problem, but to compel us to love life in all its countless and inexhaustible manifestations.' By the time he was writing socialist and religious tracts art nevertheless sometimes triumphed over polemics, in *Resurrection*, for instance, in *The Death of Ivan Ilyich*.

Not very long after this tract against sex, *The Kreutzer Sonata*, which no one could say is not a compelling read, came Bohemianism, to be intensified by the First World War and its social aftermath, Free Love and 'Live, Drink and Be Merry for Tomorrow We Die'. As early as 1907 there was a scene like a rude riposte to Tolstoy and his *Kreutzer Sonata*. Ida John dying in Paris of her fifth, of puerperal fever, lifting her glass in a toast of champagne 'to Love' with her rapscallion of a husband, Augustus John, then at the height of his fame. In the next room his mistress is looking after the children.

The Bohemians, who repudiated all conventional sexual morality as thoroughly as did Tolstoy, though from the opposite viewpoint, were then a minority which set out to shock. Epatering the bourgeoisie was their *raison d'être*. And then, not so long after that, came the Second World War, and wartime morality, and then what a witty friend used to call 'The horizontal handshake', and now young women depart from all over Europe in droves for holiday shores where they screw, presumably enjoyably, with males who wait for them like Inuits for migrating caribou.

Hedonism rules, okay?

What has happened? Birth control has.

In *Anna Karenina* Dolly, overburdened with children, visits bad Anna the outcast from society who confides that she knows how to prevent conception. She is kind enough not to point out that she is still young and pretty while Dolly is worn out with childbearing. Shock and horror is what Dolly feels. She is repulsed. And that is what Tolstoy feels about birth control. It is unnatural, says he, and women make monsters of themselves, destroying in themselves their capacity of being women, that is, mothers, so that 'men may make no interruption of their enjoyment'. Note that it is the men who are doing the enjoying.

Anna Karenina, is always talked of as the story of Anna, a society beauty, and her seducer Vronsky, a variation of the great nineteenth-century theme of adultery. Its fame as the greatest of the adultery novels (some claim that for *Madame Bovary*) tends to obscure the scope of the novel: Tolstoy portrayed a gallery of women of that time. Dolly is the unhappy wife of a bad husband. Kitty is the happy wife of a jealous and loving husband. There are court ladies, whom Tolstoy detests, and peasant women, whom he admires. One is Levin's housekeeper, more of a friend than a servant, and another the peasant woman who came to rescue Dolly from her domestic disorders. A young peasant woman shocked Dolly by saying that 'The Lord has relieved me of a burden', talking of the death of a child – one mouth less to feed. A spinster fails to get a husband and is doomed to a life of being a guest in other people's houses. A bad woman – Anna Karenina's mirror – is a prostitute and can have no future. This is a novel about the situation of women in that time. Anna now would not have to throw herself under a train. Dolly would not have so many children. Kitty perhaps would not be so content as the wife of an unreasonably jealous man. The spinster would have a career, might be a single mother. Nowhere in *Anna Karenina* does that great artist describe a wife or mistress disgusted with sex and full of implacable hatred for men's sexuality. Anna hates Vronsky at the end because he is free and she is not, but she does not hate him sexually.

There is just a hint of the conflict between the moralist and the artist in this novel, which begins with the inscription, like a curse, '"Vengeance is mine, I will repay" saith the Lord.' But there is no vengeance, the novel is irradiated by Tolstoy's love and understanding of everything.

Understanding of everything and everybody but not of himself. He said to Gorki, 'Man can endure earthquake, epidemics, dreadful diseases, every form of spiritual torment, but the most dreadful tragedy that can befall him and will remain, is the tragedy of the bedroom.'

We have the diaries of two people with a gift for complaint, invective, and a relish for recording the minutiae of the ups and downs of their love. For it was that. In between the storms were days of tranquillity. We have all the facts, or think we have, but few of us now have the experiences that could tell us what life in that family was like.

Yasnaya Polyana – which can translate as Aspen Glades, or

Bright Glades – the Tolstoys' country house, is now a shrine, and visited by thousands every year. It was the estate's manor house, a large villa, with many rooms that turned out not to be enough to accommodate all those children, and so a wing was built on. There were all kinds of sheds, outhouses and annexes. Now it has to impress us by its potentialities for discomfort, because of the numbers of people it had to house. Large, high-ceilinged rooms, which must have been hell to heat. In summer, set as it is in fields and woods, what a paradise – but there is a long Russian winter. The furniture is adequate. The sofa where Tolstoy was born and where the countess laboured thirteen times is hard, slippery, ungiving.

Fresh water did not come gushing from taps: it was brought in by the bucket and there was a bathhouse. No electric light. There is a scene of Tolstoy, an old man, writing in his study with the aid of a single candle.

The house held the parents, thirteen children, servants, nursemaids, tutors – one lived there with his wife and two children – governesses, relatives and many visitors. There were also the disciples, who expected to be fed and, often, housed, sometimes for weeks. They would fit themselves into the servants' rooms in the attic – what happened to them? – or doss down in the corridors. It was usual to have 30 people sit down for a meal. Comfort of the sort we take for granted there was none. Privacy, which we have learned to need, was not easily got. Tolstoy had his study but it was permeable by anyone who decided they had the right – Sonya, and his chief disciple, the appalling Chertkov, and people demanding spiritual counselling. Once out of his study, then he was part of everything. The quarrels of adults, the squabbles of children, the crying of babies, the arguments of the disciples must have reverberated in those wooden walls. The countess understandably complained of 'nerves' and surely Tolstoy was entitled to them too.

Thirteen children. Thirteen. *Thirteen*. Four, dead. We are not talking about a peasant woman, a farm woman, with expectations for a hard life, but an educated sensitive woman who could never have dreamed of the kind of life she in fact had to lead.

There is a tirade in *The Kreutzer Sonata* about the unhappiness that children bring, mostly the misery of the fear of them dying: the slightest indisposition could become a serious illness. In both *Anna Karenina* and *War and Peace* the difficulties of childbearing and childrearing are depicted. Tolstoy was not a father removed from the burdens of the family. How could he have been, in that house? He knew all about pregnancy and morning sickness, and milk fever and cracked nipples. He knew about the discomforts of breast-feeding and sleepless nights. His great novels accepted life's ills, as they accepted its delights, everything is in balance, in proportion; but somewhere, at some point, it became impossible for him to stand his life. A skin had been ripped off him: it must have happened. It is often enough suggested that Sonya Tolstoy was a bit demented; though we must remember that she copied out *War and Peace* and all the other novels, many times, while she was carrying and giving birth and nursing and serving her Leo who, she complained, insisted on his marital rights before she was even healed after childbirth. Surely Leo Tolstoy became a bit demented too, quite apart from the old man's infatuation with his disciple Chertkov, who was like a horrible caricature of himself.

Those of us who have known people with clinical depression, or suffering the dark night of the soul, have heard descriptions of spiritual landscapes so dreadful that attempts at consolation ring as false as badly tuned pianos. And so they are received by the sufferers who look at you with a contempt for your superficiality. 'What I am feeling now, that's the truth' they may actually spell out to the stupid one. 'When you are depressed you see the truth, the rest is illusion.' So one feels reading *The Kreutzer Sonata*. Here is a landscape of despair – no exit! Remember the cage he had made for himself, this highly sexed man. Sex – bad. Sex with a pregnant or nursing woman – bad. No sex outside marriage. A recipe for guilt and self-hatred. The wasteland he describes that lacks any joy, pleasure – one hardly dare use the word love – is the truth. So be it.

Let us imagine ourselves back in that house. It is night, supper over, the visitors and disciples in their nooks and corners. The older children are still up, studying or playing, and their voices are loud and so are their feet on the wooden floors. The little ones are in their rooms with their nurses and are as noisy as small children are.

Tolstoy wants to be a husband tonight – so he puts it. God is not coming to his aid in his battles with lust.

Sonya's newest baby is six months old. She is afraid that she is pregnant again. She has to be in a state of conflict as her Leo approaches, smiling and affectionate: carefree sex has not yet been invented in the world's laboratories. She has never known it, never, in her long married life. If she is not pregnant already then she may become so tonight. The count and countess, Leo and Sonya, make sure the doors are shut, and hope the children won't come up wanting something. The new baby is in the next room with his nurse. He is hungry and can be heard grizzling. Leo must be careful not to touch Sonya's breasts, which are swollen with milk. She tried hard at first to refuse breast-feeding, and use wet nurses, because her nipples always crack, and nursing is a torture, but Leo insisted on her breast-feeding. And he must remember that her cracked nipples sometimes bleed, if he is impatient or clumsy. The baby is really going at it now: his hungry howls will bring the nursemaid in with him if she and Leo can't get a move on. The nursemaid, a girl from the village, is singing a peasant lullaby, and the sound and the rhythms become part of Leo's thrusting, which in any case has extra vigour because he rather fancies the girl. Oh God, thinks Sonya, please don't let me get pregnant. Oh I do hope I'm not pregnant, my poor nipples will never get a chance to heal. In spite of her care, trying to shield her breasts with her hands, milk suddenly spurts all over the bed, herself, his hands. She is weeping with self-disgust and discomfort, but quite pleased she has this excuse to make Leo feel the greedy beast he is. The sheets will need washing: they were put on clean that morning. The girl who does the washing will complain again: too much washing with all these people as well as the children and it is so hard to get things dry, when the weather is bad, as it is now. Sonya's weeping infuriates Leo, and he is full of guilt and self-dislike. She is thinking that all this milk is being wasted, though she is trying to stop it flowing, while the baby's yells from next door are making it flow. The baby, who is now screaming, is a big feeder and not easily satisfied. 'I'll have to heat up a little milk for him,' she is thinking. 'I hope the children didn't finish it all at supper. They never bring up enough milk for the house, how am I to manage with all these people?' She tells Leo to get right out of bed and leave her in peace to clean up. Yes, he can come back later, if he likes, when she's fed the baby. He says he'll sleep in his study tonight. Yes, she thinks, you've got what you wanted and now you can forget me. She feels abandoned and punished.

He goes off, praying that God will answer his prayers and damp down his lusts.

This scene, or something like it, must have happened a hundred times.

No wonder prostitutes were popular, to take the strain off such marriage beds: so Leo himself once said, but now he has changed his mind and says that prostitution is wicked. Why should poor innocent women be degraded by the filthy lusts of men?

To read this book now is like listening to a scream of anguish from a hell women have escaped from, and men too. But, wait a minute: it is in what we call the West that people have escaped, or most of us. When we read that a woman in Africa, or India, or anywhere in the poor countries of the world has had eight children, and three died, then the world of Yasnaya Polyana and *The Kreutzer Sonata* is not so far away.

The Man Who Loved Children

Every family lives in an evolving story, told by all its members, inside a landscape of portentous events and characters. Their view of themselves is not shared by people looking from outside in – visitors, and particularly not relatives – for they have to see something pretty humdrum, even if, as in this case, the fecklessness they complain of is extreme. Our storyteller, Christina Stead, opens *The Man Who Loved Children*, this magnificent novel of family life, by taking us at once into the Pollit family and a child's-eye view of it, forcing us to postpone questions like, 'But are these people really so unusual?' and 'Why are their fates and destinies so important to me?' Which is rather how we feel living for a while among Eugene O'Neill's characters. Mother has just returned from one of her mysterious outings into the world, and the children, who have been hanging about waiting for her, pour into the house at her skirts, full of a gabbling curiosity about her person, her adventures, what she has bought, all portrayed with such a power of physical truth that you are forced to remember and to say, yes, that is what it was like, being small: your parents were like Fates, arbiters of all life and not only yours, and you watched them like spies and waited for revelations – a look that told of hidden-from-you happenings, a hand fidgeting like an unwilling prisoner on a chair arm or held around a teacup for the comfort of its warmth.

Henny, the mother, sits leaning her face on her head and stares into the distance, 'a commonplace habit which looked very theatrical in Henny, because of her large, bright eyeballs and thin, high-curved black eyebrows. She was like a tall crane in the reaches of the river, standing with one leg crooked and listening. She would look fixedly at her vision and suddenly close her eyes.' Henny gets up, scatters her children off her skirts – 'Oh, leave me alone; you're worse than your father' – and retreats upstairs to one of her headaches or, worse, a mood like a thunderstorm filling the house with angry electricity and danger.

'I should have been better off if I'd never laid eyes on any of them,' Henny grumbles, excluding them from her room where she dwells among cupboards full of treasures from her young-lady past, or letting them in to play with fans and scarves and dresses, and to ask her fascinated and thwarted questions; for unlike their father, she is full of secrets and dark places, and she dwells inside the musky smell of her room, 'a combination of dust, powder, scent, body odours that stirred the children's blood, deep, deep'. Or they watch her lay out the cards for her endless game of solitaire, muttering, 'A dirty cracked plate: that's just what I am!'

'I wish your mother would stop playing patience, that makes her look like an old witch or an old vixen possum,' father Sam says in a gently benevolent voice. For his benevolence is, on principle, all-encompassing. 'Mother Earth,' he whispers, 'I love you, I love men and women, I love little children and all innocent things, I love, I feel I am love itself – how could I pick out a woman who would hate me so much!' As indeed she does, blaming him for everything.

They are enemies to each other, like hostile animals, gene

enemies. The house seems like an abode of animals. Henny describes her husband's family as chickens with their heads cut off. Her children know her chameleon eye, 'the huge eyeball in its glove of flesh, deep-sunk in the wrinkled skullhole, the dark circle round it and the eyebrow far above'. When Henny mutters in her frustrated rage it is like 'the trusty stirring of some weed-grown sea animal, bottom-prisoned by blindness'. All men are dogs, she remarks, stating an obvious – to her – truth, and to her lover – if he deserves that word – she says, 'Oh! What a life! What a man! Oh, you make me sick! Bert, you're big as an elephant with the soul of a mouse.'

Sam, the father, keeps a zoo of small mammals and snakes, which he and the children cherish, but which Henny hates. For one thing, snakes bring bad luck. He has an aquarium, an aviary; he is a humanist and a lover of all life – the zoo is merely an extension of his many children, who are woken in the mornings and summoned to him by whistles they have to respond to, based on the calls of birds. When yet another babe is born, as a result of a fight between husband and wife that could easily have ended in murder, first of all the father chooses the whistle he will use to command the newcomer, a phrase from some bird's song, and then husband and wife begin a new fight over the child's name.

Sam teaches birds to sing new songs. A catbird learns the flycatcher's call to use in his own repertory, and listens while Sam and the boys school him in new calls. For Sam has to control not only his brood of children but this natural world all around him. He wakes at night, sees through the panes 'the tussle of cloud streak and sky spark' and hears that some marauder is fluttering the nestlings. 'Hist, hist!' he says – 'and reduced the twig world to silence.'

This is an ancient rattlebag of a house, and all around it are trees and shrubs and birds and birdsong, and beyond is the world of water: pond, creeks and the river. This is Sam's element, where he plays, for if what he does in the house has to be categorised as work, for it would fall down without him, he experiences it as fun, all physical enjoyment, which he shares with the children. 'The morning was hot, and Sam had nothing on beneath his painting overalls. When he waved his golden-white muscular hairless arms, large damp tufts of yellow-red hair appeared . . . The pores on his well-stretched skin were very large, his leathery skin was quite unlike the dull silk of the children's cheeks . . .' And he sings as he works and the children sing with him.

It is from inside a paradise of physical happiness that he chants his hymns to life and the beauties of his fellow man, while upstairs his bitter wife, dark and skinny like a witch, hisses out her loathing to all the world. And he says to her, 'You devil of rust and rot and boring. You will not smash my family life. You will carry your bargain through to the end. You will look after my children . . .' And she says to him, 'You took me and maltreated me and starved me half to death because you couldn't make a living and sponged off my father and used his influence, hoisting yourself up on all my aches and miseries . . .'

Our common experience, tutored by knowing psychology, insists that such enmity, such violence, bred by the venom engendered by the incongruity of these two, the parents, must damage the children, for both Sam and Henny in their various and unique ways threaten their very existence. Sam believes – it is the spirit of the times – in euthanasia for the unfit, and while the children joke, they must feel threatened, particularly the 'monster' Louie, told she looks like a gutter rat by this child-lover, her father, who proposes to weed out 'the misfits and degenerates'. And Henny says often she will kill herself and all of them. And yet it seems they are immune, experience the parental threat as no more than part of the rich emotional diet of this household.

Are they immune? 'Die, die, why don't you all die and leave me to die or to hang; fall down, die; what do I care? I beat my son to death . . .' (this to her favourite child, Ernie) 'it's no worse than what I have to endure' – and she beats him while her eyes start out of her head. 'I'll kill you children that make me go out of my mind . . .'

But the odd thing is that the reader is made to feel part of something as grand and impersonal as Greek tragedy. Easy to imagine these terrible lines declaimed in a stone amphitheatre, to silent crowds, and – yes – masks would not be inappropriate, so much are these antagonists archetypes.

'I'd drink his blood but it would make me vomit.'

Then he, 'I had long shuddering days . . . when it was as if the north wind was blowing all day, when I thought of our home here on the heights, exposed to all the winds of our anger and hate . . .'

Louie: 'What will become of me? Will life go on like this? . . . I can't live and go on being like this.'

Ernie, to his mother: 'Mother, don't, don't . . . Oh, Mother . . .'

It is like being admitted into some frightful Victorian melo-drama, reading this book, but one made ordinary and even commonplace due to the intensity and inevitableness of it. There seem no ordinary moments in this family, their element is exag-geration and hyperbole, but that is right and suitable because their natures and situation are extreme.

The children's dispositions, no different from any others', are given room by the theatricality of the parents and – here we reach the heart of the book, and this family – fed by the intemperate and inventive language to which the house resounds, day and night. Sam never uses an ordinary sentence. One feels that to say 'Let us all go for a walk', or 'It's time for breakfast', would be beyond him, precisely because it would expose him, for he is protected by his invented language, part taken from Artemus Ward and part from Uncle Remus, and full of added baby phrases and lispings. Quite sickening it has to sound to a stern modern reader, but the children delight in it. So hard is it for an outsider to penetrate, that Christina Stead translates some of it for us, but the children know it as they know the weather. 'Bin readin' a find stor-wy, Little Womey,' says Sam to his second daughter, ''bout a fine woman en a fine little girl. Good sweet story – makes your pore little Sam burst into tears.' For he feels no shame about describing himself as 'yo' po' little Dad', is not afraid of ridicule, for these children of his are his safe place where he takes refuge from the world he apostrophises as fine and ideal and full of his bothers and sisters but at which he cautiously peeps out from behind the screen of baby talk and his family.

'I married a child,' says Henny, who, whatever else she might be, is certainly not a child. This is her charitable assessment of him, in a softer moment, while she is perhaps telling her children rhymes from her plantation girlhood. But more often she sees him as 'something filthy crawling in the sleeve of my dressing gown; something dirty, a splotch of blood or washing-up water on my skirts. That's what he is, with his fine airs and don't-touch-me and I'm-too-good-to-drink. The little tin Jesus!' But he doesn't talk baby language to her, only the language of mutual loathing.

All this, don't forget, was before every home had a radio, let alone television. This was that pure and pre-Fall condition we describe as 'They made their own amusements.' Language, the enjoyment and discovering of it, was the chief employment of this family. You can fairly hear the relish in Henny's 'Silly old gobblers with their dirty hair like a haystack in a fit', or Sam's 'This Sunday-Funday has come a long way ... it's been coming to us, all day yesterday, all night from the mid-Pacific, from Peking, the Himalayas, from the fishing grounds of the old Leni Lenapes and the deeps of the drowned Susquehanna.'

Some of these passionate complaints sound like the lines of a part-song or ballad:

'The night of our marriage I knew I was doomed to unhappiness!'
'I never wanted to marry him: he went down on his knees!'
'She lied to me within three days of marriage!'
'The first week I wanted to go back home!'
'Oh Louie, the hell, where there should have been heaven!'
'But he stuck me with his brats, to make sure I didn't get away from him.'

Chants, part-songs, word-play, riddles, jokes – these are all part of everyday living. 'Ole Miss Jones, rattles her bones, over the stones: she's only a porpoise that nobody owns,' says Sam. And Henny sings,

Like his father, like his father,
He has the cut of a kangaroo ...

Probably it is this feast of words, beginning at the moment this nest of children wakes, going on all day and into the night, that insulates them against the bolts of lightning from the mother's room to strike the father dead, and the shouts of raging reproach that rise from the garden where Sam is working, to reach his wife. Words rolling off the tongue, words as an intoxicant, words as sustenance, words sonorously or rhythmically filling every room of the house, and the children waiting for them, just as they wait for their father's own special whistle for each of them – and wait, too, it is hard not to conclude, for the exuberant invective of Henny.

Surely this must be the ideal cradle and nursery for a writer? And here she is, the budding writer Louie, who must be at least a version of Christina Stead herself. Yet while seeing child Christina here, one has to think that this creation of an apprenticeship into the word is, must be, a literary artifice as well, because Louie is so much the archetype of 'the artist'. No feature of the fabled creature is lacking; from her pitiful situation of being a stepdaughter, to the wicked stepmother Henny who genuinely loathes the child even while she pities her and her clumsiness. For Louie cannot lift a cup without letting it slip, cannot take a step without turning an ankle or lift a mouthful of food without spilling it down her front.

This lumbering galumphing deformed baby elephant of a girl, hating her ugliness, dreaming of beauty – she must break the reader's heart, you would think, but no, for the power of the enchantment that lies over these pages is so great that she seems an animal who is really a princess, and she herself knows she is the ugly duckling who will be a swan. And while she is love-hungry, and Henny so cruel to her it is hard to bear, this is the child Henny relies on, sending her for her medicines and her cigarettes and, too, the little bottles of spirits, which Sam never knows about, for Louie does not betray her, and nor do the other children. Sam is a bigoted teetotaller.

The strongest of bonds, this one, between the tormented, demented Henny and the ugly child. It is their cleverness, perhaps, for they are both clever, both continually coming up against the stupid sentimentality of the man who may love children, and by extension all of humanity, but who never understands what is under his nose. Louie knows that in Henny's balefulness is a strength that feeds her too, and she is grateful to Henny for ignoring her, for solitude is what Louie craves most.

Louie is no sweet, biddable, patient little girl. There is more than a hint of what sustains her, and in what ways she colludes with Henny, when a neighbour, an old woman, asks Louie to help her kill a cat who is a burden. Louie is prepared to fill a bath with water and sit with her feet on a board that holds the struggling drowning cat under. There is a dream or nightmare quality to this sequence, precisely because of the absence of any feeling in Louie. She goes through it as if there is nothing else to be done, and no one else capable of doing the deed, and it is in fact a rehearsal or foreshadowing of her final confrontation with Henny.

In many novels from the American thirties you enter this world of language, of literature; it is often an intense poverty, lit by the imagination and by dreams. This was the Slump, and everywhere hopes were being dashed and lives cramped and spoiled. But there were books, there was poetry, and teachers who cherished talented pupils, who could see the merit in the most ugly of ducklings because of their passionate love of words. And here it is again, the schoolroom invoked so strongly you have to feel you are in it. For this is Christina Stead's most special gift; there has never been a writer who can take you so strongly into a room, or a house, or a street that you are immediately part of. Here you feel as if you might yourself start defending poor Louie against a snobbish girl, or even against Henny herself.

Henny . . . pounced on her and scolded her for her appearance, her dirty dress, her cobbled stockings and down-at-heel shoes, her loose straggling hair . . . and puffed expression ('you look

as if you spent the night in self-abuse, I'll make your father speak
to you'). She rushed into the girl's room to look out a clean
dress for her ... and suddenly came out screaming that she'd
kill that great stinking monster, that white-faced elephant with
her green rotting teeth and green rotting clothes ...

'But,' you may easily imagine screaming back, 'the girl has no
clothes, she begs for a new dress to go to school in and you
say there is no money, and what girl is going to look after
herself if she is told she disgusts her mother?'

Louie is not the only girl in this school with only one dress
and broken shoes. Many of them are very poor girls, and what
could be more touching than the way they are considerate of
each other, and how a girl who comes to school in despair
because of her dress in shreds is tended and sheltered? And
meanwhile these outcasts are drunk on language, and when
Louie has a crush on her teacher and then on a best friend she
writes

> The Indian starling, flashing in the shade
> Is like your eye, all flecked with gold and blue ...

Which the father reads and calls sickening tommyrot. The sad-
dest of ironies, for Sam has taught his tribe love for books and
words and poetry, but here is the real thing, he has given life
to a poet, and he is disconcerted, for he is unable to recognise
what he is seeing.

Louie writes all the time and we are given samples. Never
has an apprentice writer's work been so well documented. Is it
below the belt to speculate whether these romantic verses and
plays were Christina's own? Yes, probably, but all the same,
what we read is more talented than what is usually ascribed to
an aspiring adolescent. Sam is not only upset by what Louie

produces, he sees it as a threat, and he reads her hidden diaries and her poems – destroys her secret life, which she creates so as to have some kind of belief in herself. He sucks the life out of her, demanding total love and allegiance, even that she will devote her life to him. Her defence against him is cruel and final. Demanding to see what she has written down while he is delivering one of his speeches about the beauty of life, he reads only, '*Shut up, shut up, shut up, shut up . . .*' She tells him that none of his children will ever confide in him. When asked to promise that he and she will march through this cruel life together, she says, 'No, I will have nothing to do with you.'

What are the bones of fact here? – for it is easy to experience this novel as submission to a wonderland of language and events. The first and most surprising fact is that it was an Australian writer – Christina Stead, brought up in Sydney – who created this novel which is as American as Steinbeck's or Faulkner's. Surely Faulkner himself would applaud Henny, the gimcrack southern belle from Baltimore, with her genteel dreams and pretensions, who had expected so much better for a husband than a minor bureaucrat – it does come as a surprise that Sam actually has an office job, does not spend all his time on his house and his garden and his animals. And his children. Sam knows, the children know – they are continually being reminded – that this abounding family life of theirs is a descent from a high estate, that their mother was once beautiful, a dark thin young lady in a ruffled silk dressing gown, but this beauty has disappeared, and in her place is this witch, an angry grubby Henny who screeches and drudges. No fairy story has ever told of a more powerful transformation than this of Henny's, the beauty from Baltimore.

Henny's father has always given her money, and she has always begged for more. What do you do with it? he complains. She is a spendthrift he says, why can't she manage? But how can a woman manage with seven children and a husband who despises money, admires poverty? The great draughty old house is not paid for by her unworldly husband but is her father's. She begs and borrows, she uses money-lenders, she is forever in debt, she sells her body to a rich friend, a businessman, who finally tires of her perpetual money troubles. All this to keep food on the table and her children clothed. Meanwhile the family live in confidence of future plenty, for when the father dies of course Henrietta, his favourite, will be left not only this house but a fortune. When the old man does die he is proved to have been as improvident as his daughter, for there is no money, and even this poor house has to be sold to pay debts. The man who loves children and thinks poverty is beautiful takes them to an even seedier house, in a neighbourhood so low Henny knows she has reached the worst. Now nothing is left of her gracious southern-lady self, her pretty ways are all gone, and the treasures in her secret drawers which the children loved so much are sold – laces, ribbons, flowers, jabots, belts, hairpins and combs, buckles and false jewels, stockings and the little pots of rouge and mascara – which Sam anathematises – all gone, and, too, the last of Henny's silver and valuables.

Meanwhile Sam is still happy as the day is long, for he has kept belief in a beautiful world to come. The idealistic dreams of the political thirties do seep down here, but in Sam Pollit they are not contained in a political party but float wide and free, in these nets and webs of words. 'When the time for man comes . . . he will see and rise to the light – there is no need of revolution, but only of guidance, and . . . we will reach the good world, the new age of gold.'

He has a stroke of luck – so he thinks. His department sends him to Malaya, to the glamorous East, where he amazes all the locals, who see themselves as oppressed by the white man and his ways, by apostrophising the brotherhood of man. 'You are but an ebonized Aryan ... and I am the bleached one that is fashionable at present.' And he congratulates himself thus: 'What a gift he has been given ... to love and understand so many races of man! – and why? His secret was simple. They were all alike ...' Meanwhile the representatives of the brother races in question are puzzled by him. He is a good man, they think, but they do not seem able to get the simplest fact about the life they lead into his head. His superiors are not puzzled, they are furious. Sam Pollit, floating on clouds of elation inflated by love, offends white people, and does not know it, for are not his views so obviously true and good? He has never known, either, that he has had enemies who resent him, because of his 'socialist' views and his contempt for everything they value. His behaviour in Malaya gives them an excuse to unseat him. And indeed his behaviour is inexcusable – for anyone but a grown-up child who has never been able to see himself as others see him. His enemies not only use the obvious excuses to get rid of him but attribute to him all kinds of dark financial dealings. Now indeed he is 'po' little Sam' but he is too high-minded to defend himself against the scandal. When asked why not, when begged to fight for himself for the sake of his wife and family, he says he will not lower himself by descending to the level of his enemies.

How can things possibly get worse for this family? They do. In the end it has to collapse. Meanwhile, do they understand how very badly off they are? Henny does, for she has always understood exactly how the family stands, and how her husband is seen. But Miss Aiden, Louie's beloved teacher, comes to visit and finds a poverty that is incredible to her. The Pollits lack everything, she thinks: 'I had no idea that there was a place as primitive in the whole world.' She had expected a decayed gentility, nothing like this threadbare misery – which, strangely, the family do not seem to see. But what Miss Aiden does not understand is that beyond the ugly home-cemented back porch is an orchard wilderness, and birds, and creeks and a river – the wildness that has been the children's safe place and is their heritage.

Not long ago a camera team in some frightful South American urban slum handed over a camera to children, so they could photograph their infinite deprivation from their own point of view and their situation would not always be seen through the eyes of rich visitors from the fortunate world. But what the children chose to film were scenes of themselves and their friends playing in the water of an old cracked fountain – a joyous scene. They did not know their poverty was extreme, and wanted to commemorate happiness. Louie is sent every year for the summer to her mother's family, the Bakers, another once well-off, now impoverished, clan. We are ready to be sorry for her, immersed for weeks at a time with these mean, sternly religious people, who resent the improvident Pollits, and resent her, for they know she is there because Henny wants to get rid of her and sees these visits as a way of having one less mouth to feed. But Louie is happy with all the family pressures off her, she chooses not to notice the ungenerous mutterings. For her this other family is a paradise she longs for all the year, and when at last they refuse to have her, it is a tragedy for her.

So insistent a claim do Henny and Sam make on the tale that it is easy to overlook the prodigal variety of the other Pollits and the Collyer relatives who come and go, each of these lives written and offered to the reader with the same sense of epic importance that lives do have to the livers of them. A visit from any one of these people brings into the story that sense of the extraordinariness, the mysteriousness of existence which so easily gets lost as the days go round. Even a tiny scene of a servant girl talking with Louie suggests so much more than the important (to them) exchanges of two little girls competing to sound interesting, for here, though only suggested, is the tragedy of the young girl Nellie, who is thrown out in disgrace, turned out like a dog, because she has told Louie she is a bastard, herself hardly knowing what the word means. Where did this 'sloppy and cheerful' little girl come from? A reformatory, for that's where people got their servants. 'A love-child,' mutters Henny, disgustedly imagining sordid couplings. And where did she go? What happened to her?

Or three women, Henny, her sister and Sam's sister, sit gossiping through a long afternoon, creating worlds of lives and people, while Louie listens – but they do not know she is there. This is how talk is used in *Ulysses* (the Irish one) to create a matrix of events, thick and complex, painting a picture of a culture, a society.

Aunt Bonnie, Sam's sister, is a minor character. She is used by the Pollits as a servant, but her life is explosive with drama. When she scorches, as she irons it, Henny's only decent blouse, a relic of her gracious living, it is a crisis like a war or an earthquake. She gets thrown out too, only to become pregnant. It is Sam, who loves children, and wishes he could have a hundred, who defends the disgraced woman while the other Pollits draw aside their skirts.

The children are each one an individual. Of them all, apart from Louie who pervades the story as thoroughly as Henny and Sam, little Ernie is the one with the power to make you think about his future. He is obsessed with money, because his mother is obsessed. He knows exactly what is in her purse, demands to know what she has spent it on if there are a few cents gone after a trip into town, and saves up his pocket money, such as it is, in a hiding place under the floorboards. But his mother steals it from him, one day when she is desperate. Will she put it back? he begs, he demands, and she says she will . . . Evie, the other daughter, 'Little-Womey', is being tutored by her father into being the perfect female, but we feel she will survive. The twins and Thomas are very much themselves – we can imagine their futures as adults. The new baby is a hate-child if ever there was one, but not much is made of his unfortunate beginnings, and he seems to survive adequately on no nurturing at all, or none that is recorded.

When you put down this book at last and emerge into the light of a day very dull by contrast, as is as if you have left not only this densely imagined swarming world of Pollits and Collyers but your own childhood too, where a smashed cup or a burned blouse or an overheard matter of gossiping women is a revelation of life's dangers and richness.

And when these children grow up, will they remember the preposterousness of po' little Sam, and poor clever demented Henny, and the poverty so extreme a teacher could not believe what she saw, or will they know they were in an Eden where children ran about naked among animals and birds, where their ears were filled with shouts of rich and resounding language, where it was only an exuberance of temperament for mother and father to scream insults and threats of death, and where a sister, as ugly as a crippled beast, wrote verses 'after Confucius':

> A yellow plum was given me and in return a topaz fair I gave,
> No mere return for courtesy but that our friendship might
> > outlast the grave.

Well, there are no households, no families, like that now, intoxicated with words, for poetry has been silenced by television, and poverty is no longer redeemed by the world of imagination entered by opening a book.

The Man Who Loved Children may be read for its evocation of a lost world as much as for its great virtues. For it is a great novel, one that is always being rediscovered and then for some reason slips away out of sight, and then is found again. Christina Stead is a great writer. Beside her name is a list of novels, each one unlike the work of any other writer and unlike each other, and perhaps that is why she is not finally accepted into the company of great writers. It is hard to understand, though. There are formally accepted canons of Best Books, Best Writers, for that time – the thirties and forties – and some of them are nowhere near her size in scope and magnificence.

For Love Alone continues the story of the ugly duckling, under another name, with a different family, and in a different country – Australia. But here she is, love-hungry, lonely, stuffed with talent and ambition, tormented by the penny-pinching poverty of the thirties, longing to escape to London and the company of fellow spirits – which she eventually does. Now the picture is the same in 'feel' and atmosphere as D. H. Lawrence's evocation of talented, poor and fiercely independent souls. *The People with the Dogs* so strongly creates New York it is easy to believe you have lived there yourself even when, like myself, you have not lived there more than a few days at a time. I could walk into one of these rooming houses as if I had never left it, a friend of these people and their dogs. *Letty Fox: Her Luck* is about the anarchic relationships in New York in a time of sexual revolution. These women are 'free', but really a woman's luck still depended on men: if she was going to live well, she needed a well-heeled man.

Every one of Christina Stead's novels is unique and unforgettable. This one, *The Man Who Loved Children*, is reckoned her best. And it is. But sometimes it seems that the last one of her novels you have read is her best. This may happen with a great writer. As I look along my shelf of her books, it is difficult not to write eulogistically about every one of them.

Kalila and Dimna – The Fables of Bidpai

The claim has been made for this book that it has travelled more widely than the Bible, for it has been translated through the centuries everywhere from Ethiopia to China. Yet it is safe to say that most people in the West these days will not have heard of it, while they will certainly at the very least have heard of the *Upanishads* and the *Vedas*. Until comparatively recently, it was the other way around. Anyone with any claim to a literary education knew that the *Fables of Bidpai*, or the *Tales of Kalila and Dimna* – these being the most commonly used titles with us – was a great Eastern classic. There were at least twenty English translations in the hundred years before 1888. Pondering on these facts leads to reflection on the fate of books, as chancy and unpredictable as that of people or nations.

The book's history is as fascinating as its contents, and would make a pretty volume on its own.

The first English translation was done in the sixteenth century by Sir Thomas North – he who translated Plutarch into a work which was the source of Shakespeare's knowledge of the Roman world. North's Plutarch was popular reading: so was his version of *Bidpai*. In the introduction to the reissue of this translation in the nineteenth century, Joseph Jacobs of Cambridge (Jews have been prominent in the movement and adaptation of the book) concludes: 'If I go on further, I foresee a sort of mental dialogue which will pass between my reader and myself: "What," the reader will exclaim, "the first literary link between India and England, between Buddhism and Christendom, written in racy English with vivacious dialogue and something resembling a plot. Why, you will be trying to make us believe that you have restored to us an English Classic!" "Exactly so," I should be constrained to reply, and lest I be tempted into this temerity, I will even make a stop here.'

And he did stop, but by then he had written a very great number of pages. I have been handed over by Ramsay Wood a vast heap of many versions of the *Fables of Bidpai* – some of them rare and precious – to aid me in this task of doing an introduction, and the first thing to be noticed is that the introductions tend to be very long: it is clear that the authors of them have become beguiled and besotted with the book's history. As I have. For one thing, it has lasted at least two thousand years. But it is hard to say where the beginning was – suitably for a book whose nature it is to accommodate tales within tales and to blur the margins between historical fact and fiction.

One progenitor was the Buddhist cycle of Birth Tales (or Jātaka Stories) where the Buddha appears as a monkey, deer, lion, and so on. Several of the Bidpai tales came from this cycle. Incidents that occur in *Bidpai* can be seen in sculptures around Buddhist shrines dated before 200BC. The Buddha himself took some of the Birth Tales from earlier folktales about animals. But there is no race or nation from the Egyptians on – or back, for we may surely no longer assume that current information regarding ancient history is all there is to be known, or all that we will come to know – that has not used beast-fables as part of its heritage of instructional material. And so the genre is as ancient as mankind itself. Sir Richard Burton, who like all the

other orientalists of the nineteenth century was involved with
Bidpai, suggested that man's use of the beast-fable commemor-
ates our instinctive knowledge of how we emerged from the
animal kingdom, on two legs but still with claws and fangs.

Another source or contributor was that extraordinary book,
the *Arthaśāstra* of Kautilya, which is suspected of dating from
about 300 BC. It is not easy to lay one's hands on a copy, and
this is a pity: at a time when we are all, down to the least
citizen, absorbed, not to say obsessed, with sociology and the
arts of proper government, this book should take its place, not
as the earliest manual on the subject, but as the earliest we
know of. It describes in exact and even pernickety detail how
properly to run a kingdom, from the kind of goods that should
be available in the market-place to the choice of kingly advisers;
how one should go about creating a new village, and where;
the right way to employ artisans to manufacture gold and silver
coins; disputes between neighbours about property and boundaries; how to keep accounts; the legal system; the use of spies.
It is all here. And to our minds, what a mixture of humanity
and brutality! It was forbidden, for instance, to have sex with
a woman against her will, even if she was a prostitute, but
there are also lengthy instructions about the use of torture as
a punishment. Kautilya was a very cool one indeed; surely this
book must have influenced Machiavelli when he wrote *The
Prince*. If not, then the books come from the same region of
human experience. Candid, unrhetorical, infinitely worldly-
wise, the tone is more like that which one imagines must exist,
let's say, between a Begin and a Sadat when sitting together
facing the realities of a situation unobserved by slogan-chanting
supporters, or between a Churchill and a Roosevelt meeting
in the middle of a war. There is nothing in the *Arthaśāstras*
that minimises the harshness of necessary choices. It was by
no means the first of such handy guides to statesmanship, for

Kautilya says it is a compendium of 'almost all the *Arthaśāstras* which in view of acquisition and maintenance of the earth have been composed by ancient teachers'. In other words, this to us so ancient book was to him the last in a long line of instructive tracts, stretching back into antiquity. Throughout he quotes the view of this one or that, sometimes up to ten or more, and then adds at the end, 'My teacher says . . .' but usually disagrees with them all, including his teacher, with 'No, says Kautilya . . .' or 'Not so, says Kautilya . . .', setting everything and everyone right, so that the book has about it the air of a young man refusing to be impressed by tradition – rather like students in the sixties bringing their own books to class and insisting on choosing their own curriculum.

The cycle called *The Fables of Bidpai* came into existence in this manner . . . but let us choose a version that, typically, tries to set fiction on a base of fact. Alexander the Great, having conquered India, set a disliked and unjust governor over the vanquished ones, who were at last able to overturn this tyrant, and chose a ruler of their own. This was King Dabschelim, but he turned out to be no better than his predecessor. A wise and incorruptible sage named Bidpai, knowing that he risked his life, went to the no-good king to tell him that the heavens were displeased with him because of his depredations, his cruelties, his refusal to be properly responsible for the welfare of the people put in his care. And sure enough, Bidpai found himself cast into the deepest and foulest dungeon; but the king, attracting to himself heavenly influences because of his inner disquiet over this behaviour of his, was caused to think again and . . . Thereafter the tale unfolds in the characteristic way of the genre, stories within stories, one leading to another. We in the West do not have this kind of literature, except where it has come to us through influences from the East: Boccaccio and Chaucer, for instance. What this method of storytelling, or this design, is supposed to illustrate is the way that in life one thing leads to another, often unexpectedly, and that one may not make neat and tidy containers for ideas and events — or hopes and possibilities — and that it is not easy to decide where anything begins or ends. As the history of the book itself proves. When the 'frame' story stops, temporarily, and a cluster of related tales is told, what is happening is that many facets of a situation are being illuminated, before the movement of the main story goes on. There may be even more than one 'frame' story, so that we are led gently into realm after realm, doors opening as if one were to push a mirror and find it a door.

Another version of the book's origin is that there was once a good and honest king who had three stupid and lazy sons. Many educational experts came forward with suggestions as to their proper instruction, but the king was in despair, knowing that to give them the foundation of information they needed would take years, by which time the kingdom would be ruined. And then came a sage who said he would impart to the three princes the essence of statesmanship and sensible conduct in the form of instructive fables, and the process would be accomplished in a very short time, if the princes could be persuaded to pay attention. Thus the book has been known as *A Mirror for Princes*, and we are told that it was given to princes as part of their training to be monarchs.

The original Sanskrit version vanished, though later the material was translated back into Sanskrit from other languages, and India has produced as many versions 'as there are stars in the sky'. The ancient Persian King of Kings, Nushirvan, heard of the book, and sent embassies, and it was translated into the ancient Persian tongue of Pahlavi, which event was thought of such importance that Firdausi celebrated it in the *Shahnama*. The incidents of the tales were infinitely illustrated in this book and in very many others, and anyone at all interested in Persian art will certainly have come across them in miniatures and otherwise. Not only Persian art – I have here a postcard from the British Museum of a turtle being carried through the air on a stick by two geese: the friends who could not bear to be parted. It is from a Turkish manuscript. The British Museum has this and many other ancient manuscripts so precious one may view them only through glass, like jewels, which they resemble.

When the Arabs conquered the old world, after the death of Muhammad, poets and scholars arrived in India, enquiring for the famous book they had heard so much about. The way they tracked it down, like the account of how the old Persian envoys found their copy, makes an attractive story full of suspense, mystery and drama, so that one has to suspect that the storytellers of the time took their opportunity to honour even further this honoured book by copious invention; while some of them made 'quest tales' from the material, in which the book becomes a hidden treasure. The most famous translation into Arabic was by a Zoroastrian who converted to Islam. Another was probably by an honoured Jewish scholar. In those comparatively flexible days, scholars were able more easily than now to appreciate each other and work together across boundaries. There were religions then, not nations – a fact it is hard to remember in its dimensions when considering how things were in those days. For instance, to read the biography of Muhammad by ibn-Ishaq, the Muslim equivalent of the New Testament, where nations and national feelings are absent, and men and women are known as Muslims, Jews, Christians, Zoroastrians, and there were no Arabs and Jews in our sense, since that is a division of modern times, to read this book is hard for a modern Westerner because of how we see everything in terms of nations and nationalism. So strange is it that the mind keeps seizing up and you have to stop, and start again.

The query has been raised: What was the 'secret ingredient'

of this Bidpai book, 'this ocean of tales', that enabled it to be absorbed without resistance, and to be loved by Buddhists, Zoroastrians, Christians, Muslims, Jews? One answer was that in all these traditions it is established that tales and parables are for instruction and illustration as well as for entertainment. Medieval Europe rushed to translate the book because its fame was known, and they wanted its aid in learning how to live better. But nowadays we use this phrase in a different sense.

One of the best-known and most influential of the old versions was *Anwar-i-Suhaili*, or *The Lights of Canopus*. There had been earlier Persian versions, but these were considered inadequate and even elitist. An emir, or general, called Suhaili (of Canopus) invited one al-Kashifi to make a new version. I was interested that Canopus was being used as a name in a culture and at a time when names were often chosen to describe qualities, or as an indication of qualities a person hoped to acquire. People were expected to regard names as signposts, as it were. Round about that time there came into existence a cluster of Persian classics, all of Sufic origin and inspiration. *The Lights of Suhaili* is one of these. It is the same in 'feel' and format as, for instance, Saadi's *Rose Garden*, using the Bidpai tales as a frame, or lattice, around which are woven associated tales, anecdotes, reminiscences, current scientific information, and verse of different kinds. It is worthwhile insisting that this great classic, now regarded with a truly horrible reverence and solemnity, was a popular book, meant for entertainment, as well as instruction. But who was this general or governor whose name became the name of the book, so that he was, in the way of those times and regions, place, person, tradition – all at once – and was able to bring about the creation of a new Sufi classic, using the ancient Bidpai material to do it? And who was al-Kashifi, whose name means 'that which is manifested', or 'shown', or 'demonstrated'?

Canopus the star is much embedded in the mythology of ancient times and when you trace it to this country or that it melds and merges into other names, places, personages. To illustrate the remarkable law known to all researchers, but not yet acknowledged by science – that when one is becoming interested in a subject, books formerly unknown and unsuspected fly to your hand from everywhere – while I was speculating about Canopus, and what it could mean in this context, if it meant anything, there came my way *Astronomical Curiosities*, published in 1909, and one of its main sources of information was one al-Sufi, an Arabian astronomer of the tenth century. Much is said by al-Sufi about Canopus of the constellation Argo. Argo was associated with Noah's Ark. It represents, too, the first ship ever built, which was in Thessaly, by order of Minerva and Neptune, to go on the expedition for the conquest of the Golden Fleece. The date of this expedition commanded by Jason is usually fixed at 1300 or 1400 BC. Canopus was the ancient name of Aboukir in Egypt, and is said to have derived its name from the pilot of Menelaus, whose name was Kanobus, and who died there 'from the bite of a snake'. The star is supposed to have been named after him, in some traditions, and it was worshipped by the ancient Egyptians ... but Canopus is also the god Osiris, and is in the most remarkable and ever-changing relationship with Isis, who was the star Sirius ... and thus is one enticed into all kinds of byways, from which it is hard to extricate oneself, and harder still to resist quoting, and thus joining the immoderate preface-makers whom I can no longer in honesty condemn.

The *Iliad* and *Odyssey* are linked with Bidpai in another way too: a Greek called Seth Simeon translated it in the eleventh century, adding to it all kinds of bits and pieces from these two epics – another illustration, if one is needed by now, of the way such material adapts to new backgrounds and new times. In

Hebrew, Turkish, Latin, Russian, Malay, Polish – in almost any language you can think of – its naturalisation followed the laws of infinite adaptability. It is not possible to trace its influences: as is always the way when a book's seminal power has been great, it was absorbed and transformed by local cultures. Certainly the Bidpai tales can be found in the folklore of most European countries, almost as much as they can in the East. Some were adapted by La Fontaine. Beaumont and Fletcher are supposed to have used The Dervish and the Thief as a germ for *Women Pleased*. Aesop's fables as we know them are indebted to Bidpai.

There has not been an English version for a long time. The existing ones have become stiff and boring. Many consider Sir Thomas North's still to be the best, but what for the Elizabethans was a lively new book is for us a museum piece.

This fresh creation by Ramsay Wood follows the more than 2,000-year-old precedent of adapting, collating and arranging the old material in any way that suits present purposes. It is contemporary, racy, vigorous, full of zest. It is also very funny. I defy anyone to sit down with it and not finish it at a sitting: his own enjoyment in doing the book has made it so enjoyable.

And there is another good thing. The original, or perhaps I should say some arrangements of the original, had thirteen sections: The Separation of Friends, The Winning of Friends, War and Peace, The Loss of One's Gains, The Rewards of Impatience, and so forth. This volume has only the material to do with friends, artfully arranged to make a whole. And so we may look forward – I hope – to the rest.

Speech at Vigo on getting the Prince of Asturias Prize 2002

Once upon a time, and it seems a long time ago, there was a respected figure, The Educated Person. He – it was usually he, but then increasingly often she – was educated in a way that differed little from country to country – I am of course talking about Europe – but was different from what we know now. William Hazlitt, our great essayist, went to a school, in the late eighteenth century, whose curriculum was four times more comprehensive than that of a comparable school now, a mix of the bases of language, law, art, religion, mathematics. It was taken for granted that this already dense and deep education was only one aspect of development, for the pupils were expected to read, and they did.

This kind of education, the humanist education, is vanishing. Increasingly, governments – our British government among them – encourage citizens to acquire vocational skills, while education as a development of the whole person is not seen as useful to the modern society.

The older education would have had Greek and Latin literature and history, and the Bible, as a foundation for everything else. He – or she – read the classics of their own countries, perhaps one or two from Asia, and the best-known writers of other European countries, Goethe, Shakespeare, Cervantes, the great Russians, Rousseau. An educated person from Argentina would meet a similar person from Spain, one from St Petersburg meet his counterpart in Norway, a traveller from France spend time with one from Britain, and they would understand each other, they shared a culture, could refer to the same books, plays, poems, pictures, in a web of reference and information that was like a shared history of the best the human mind has thought, said, written.

This has gone.

Greek and Latin are disappearing. In many countries the Bible, and religion – going. A girl I know, taken to Paris to broaden her mind, which needed it, though she was doing brilliantly in examinations, revealed that she had never heard of Catholics and Protestants, knew nothing of the history of Christianity or any other religion. She was taken to hear mass in Notre Dame, told that this ceremony had been a basis of European culture for centuries, and she should at least know about it – and she dutifully sat through it, rather as she might a tea ceremony in Japan, and afterwards enquired, 'Are these people some kind of cannibal then?' So much for what seems enduring.

There is a new kind of educated person, who may be at school and university for twenty, twenty-five years, who knows everything about a speciality, computers, the law, economics, politics, but knows about nothing else, no literature, art, history, and may be heard enquiring, 'But what was the Renaissance then?' 'What was the French Revolution?'

Even 50 years ago this person would have been seen as a barbarian. To have acquired an education with nothing of the old humanist background – impossible. To call oneself educated without a background of reading – impossible.

Reading, books, the literary culture, was respected, desired, for centuries. Reading was and still is in what we call the Third World a kind of parallel education, which once everyone had, or aspired to. Nuns and monks in their convents and monasteries, aristocrats at their meals, women at their looms and their sewing, were read to, and the poor people, even if all they had was a Bible, respected those who read. In Britain until quite recently trade unions and workers' movements fought for libraries, and perhaps the best example of the pervasiveness of the love for reading is that of the workers in the tobacco and cigar factories of Cuba whose trade unions demanded that the workers should be read to as they worked. The material was agreed to by the workers, and included politics and history, novels and poetry. A favourite of their books was the *Count of Monte Cristo*. A group of workers wrote to Dumas and asked if they might use the name of his hero for one of their cigars.

Perhaps there is no need to labour this point to anyone present here, but I do feel we have not yet grasped that we are living in a fast fragmenting culture. Pockets of the old excellences remain, in a university, a school, the classroom of an old-fashioned teacher in love with books, perhaps a newspaper or a journal. But a culture that once united Europe and its overseas offshoots has gone.

We may get some idea of the speed with which cultures may change by looking at how languages change. English as spoken in America or the West Indies is not the English of England. Spanish is not the same in Argentina and in Spain. The Portuguese of Brazil is not the Portuguese of Portugal. Italian, Spanish, French grew out of Latin not in thousands of years but in hundreds. It is a very short time since the Roman world disappeared, leaving behind its legacy of our languages.

One interesting little irony about the present situation is that a lot of the criticism of the old culture was in the name of

Elitism, but what is happening is that everywhere are enclaves, pockets, of the old kind of reader and reading and it is easy to imagine one of the new barbarians walking by chance into a library of the old kind, in all its richness and variety, and understanding suddenly what has been lost, what he – or she – has been deprived of.

So what is going to happen next in this tumultuously changing world? I think we are all of us fastening our seat belts and holding on tight.

I drafted what I have just read before the events of 11 September. We are in for a war, it seems, a long one, which by its nature cannot have an easy end. We all know that enemies exchange more than gunfire and insults. In this country Spain you know this better perhaps than anyone. When feeling gloomy about the world I often think about that time here, in Spain, in the early Middle Ages, in Cordova, in Toledo, in Granada, in other southern cities, Christians, Muslims, Jews lived harmoniously together, poets, musicians, writers, sages, all together, admiring each other, helping each other. It went on for three centuries. This wonderful culture went on for three centuries. Has anything like it been seen in the world? What has been, can be again.

I think the educated person of the future will have a wider basis than anything we can imagine now.

Censorship

Towards the end of the reign of the late unlamented Shah of Iran a certain lowly citizen named his beautiful cat Shah-in-Shah, King of Kings, a title claimed by this king who was the son of a common soldier. The culprit was arrested, and disappeared into Iran's system of prisons, tortures and hangings. It is safe to assume that the Shah, while a petulant tyrant, could not have approved of the unfortunate being executed for calling a cat a king, but then he would not have known about it. Rulers more than anyone else may complain that they really cannot be expected to keep an eye on everything. Our age of terrors is often characterised by the grotesque, the inconsequent, the simply silly, and this incident is such a perfect example it must be cherished by connoisseurs of the politically surreal. But surely what must interest us is not the Shah, nor even the victim, whose fate is too familiar to merit much notice, but the state of mind of the man responsible. If, as is usual, the machinery of the secret police was simply transferred from shah to ayatollahs, then the same official was probably at it for years, but he must have retired by now, growing roses and generally cultivating his garden. How does he see himself? Is he secretly thinking, but what got into me? *What got into me* is the secret theme of the thinking of successive waves of people who were part of persecution's machineries, but later became appalled at the past – at themselves. As for the many citizens who thought, 'And quite right too, he shouldn't have insulted our dear Shah', then there isn't much to be done about them, for the lovers of authority, no matter how cruel, will always be with us. And they will have forgotten about it by now, as the white supporters of apartheid may now murmur, 'I was always a bit of a liberal you know.'

Direct and unambiguous censorship, as part of state control, is easier to combat than the indirect results of it. Books, works of art, and their authors, may be banned, reviled, made non-books and non-people, but what is hard to see is a prevailing wind of opinion, most particularly if it blows fitfully. Jack Cope, the writer, having been a communist, wanted a passport to leave South Africa, where he was under threat. At last he found himself sitting opposite the relevant official. 'Ach, hell, Mr Cope, look at it from our point of view. How can we give you a passport? You are a commie and you are a liberal too.' Impasse. Recently Jack had written a little tale about a bird caught in power lines. A linesman saw it, notified base, the machinery for power was shut down for the district, a man climbed up and rescued the bird, and with tears in his eyes watched it fly away. The official with life and death in his hands – passports were that then – confessed he hadn't read Jack's books, he didn't read commie books, but he remembered a nice little story, and he told Jack the tale of the sparrow. 'I wrote that story,' Jack modestly confessed. 'Ach, hell, man, but that is a nice story.' And he gave Jack his passport. Never say that literature cannot have practical uses. Meanwhile South Africa's prisons, some of the cruellest in the world, continued to flourish, and so did censorship, which was arbitrary, to say the least. For instance, *Black Beauty* was banned, for reasons obvious to the white censor. Many writers' books were banned, mine among them, and then we authors might hear they were on sale somewhere, but then banned again, all this giving rise to much satirical laughter. If you are white – and privileged, or privileged anywhere, then it is easier to maintain a stoical attitude towards persecution, petty or otherwise, and easy to make jokes. The white progressive writers could fight with ridicule, but the appealing little scene of the white immigration official, white writer and released bird could never have happened with a black writer, and they fled from the country when they could. But I wonder about the books not written, and here I come to my concern. When certain winds blow they wither everything that is unprotected. Let us imagine a poor black man – these days it could be a woman – who has managed because of frightful sacrifices by his parents, and then himself, sometimes walking miles to school every day, to get himself some kind of certificate, and with that, a clerk's job. He has read enough to know that his everyday experiences could make tales that would be printed and admired. He dreams of writing them. But he lives, let us say, in old Soweto, and his working conditions make it hard for him to sustain creative energy, and then he cannot help observing how the black writers still in South Africa are treated. Those who have fled, sometimes a few steps in front of the police, are in exile in London and New York and in universities which these days so often give shelter to victims of persecution. He heard some are drinking too much, dying young, often not writing much. In the evenings he sits at a table where his mother and then his wife have cleared the supper things, he lights the oil lamp, he gets out his exercise book, he takes up his biro, and then – he stops. What he would like to write about are his daily struggles, the miseries of poverty, the attentions of the police, the efforts of his women to feed him and the children, how it feels to watch and – this is the worst – how his talented children are going to waste. He knows that simply to describe his life could be seen as an act of sedition; these days everyone knows what the daily lives of people are in luckier countries. He sits on, staring at the bricks of his wall, which he may have built himself. Would he have to leave his home, his family? Who would look after them? His exercise book remains empty. His own talents, let alone his children's, will remain unfulfilled.

How many of such people were there? How many now in various parts of the world? In Zimbabwe the police may sit in on writers' meetings, nothing secret about it; or they harass writers, or influence reviewers and editors against them. They drop in to say to a writer they hear such and such a book is being planned, but it would be better to think again. At this very moment, everywhere from China to Indonesia to South America to parts of Africa, a woman or man is thinking, But I daren't write it. Talent is not necessarily allied to a readiness for martyrdom, or even courage. Why should it be? Such is our time's history that our paradigm has to be an Ernst Toller, Solzhenitsyn, the killed or persecuted writers of some Muslim countries. A good thing for writers to be talented, but to be noticed it is even better if they are in prison or fighting cancer or, like Rushdie, sentenced to death. Writers as victims, that's our mental set, but we scarcely notice the wasted or disappointed ones.

There are times and places when we collude with tyranny, in ways more direct than simply not noticing what goes on. In the old Soviet Union writers might claim proudly that they were developing censors that stopped them writing anything critical about communism. A shocking thing: but we all have inner censors, and often don't suspect it. It is hard to step outside a prevailing way of thinking, particularly when you are convinced you are living in a free society. If you travel outside your culture, let's say to the Fat East, or to a Muslim country or even somewhere in the United States, you may catch a glimpse of how we seem to others – or are not seen at all. In Iowa or Dakota for many people a state boundary can be their horizon. Britain – what's that? In China Europe seems simply to drop over the edge of the world. If Europe ceased to exist tomorrow millions of people would not even notice.

An interesting indication of how we think is books that do not get published, or, if they do, are scarcely noticed. One example, among many: Arthur Deikman's book *The Wrong Way Home*, about cults and their characteristics. By now we are pretty well informed about cults, but Deikman went on to point out that many of our institutions, from big businesses to gentlemen's clubs, share the characteristics of cults. Surely there could not be a more useful tool for examining our culture – but no. It was ignored. Perhaps it was too close to the bone.

The most powerful mental tyranny in what we call the free world is Political Correctness, which is both immediately evident, and to be seen everywhere, and as invisible as a kind of poison gas, for its influences are often far from the source, manifesting as a general intolerance. The history books will say something like this: 'When the certitudes of communism began to dissolve then collapsed with them – but slowly in some countries – the dogmas of Socialist Realism; but at once stepped into the vacuum Political Correctness. This began as a sensitive, honest and laudable attempt to remove the racial and sexual biases encoded in language, but it was at once taken over by the political hysterics, who made of it another dogma. In no time, from one end of the world to the other, everyone was saying, "It is Politically Correct", "I am afraid it isn't Politically Correct", as if ordered to do so. There could hardly be a conversation without it, and PC was used often as the Victorians used "It isn't done", meaning socially improper, or to bolster the orthodoxies of "received opinion", or even to criticise the eccentric. The new tyranny soon took over whole universities, particularly in the United States, departments of universities, colleges, schools, dictating habits of criticism, suffocating thought in some areas of scientific research, dimming the natural ferments of intellectual life. The submission to the new creed could not have happened so fast and so thoroughly if communist rigidities had not permeated the educated classes everywhere, for it was not necessary to have been a communist to absorb an imperative to control and limit: minds had already been thoroughly subdued to the idea that free enquiry and the creative arts must be subject to the higher authority of politics.'

Truly, we cannot stand being free. Mankind – humankind – loves its chains, and hastens to forge new ones if the old ones fall away.

The trouble is that people who need the rigidities, dogmas, ideologies, are always the most stupid, so Political Correctness is a self-perpetuating machine for driving out the intelligent and the creative. It is forming a class of people – researchers, journalists, particularly educators – who are exiles in their own culture, sometimes kept in inferior work, or even unemployed, and yet they are often the best, the most innovative, the most flexible.

In a certain prestigious university in the United States two male faculty members told me they hated PC but did not dare say so, if they wanted to keep their jobs. They took me into the park to say it, where we could not be overheard, as used to happen in the communist countries. Militant feminists were in charge.

In a good school in California I was taken to task by pupils for Political Incorrectness, in *The Good Terrorist*, which they were being 'taught' in class. Being 'taught' meant going through it to find incorrect thinking. Again, a young teacher took me aside to say she hated what was going on, and she was leaving teaching altogether, because this was what teaching had become.

In Wales I heard of a teacher, much loved by the pupils, who taught literature as it should be, out of her own love and enthusiasm, but she had been eased out of the department. Her ideas were considered old-fashioned. She was the kind of teacher of whom you hear people say: I was so lucky, I had this teacher who taught me to love books.

The sad question has to be, with this pattern so firmly established in our minds, when we do succeed in driving out the nasty new tyranny – if we do – what will replace it? The intolerances of religion were succeeded by communism, their mirror image, which set the stage for Political Correctness. What next? What should we be looking out for, what should we be guarding against?

The Forgotten Soldier, Guy Sajer

This book was put into my hands by a veteran of the campaign in Burma, a particularly nasty theatre of the Second World War. 'You'll never read a better book about being an ordinary soldier. Pity they were Nazis.' I read it with awe at what human beings can stand, and rereadings have not dulled my reactions. Many books are written about war, few by the men who do the bloody work. We are far here from the balanced reports of war correspondents, from the plans of generals, let alone the demented schemes for world conquest of Stalin and Hitler.

Guy Sajer, not yet seventeen, with a French father and a German mother – a First World War alliance – fell in love with military excellence, as he puts it, and joined Hitler's armies. He then had to become all German, and fought with the German armies into and across Russia, retreated, pursued by the Russians and, starving, the only one left alive of his comrades, was advised by a kindly French officer that since his mother was German, not his father – which would have meant him becoming a prisoner – he could join the French administration supervising the collapse of Germany. The German boy, twenty years old, had to reverse his efforts to suppress his French self, was fed and clothed and rehabilitated – his body, not his mind – but not surprisingly became very ill. Which reminds me of a friend who, having survived four years of horror in a Japanese prison camp, people dying all around him of starvation and disease, arrived skeletal but healthy in England, but nearly died of a mild flu.

Could there be an apter symbol of Europe, of Europe's mingled and mangled fates, than this young man? Or a more painfully racked person than Guy Sajer at the Victory Celebrations in Paris, which celebrated the defeat of his Germany, reciting under his breath the names of his dead comrades whose heroism was certainly not being applauded that day, and who were soon to be deliberately forgotten by the new Germany who had to find them an embarrassment?

Years ago I was told that this Guy Sajer was living in Paris, solitary, and bitter that the men, or rather, boys – we have to remind ourselves that we are reading about 18-year-olds, 19-year-olds – had never been credited for their bravery. He has consecrated his life to bearing witness, says that as far as any personal life is concerned, he was burned out. This book could have been called 'A Dead Man Bears Witness'. I think he would have approved. A person may flare like a match and be left a blackened twisted wraith of himself.

They started off, as young men do, high on adventure and patriotism. Sieg Heils and Heil Hitlers are recorded but not made much of. The cloudy patriotic idealism of Nazism does emerge in the speeches of officers trying to justify the war, and Sajer records that he rebuked comrades for lapses in patriotism. What immediately emerges as a major theme is that soldier's preoccupation, food. These youths, at an age when no amount of food can ever be enough, were on rations, and it all gets worse as the war goes on and Germany frays apart: ersatz food, ersatz clothes, and the supply convoys uncertain, or not coming at all. These always hungry young men were fighting like wolves, on air, sometimes for days, then weeks at a time.

The author says that we, sitting comfortably and reading his words in safety, can never understand what he is describing. That is true. 'I cannot find words to describe what I saw. Words and syllables were perfected to describe unimportant things.' This plea to our imaginations repeats throughout his pages.

A comparison presents itself: Solzhenitsyn's *1914*, that account of the confusions of war, masses of men being moved about, chaos everywhere, no one knowing what is going on. These soldiers, making impossible sacrifices, urged on by officers to find in themselves yet another ounce of effort, thought they were supplying the soldiers fighting at Stalingrad, but that front had collapsed. They were being killed in their thousands to support men already dead or taken prisoner. And the tale is told again, again; when the German front was collapsing every-where and the Russians advancing, Sajer and his mates were making efforts to retake a certain sector. Starving and in rags, they were met by starving men in rags. 'Our shock at meeting our combat troops in such a state was equal to theirs finding us as we were.' Two officers confer: 'Where do you think you are going . . . what are you talking about . . . what sector, what hill? – are you dreaming? There is nothing left, do you hear me? Nothing but mass graves which are blowing apart in the wind.' 'You can't be serious . . . you are a little light in the head and you are hungry. We, too, have been keeping ourselves alive by miracles.' 'Yes, I'm hungry, hungry in a way the saints could not have imagined. I'm hungry and I'm sick and I am afraid. I feel like devouring you. There were cases of cannibalism in Stalingrad and soon there will be here too.'

An account of the battle to take a position at Belgorod, ten days of fighting, which Sajer rightly says it is impossible to imagine, must surely be a classic of war. They took it and then the Russians retook it. A third of the German soldiers were killed. Futility, unless heroism is its own justification – and what else can soldiers believe, when there is nothing to show for such efforts? 'There is no sepulchre for the Germans killed in Russia. One day some mujik will turn over their remains and plough them under as fertiliser and sow his furrow with sunflower seed.'

There are rewards of insight into the human condition which it seems the author only too painfully understands.

The famous regiment, Gross Deutschland, for which Sajer volunteered, was trained by a certain Herr Hauptman. We may have read, or seen, how raw youths in this army or that are bullied and bludgeoned into being good soldiers, but all these accounts are like the descriptions of first days in infant school compared with the regime of Herr Hauptman, which we read disbelieving. He killed four men and incapacitated others, and at the finish this sadist said he felt satisfied with his men and with himself. 'It seems scarcely possible that by the time we left we all nourished a certain admiration for Herr Hauptman. Everyone in fact dreamed of someday becoming an officer of the same stripe.'

There is a key question that has to nag and intrude. Nowhere, not once, are Jews mentioned. Yet we know how Hitler's armies were ordered to treat Jews. Is it likely that Gross Deutschland did not follow Hitler's orders, or had not heard of them? There are accounts of cruelties by the German side and by the Russians. Both killed or abandoned prisoners and the wounded, sometimes their own. There are also incidents showing compassion. A starving soldier rescued a bottle of half-sour milk that was the only food of a baby, only to be killed by enraged comrades. But never a mention of Jews. What are we to believe? Yet there are surprises you would think were impossible. Throughout the Ukraine in the early days of the war the Germans were welcomed as deliverers, fed, given shelter, found girlfriends, among people who hated the communists. Captured partisans shouted that they were anti-communist and on the same side as the Germans. But here is another surprise.

The Germans did not seem to hate the Popovs, the Ivans, the Russkies, as much as they did the partisans, who aroused in Sajer paroxysms of hate. They were unfair, played dirty, were treacherous and generally disgusting. No mercy for partisans, only loathing. There is no end to the sheer irrationality of – well, of us, of humans.

'Russian excesses do not in any way excuse us for the excesses of our own side. War always reaches depths of horror because of idiots who perpetuate terror from generation to generation under the pretext of vengeance.'

The long finale of this account of every kind of excess is the retreat into Germany, before the Russian armies. No food. Uniforms in rags. One after another Sajer's friends were killed. 'To watch a friend die is like dying oneself.'

And in the middle of this long nightmare notes of pure farce. If Sajer and his comrades hated the partisans, they hated even more their own military police, who would appear fresh and fed to punish half-crazed men more dead than alive just emerged from days of battle – for having lost a bit of equipment.

Soldiers who had not eaten for days and could hardly stand, saw an abandoned supply vehicle and raided it. Two were hanged by the police with a label around their necks, 'I am a thief and a traitor to my country.'

The battles to preserve bridgeheads along the Baltic and North Sea coasts so that refugees and surviving soldiers could be taken off in boats were as terrible as any that had gone before. At last Sajer was rescued and became French, repeating under his breath the names of dead comrades who by now would be old men honoured in anniversary Victory parades if the infamous history of Hitler's Barbarossa permitted it.

Sajer never says that he admired the Nazis and that is why he found his way to the German side. He was not seventeen, and both France and Germany were afflicted by every kind of extremist idea, communist, fascist, anarchist. In peacetime early errors of judgement are put down to youthful fervour and forgiven, but his error was unforgivable and nearly finished him for good. He does not say anywhere that he made a mistake; probably the memories of his dead comrades forbid, but when he repeats the names he will never forget, Hals, Lindberg, Pferham, Sollers, there is another name he says he must forget, and that name is Guy Sajer.

'People who hated me pursued me with vindictiveness, seeing in the past only cupidity and culpable error. Others might some day understand that man can love the same virtues on both sides of a conflict, and pain is international.'

I cannot think of another book that is such a protest against human destiny, and which succeeds so well in what he attempted. 'To reanimate with all the intensity I can summon, those distant cries from the slaughterhouse.'

His achievement is that it is not only the German soldiers we see as we read, but the Russians he was fighting, and all the soldiers of the great battles and wars of our time. Verdun and Passchendaele, Stalingrad, Kursk, Vietnam . . . but the list would fill pages; so that it seems in our imaginations take shape millions, multitudes, of very young men, dead young men, who stand, ironical ghosts, watching us scratch around in our dusts.

Sajer says he has learned the power of forgiveness. Is it the Führer he has to forgive? The Russians who ploughed their tanks again and again into the retreating crowds of civilians, mostly old people and women and children, along the shores of the North Sea? The military police who hanged his two comrades for stealing a couple of tins of ersatz food? But probably it is History itself – for in the face of such enormities it is comforting to take refuge in abstractions.

Preface to *Ecclesiastes*, King James Version

It is something of an undertaking, to write even a few words about a text that has inspired mountains of exegetics, commentaries, analyses, over so many centuries, and in so many languages: and you have not read one word. Immodesty, it could be called, and when I allow myself to think about my audacity, I do feel a little breeze of elation which, considered, turns out to be a mild attack of panic. But most readers will be in the same innocent condition, if they have read Ecclesiastes at all. Once, and not so long ago, everybody in Britain, and for that matter everyone in the Christian world, was subjected to that obligation, going to church, where every Sunday was heard the thundering magnificence of this prose, and so, ever after, they would have been able to identify the origin of phrases and sayings which are as much a part of our language as Shakespeare. These days, if someone hears, 'There is a time to be born and a time to die . . .' they probably do think it is Shakespeare, since the Bible these days is the experience of so few. Ecclesiastes? Who's he! But an innocent, even an ignorant, reader may discover a good deal by using simple observation.

The book begins with a description. 'The words of the Preacher, the son of David, king in Jerusalem.' That is to say, the words have been collected from notes, or memories, of the Preacher, by disciples or pupils or friends, and made into a whole: probably after he was dead. He did not himself make this book, and it is tempting to remember that he said, 'Of the making of books there is no end, and in much study is a weariness of the flesh.' Other great teachers, such as Socrates, Jesus, Confucius, many others, refrained from making books and testaments, leaving this task to other people. Why did they not see the necessity to preserve their 'image' or to edit a testament to make sure that posterity would see them as they saw themselves? Was the reason that they knew their influence – what they said, how they lived – had impressed their pupils and their contemporaries so strongly in their lifetime that written records were superfluous? I think it is worthwhile to at least consider this possiblity.

It is not until the twelfth verse that we hear his own words, with 'I, the Preacher, was king over Israel, in Jerusalem.' He tells us he devoted himself to the acquisition of wisdom, which is the task given to the sons of men by God, but there was pain in it. 'For in much wisdom there is much grief; and he that increaseth knowledge increaseth sorrow.' So then he decided to experience pleasure and the satisfactions of worldly accomplishment. He built houses and planted gardens and vineyards and orchards; he made pools and streams; he acquired male and female servants and all kinds of possessions, and silver and gold, and male and female singers. Whatever he had a fancy to have – so he tells us – he got; he was like the people now who decide that they are going to have a good time and not care about serious things. But then, having done all that, he had a good long look at his life and his property and his riches and knew it was all vanity and vexation of spirit (vanity in the sense of futility, illusion) and that happiness is not to be found in pleasure and that wisdom is better – making a full circle, one might say, if it were not that even a casual reading reveals that verse by verse this is contradictory stuff, a confusing message – if he ever intended what he said to be considered as a message. What we have here is sayings from different occasions, and different contexts, and with different people. There is a deep and terrible need in us all to systematise and make order, and perhaps it is helpful to imagine this material in a pre-book stage, when it was scribbled notes made when listening to the Preacher; or what happened when pupils met after he was dead: 'What do you remember of him? And you? And you?'

What unites the book is precisely that this is some of the most wonderful English prose ever written. My father, young at a time when not to accept church religion was to invite persecution and social ostracism, said that Sunday, when he had to go to church three times, and also to Sunday school, was like a great black hole every week, but later said that it was listening to the prose of the Bible and the prayer book that taught him to love language and good literature. Generations of writers have been influenced by the rhythms of the Bible, which may be observed in the prose of the best of them – as well as the worst – and we are very much the poorer because the Bible is no longer a book to be found in every home, and heard every week.

From the very first verse of Ecclesiastes you are carried along on a running tide of sound, incantatory, almost hypnotic, and it is easy to imagine yourself sitting among this man's pupils, listening to, for instance, 'Remember now thy creator in the days of thy youth, while the evil days come not, nor the years draw nigh when thou shalt say, I have no pleasure in them.' Your ears are entranced, but at the same time you are very much alert. You have to be old to understand that verse, to see your whole life, from early heedlessness to present regret for heedlessness; you find yourself drifting off into speculation. Was this particular admonition addressed to young people, to remind them that old age will come for them too? Or reserved for grey heads who would hear it with the ears of experience? Or flung out in an assembly to be caught by anyone who could – who had the ears to hear, as Jesus put it.

Towards the end, verse 9 of chapter 12, suddenly it is not his voice, not 'I' speaking, and we are back to description; '. . . because the Preacher was wise, he still taught the people knowledge; yea, he gave good heed, and sought out, and set in order many proverbs'. That is how one contributor to the book saw what Ecclesiastes was doing. And, yet again, we are reading a document that to us is ancient, but it records people who saw themselves as successors in a long line, stretching back into their antiquity.

Between the man, Ecclesiastes, and ourselves, are many veils. One is translation. Over the exact meaning of a word or phrase scholars have laboured and many sermons have been delivered in churches. That word 'Preacher' for instance. In what other ways could the original have been translated? 'Preacher' is so much a concept from organised Christianity, which spawned preachers by the thousand men (and now women) standing in pulpits to expound their views of life to a congregation, and their quite amazing intimacy with God's thinking. Should that 'Preacher' have been 'Teacher'? – a very different thing.

Another barrier is the nature of the people who recorded the words, or who remembered them. We all know that what we say to a friend will be filtered through the character and experience of that person, and it is safe to assume that Ecclesiastes' pupils were not on the same level as he was, any more than Jesus's disciples were on his level, and that they, like us, had to strain to understand a nobility of mind that was beyond their ordinary selves. There is a little cry of despair in this text, the tale of a small city, besieged by a great king; a poor wise man saved the city, and yet no one remembered the poor man. 'Wisdom is better than strength' is the conclusion, 'nevertheless, the poor man's wisdom is despised and his words not heard.'

There is an interesting deduction or two to be made. This man was the son of David, that is to say, of the Royal House of David, at a time when kings were considered to be God-chosen and God-inspired. The word 'ecclesiastic' now means a clergyman, or describes a clergyman, or what appertains to churches. There is a little encapsulated history here: this 'Preacher' was no churchman, and nowhere does he mention a church: thus do the living springs of knowledge, of wisdom, become captured by institutions, and by churches of various kinds.

Writing Autobiography

At the very end of his life Goethe said that he had only just learned how to read. He was the most distinguished man of letters in Europe, one of a galaxy of literary eminences, so he wasn't talking about his ABC. So what was this very old man talking about, when he said he had only just learned how to read?

I have put this at the beginning of my essay because it illustrates what a long time it sometimes takes to learn things. Writing volume 1 of my autobiography I learned a good deal I didn't expect, and I was amazed at myself because it had taken so long. You always learn when writing a book. It is a fact as yet unknown to science that when you tackle a new subject then suddenly it is everywhere, on the television, in the newspapers, on the radio, people start talking about it, an overheard conversation on a bus – there it is again, and a book falls open at just that relevant place. This is a quite astonishing phenomenon, but, like many others, we take it for granted. I am not however talking about that kind of learning, but what happens when you say, 'Good God, how was it I didn't see that before! It's perfectly obvious!' I have been reading biographies and autobiographies all my life, yet I have never actually sat down to think about the differences between them, nor the differences between them and novels. Yet the very moment I began to think seriously, the problem began to bristle with difficulties.

One reason I didn't expect anything different *in kind* was that I had written autobiographical pieces before, for instance, *In Pursuit of the English*. That little book has a good deal in common with a novel. Not that it isn't true – it is true enough except for some things changed for libel purposes. It is more a question of a tone, a pace. It has the feel of a novel. And this raises such questions that I shall have to leave it right there. The tone, or 'voice' of a novel – what it is, why it is – is probably the most important thing you can say about it. Certainly the book has a shape like a novel. I'll come back to shape.

The fact is, novels, autobiographies and biographies have a lot in common. One thing is something we take for granted: they are all written down. What we take for granted is often the most important thing and we don't examine it. We take for granted that novels, autobiographies and biographies are sitting up there on a shelf, tidy, self-contained books, complete – *written down*. The truth.

For many thousands of years we – the human race – told stories to one another: tales told, or sung. Not written down. Fluid. Biography of our kind is quite new; I suppose Boswell's *Life of Johnson* is the first. Autobiography of our kind? Cellini, Casanova were the first, I think: fixed and permanent records, something you can lift from a shelf, and quote from. Extracts that appear in think-pieces and theses, and then travel to other theses and books: immutable – the Truth.

The reason why people feel uneasy and disturbed when their lives are put into biographies is precisely because something that is experienced as fluid, fleeting, evanescent, has become fixed, and therefore lifeless, without movement. You can't appeal against the written word, except by more written words, and then you are committed to polemic. Memory isn't fixed: it slips and slides about. It is hard to match one's memories of one's life with the solid fixed account of it that is written down. Virginia Woolf said that living was like being inside a kind of luminous envelope. I would add to that 'inside a moving, flickering luminous envelope, like a candle flame in a draught'.

Our own views of our lives change all the time, different at different ages. If I had written an account of myself aged 20 it would have been a belligerent and combative document. At 30 – confident and optimistic. At 40 – full of guilt and self-justification. At 50 – confused, self-doubting. But at 60 and after something else has appeared: you begin to see your early self from a great distance. While you can put yourself back inside the 10-year-old, the 20-year-old, any time you want, you are seeing that child, that young woman, as – almost – someone else. You float away from the personal. You have received that great gift of getting older – detachment, impersonality.

Once I read autobiography as what the writer thought about her or his life. Now I think, 'That is what they thought *at that time*.' An interim report – that is what an autobiography is. Would Cellini, would Casanova, would even Rousseau, later have agreed with what they said about themselves in those books that we assume is the fixed truth about what they thought?

It was much easier when the talk about each other or about ourselves was oral. For thousands of years, when storytelling was oral, there was autobiography, but very different from ours, just as biography was different. Here is a fragment of autobiography from just over a thousand years ago.

Egil Skalla Grimsson wrote the poem which will be found in his saga, an old man, lonely, despondent, after all the activity of his life. His sons were dead, his god had betrayed him. Poetry, he said, wasn't easily drawn any more 'from the hiding-place of thought' but he composes, he mourns, and can say for himself, and for others, in conclusion:

> It is bad with me
> now, the Wolf, Death's
> sister, stands on the headland,
> but gladly, without fear
> and steadfast shall
> I wait for Hel,
> goddess of death.[1]

This little verse, part of a long saga, must have been told or sung by dozens of storytellers or singers, in the halls of queens, kings, chieftains, or in gatherings of robbers in the forests. They felt no need to stick to an exact pattern of words.

Between those story-tellers and us is a great gulf, and that *is* the gulf. Many different kinds of men and women were described by that verse. The man whose words I read is strongly characterised. He is stoic, brave, full of self-respect. Now let us imagine a different kind of man – nervous, fearful. The people listening will have known the saga by heart, and while they listen their brains are doing two different things, checking for the familiar, but delightedly anticipating the new – what this teller will do with the old words, on this occasion.

> Oh dear, I don't feel well,
> I saw the wolf today,
> We all know what that means,
> I have bad dreams.
> I am afraid of the goddess of death.

---

1 Quoted from Geoffrey Grigson, *A Private Art: A Poetry Notebook* (London: Allison & Busby, 1982), 82.

I am a child of our culture, which has depended for some hundreds of years on print, and so I feel guilty when I change sacred print. I have to set aside guilt to do what storytellers and singers did as a matter of course. Let us try another kind of person.

> Guess what!
> I saw the wolf today.
> You don't have to tell me what *that* means.
> So what! I'm not scared of that old bag
> the goddess of death.

These old people depicted themselves in broad bold strokes. They didn't go in for our kind of psychologising – no subtlety, no complexity. That would not have suited the sweep of the saga, the epic, the kind of story that had to hold the attention of listening serfs and soldiers and servants as well as the lords and ladies who were more educated, though probably not much more.

Psychology came in with print, with the explosion of the written word: Proust, Mann, Woolf, Joyce were the products of the print revolution.

There must have been a great change in the structure – the physical structure – of our brains when print was invented. Suddenly books were being printed by the thousand all over Europe by printing presses we now think of as primitive, yet they made some of the most beautiful books ever created. We haven't yet come to terms, I think, with that revolution. Have we ever asked *what* changes took place in our brains then, when people began to read instead of to listen? It was a process that went on in stages. People did not just pick up a book and begin reading in the way we do. St Augustine describes how he was reading, and suddenly thought, 'but I don't have to mouth the words as I read, I can read silently'. Monks read aloud, as did anyone who actually owned books. Then they read silently but mouthed the words. Then they realised they did not have to shape the words with their lips. The process was complete.

We are on the verge of another revolution as powerful – we are living through it in fact – the electronic revolution. This is evidently affecting our brains. I can observe the process in myself: my attention span is shortening. Probably it is because of television, the way we constantly switch attention from one channel to another, but we don't really know the reason. We have no idea what the end of it all will be, any more than the people knew who lived through the print revolution. We can say either that we are a very careless species, recklessly undertaking great changes without asking what the result will be, or that we are helpless in the face of our own inventions.

To return to the immediate problems of novels, autobiographies, biographies. There is one way autobiographies have to differ from novels. Novels don't have to be the truth. Autobiographies do have to be. At least the attempt must be made. And this brings us to Memory. What memories can we trust? Only the slightest of thoughts on the subject shows that memories are about as dependable as soap bubbles. I think there are two kinds of memory that we can rely on.

One. You are very small. You are looking up at enormously tall people. The door handle is out of reach. Chairs and sofas are great cumbersome obstacles. A cat is almost as big as you are. The dog is much bigger. The ceiling is almost out of sight. Everything is an assault on your senses. Smells are very strong. Every surface has a different texture, a different world. Sounds are so various you spend a lot of your time trying to understand them. You are inside a whirlpool of sense impressions, an assault. This is the world of a small child. No adult lives in that world. We have blocked most of it out long ago. No adult could live in that world: they wouldn't be able to do anything else but try to remain steady while sounds, scents, sights, insist on being understood. These are reliable memories: the hot slippery surface of a horse's neck, the strong smell of the horse. The sharp cutting edges of stone steps, where you descend, as if going down a mountain side.

Two. The other class of memory I think you can rely on is events that have happened repeatedly, day after day.

The memories that are not reliable are probably most of those about our older childish selves. Parents create memories for their children. 'See this photo? That's you, there. Do you remember, we went down every weekend to the park, and you fed the ducks, and then we had a picnic under the trees. Do you remember?' And the child remembers, the memory has been made for him or her.

The moment I was suddenly informed how utterly unreliable memories can be was when I met, after years, someone with whom I had been on a trip to Russia, early in the 1950s. This was two weeks of intense experience, and I have strong memories of it. But when I said to this woman, 'Do you remember – this or that', she didn't. She remembered quite different things. We might have been on two quite different trips. Or when I met my brother after many years, and he did not remember things we did together that are among the most powerful memories I have.

Now, in a novel, it doesn't matter: memories true and false become part of the fabric of the story and for a while you become one with the psychotherapists and psychiatrists who say that it doesn't matter if your fantasies are not true: they are diagnostic of your condition. They are the product of your psyche. They are valid. If you are writing autobiography that won't do at all. So you sit there for hours, wondering. Is that true? Did I make it up? What is the truth? Immediately other questions come up and you have to deal with them before getting on with your task, which is writing your autobiography.

And not sitting brooding about all these ideas, for it is not getting the work done.

Why do you remember this and not that? You might remember a weekend, or an hour, or a month in the greatest possible detail, and then there are weeks or months of blank. What you remember so clearly might easily be unimportant. The experts say you remember a certain event or time because something very important was going on. They also say the opposite, that if you forget something – a person or event – it is because it was all very important, but stressful: it is repressed. I think that what makes you remember something, important or unimportant, is that you were particularly awake at the time, paying attention. Most of the time we are in a sort of trance, not noticing much. We are probably thinking about what we will have for our supper or that we must buy medicine for the cat.

If memory is identity then we are indeed in a bad way. Can you remember what you did yesterday? Perhaps yesterday, yes. Three days ago? This time last week? This time last month? Very hard to remember: most of it has gone.

This business of identity I wrote about in my book *Briefing for a Descent into Hell*. A young woman, a friend of mine, was in the psychiatric ward for the local hospital where I was visiting her. Very late one night, she told me, a man was brought in who had been found wandering on the Embankment. He had lost his memory. But so much 'together' was he that the doctors at first thought he was putting on an act, was pretending. He was well dressed and clean. He was obviously educated. He engaged in long conversations about literature and art. If you hadn't been told, you would never have known he had lost his memory. Yet he had. He had no idea who he was, and it took something like six weeks before he remembered. During those six weeks he was all there, a strong, intact presence. Yet he had no memory.

In any case it is such a flickering, fleeting record. Sometimes I feel I could wipe it all away with one sweep of my hand, like brushing away a kind of highly coloured veil or thin rainbow ... and there still sits the autobiographer, uneasy about her memories, about the truth, and the book is not being written.

Why a book at all? Why do we have this need to bear witness? We could dance our stories, couldn't we?

In Binga on the shores of Lake Kariba is a shop where you can buy highly carved sticks on which are carved the histories of the local tribe. There have been cultures that wove stories and histories and information into carpets.

But we tell stories, we have to.

Why? Why a story? We must have a pattern in our minds, and we tell stories because we have to conform to that pattern. We need a shape for the tale. A beginning, a middle and an end. What is the template for that pattern? Only one that we can immediately see: we are born, we grow older, and then we die. Perhaps that is the template. Perhaps that is why we need to know what will happen next when we read or hear a story. This is so strong that even if you are in, let's say, a dentist's waiting room, and you are reading some truly rubbishy tale, you still need to know the end and hope it will not be time to be called in to the dentist until you have finished it. Yet you don't care at all for the actual tale: you have to know what is going to happen next.

So, when you are shaping an autobiography, just as when you shape a novel, you have to decide what to leave out. Novels are given shape by leaving out. Autobiographies have to have a shape, and they can't be too long. Just as with a novel, you have choice: you have to choose. Things have to be left out. I had far too much material for the autobiography. Yet it should be like life, sprawling, big, baggy, full of false starts, loose ends, people you meet once and never think of again, groups of people you meet for an evening or a week and never see again. And so as you write your autobiography it has to have a good deal in common with a novel. It has a shape: the need to make choices dictates that. In short, we have a story. What doesn't fit into the story, the theme, gets cut out.

I wrote a novel once called *The Marriages between Zones Three, Four and Five*. I had the material for that novel for years, but could not find the way to do it. Suddenly I found it. The solution was simple, as solutions usually are. I decided I had to use the storyteller's voice. The storyteller is in everyone and we tell stories all the time. When we come back from the supermarket and say to whoever is here, 'You'll never guess what I saw. Bridget was in the supermarket, and she wasn't with her husband, she was with that young fellow from the hotel . . .', and you're off, and your listener wants to know what happens next, even if she or he cares nothing about Bridget, nor about the young fellow from the hotel. The storyteller is sexless, ageless, timeless, is thousands of years old, and not culture-bound. Folk tales and jokes travel across frontiers, always have, always will.

There is another interesting little paradox when you think about novels and autobiographies. We are now familiar with the idea that in each one of us live several personalities. This is easier to see in other people than in ourselves. The extreme case was Sybil, about whom there was written a book, and there was a film and television. She had, it seems, up to thirty-odd separate personalities. I am not talking about roles. A man is a brother, husband, son, father, etc. A woman is a sister, wife, daughter, mother, and so on. Roles are not personalities.

One of the ways one can use novels is to see the different personalities in novelists. Dickens is very useful for this. You can see the same personalities appearing in novel after novel, perhaps different sexes, different ages, but obviously the same. These are the personalities that make up Dickens. You are looking at a map of Dickens – what he is. And the same with other novelists. Now here is the paradox. It is easier to see this map of a person in their novels than in the autobiography. That is because an autobiography is written in one voice, by one person, and this person smooths out the roughness of the different personalities. This is an elderly, judicious, calm person, and this calmness of judgement imposes a unity. The novelist doesn't necessarily know about her own personalities. But when the same character keeps popping up in novel after novel, then you have to think. In me somewhere is a delinquent girl or boy, or at least defective in some way, if not young, a non-coper, and clearly this creature is lurking or latent. 'Oh there you are again,' I say, as there is yet another appearance, and you have to be somewhat fearful: under what circumstances would this inadequate person appear in life, come off the page into reality? And you think, 'Well, I wouldn't like *you* very much, if I met you.'

An autobiography – or for that matter a biography – uses a lot of novelist's tricks. These are not necessarily used consciously – if you have been at it for decades, you have learned the tricks so thoroughly the material demands them and you use them, and only afterwards, reading what you've written, think: 'Oh, that was what I was doing, was I!'

For instance, in *Under my Skin* I have a piece about a small girl – me – lying down in the afternoon, and her mother – my mother. It is about time, the different ways children, young people, middle-aged people, old people, experience time. I sometimes say 'I, me', and sometimes say, 'the child'. I say 'my mother', but sometimes 'she'. And there is a point where I suddenly change tone, and say 'the woman'. My mother is writing a letter home to England, as, at that time, the wives of farmers did: when they wrote letters to England they were writing *home*. And I say, 'the woman who' – and when I did that I made it general: she becomes all the farmers' wives writing letters home. This whole section could be a novel, one of the big loose novels, like Dreiser's or Thomas Wolfe's (the old one, not the journalist), some of Christina Stead's, Faulkner's.

There is another problem, a major one. It is a question of the first person, and the third person – when to use what. The first person, autobiography, the 'I', in fact holds the reader at a distance, and this is strange, since on the face of it 'I' should be – surely – an invitation to the reader: 'Come on, nothing is being held back, here I am, no disguises.' But really it is much harder to identify with an 'I' than with 'he', or 'she'.

Let us get back to that little verse.

> Things don't go well with me now.
> The wolf, death's sister,
> Stands on the headland,
> But bravely and with a stout heart
> I am waiting for the goddess of death.

I wouldn't find it all that easy to be familiar with that 'I': a self-contained and dignified man. But let us make it 'he'.

> Things aren't too good for him now.
> The wolf, death's sister,
> Stands on the headland,
> But bravely and with a stout heart
> He waits for the goddess of death.

This man is much easier to approach. The 'I' distances you, insists on a sort of privacy. 'He' could be you.

And when you change it to 'she', then suddenly you are in a most contended-for area.

It's not too good for her now . . .
Bravely and with a stout heart
She waits for the goddess of death.

At once we are in a quite different kind of story. As soon as you use the word 'she' the associations crowd in, in this case, probably a wise woman with her herbs and friendly attendant crow, or a woman warrior, or some beautiful but ageing queen. And from each of these spring all kinds of ideas that have nothing to do with the situation of an old person waiting for death.

Suppose it went:

I, an old woman, find life hard,
The wolf –

That 'I' defines, excludes, makes exact.

A quotation from Goethe – Goethe again – seems to me to go to the heart of the problem, of how we judge, how we read. It is from his autobiography.

Hence it is everybody's duty to inquire into what is internal and peculiar in a book which particularly interests us, and at the same time, above all things, to weigh in what relation it stands to our own inner nature, and how far, by that vitality, our own is excited and rendered fruitful. On the other hand, everything external that is ineffective with respect to ourselves, or is subject to a doubt, is to be consigned over to criticism, which, even if it should be able to dislocate and dismember the whole, would never succeed in depriving us of the only ground to which we hold fast, nor even in perplexing us for a moment with respect to our once-formed confidence.

This conviction, sprung from faith and sight, which in all

cases that we recognise as the most important, is applicable and strengthening, lies at the fountain of the moral as well as the literary edifice of my life, and . . .[2]

And, with Goethe, back to the beginning of this essay, when he said he was an old man and had only just learned how to read. What did he mean? I think that he had learned a certain passivity in reading, taking what the author is offering, and not what the reader thinks he should be offering, not imposing himself (herself) between the author and what should be emanating from the author. That is to say, not reading the book through a screen of theories, ideas, political correctness, and so forth. This kind of reading is indeed difficult, but one can learn this sort of passive reading, and then the real essence and pith of the author is open to you. I am sure everyone has had the experience of reading a book and finding it vibrating with aliveness, with colour and immediacy. And then, perhaps some weeks later, reading it again and finding it flat and empty. Well, the book hasn't changed: you have.

---

2 *Poetry and Truth: From my Own Life*, part III, bk XII, trans. John Oxenford, 2 vols. (London: H. G. Bonn, 1848–9), II, 131–2.

The Amazing Victorian: A Life of George Meredith

We all know the Victorian writers, Dickens, Thackeray, George Eliot, Trollope, Hardy, even Gissing. But there is one, in his time as celebrated as any of them, who is forgotten. George Meredith was admired by his peers. Stevenson, for instance, said that he was 'out and away the greatest force in English letters'. He was commended by most critics, even while some complained of his difficulty. He had fervent readers. Yet now the literary departments hardly know his name. Mervyn Jones's fine book is an attempt to rescue a great writer from undeserved oblivion. It is a fascinating read, and solid, well researched and reliable.

Meredith was the son of a tailor, but as befits a time of social mobility, his relatives married up and down the social scale. He described his childhood with bitterness and pain, his father as a muddler and a fool, his mother as handsome, refined and witty. She died when he was five and he became a ward in Chancery, his father being unable to support him. At fourteen, already expected to be an adult, he was sent to school in Germany. This was a period when English intellectuals knew German, and read German literature and philosophy. Meredith was always a European, cosmopolitan in his books and in his thinking.

He doggedly prepared himself to be a writer. His first book was *The Shaving of Shagpat*; influenced by *The Thousand and One Nights*, it was madly idiosyncratic. It was applauded, by George Eliot for one. His second, *The Ordeal of Richard Feverel*, announced his preoccupations. It entrances some, others loathe it (Katherine Mansfield, for instance, whose vehemence seems to me suspect). In the 1960s, I watched a houseful of teenagers snatching this novel out of each other's hands. It is about a well-meaning father, autocratic, sententious, who intends to produce a perfect offspring – his son. He destroys him. The youngsters admired its wild, exaggerated language, its swoops into farcical comedy, the Dickens-like housekeeper, Mrs Berry, whose advice to young brides is 'kissing don't last, cookery do'. They loved the cast of eccentrics commenting like a chorus on the father's follies, and above all they wept over the young lovers, immured in separate rooms, heartbreakingly calling to each other.

This pattern – the obtuse idealistic bully, his female mentor, the ironic observers – recurs, as does the lively brave young woman who defies Fate (which then had to be an unlikeable marriage). Here is a gallery of attractive heroines. No simpering, modest girls in Meredith's work; they defended themselves with wit and with courage, were clear-eyed about the situation of women, and critical of marriage as an institution.

The Egoist is, for me, the distillation of Meredith, a cool, witty, intelligent novel. I could in another mood say *The Amazing Marriage*, which includes almost as much of socialist politics as it does of the logics of the heart. Some people prefer *Diana of the Crossways*, because of its spirited heroine.

Meredith was much admired as a poet: some believed that as a poet his name would survive. He was influenced by Darwin, and his long poem *Modern Love* was seen as pioneering thought on love and marriage, both in rapid evolution. What he has left behind are poetic phrases whose origin we have forgotten. 'Ah, what a dusty answer gets the soul / When hot for certainties in this our life.'

He became a reader for Chapman, quietly influential, encouraging young writers, women, too. He believed women could and should write as seriously as men, and was scornful of those who wrote sentimental romances, rejecting *East Lynne*, and Ouida's first novel, thus losing a fortune for Chapman.

A novel that has been unfashionable and 'too reactionary' through much of its existence is *The Tragic Comedians*. A notorious revolutionary, Alvan, based on Ferdinand Lassalle and, some say, Marx's appalling son-in-law, loves an aristocratic girl, Clothilde. So far, conventional enough. The story is really a description of an emotional power struggle. Alvan wants her to elope with him – she refuses. Later, when she is locked up by her parents and is ready, not to say anxious, to elope, he refuses, insisting that he has to be recognised by her circle and her society, thus revealing himself as a poseur and an opportunist. Surely now this novel's cool hawk's viewpoint could be admired as it deserves: it is a true comic novel. It is out of print. Those critics who complained that Meredith's writing was too rich a mix have triumphed. Virginia Woolf said, 'He will be forgotten and discovered and again forgotten and discovered, like Donne and Peacock and Gerard Hopkins.'

You might think that the women's movement of the 1960s would have noticed this passionate partisan of women, this creator of heroines so far in advance of their time . . . but no. He is dead. He is white. He is male. Too bad.

Mervyn Jones has provided summaries of the plots, which are useful, particularly in showing the capacious landscapes of Meredith's mind, but they cannot convey any of the flavour of this most civilised of novelists.

Bulgakov's *The Fatal Eggs*

There were glorious writers in the Stalin period, and some people think Bulgakov was the greatest. *The Master and Margarita* and *The White Guard* are the best-known of his works, but this tale, *The Fatal Eggs*, is unfamiliar even to people who love Russian literature and its continuing vitality and inventiveness. Here we have science fiction, pure and simple, but it owes more to the early days of sci-fi and H. G. Wells, whom he admired, than to the spirit shortly to inform the American golden age of science fiction. In the very first line of *The Fatal Eggs* we are told the date of the events is 1928; more precisely, 16 April. What happening is being commemorated here? – 1928 was not the jolliest of years. A lot of American sci-fi was social criticism or disguised political comment: it has been exasperating to read comments to the effect that science fiction is 'escapist'. It has often foreshadowed real scientific discovery, and sometimes the horrific regimes it describes have been only too real. *The Fatal Eggs* can be seen as a parable about the nature of Soviet communism, though the frame of the tale is a mad scientist of genius and a ray – not a death ray, but one that vitalises – engendering swarms of reptiles, instead of beneficent beasts, because of some mix-up in the laboratory. This is a device much loved in the genre. At the end, when Moscow is about to be destroyed by the monstrous swarms, it is saved because of a cold snap that destroys the tropical creatures, in the nick of time, just as in *The War of the Worlds* the aliens were opportunely destroyed by a virus they had no defences to, like natives of South America and other innocent places after the coming of the Europeans bearing deadly diseases. No aficionado of the genre could fail to be enchanted by this so perfect example. When it was written mad professors of genius and deadly rays were still novelties, embodying the secret fears of ordinary people about what might be going on in the laboratories. This at least hasn't changed, if nowadays our professors are so urbane and their technologies so confident.

How Bulgakov did enjoy writing *The Fatal Eggs*: the exuberance of it, the enjoyment, has to enliven the reader, and make us laugh. His relish in the tale is like what he brings to *The Heart of a Dog*, a more sophisticated story and one which – at least to me – is almost unbearable. Bulgakov was horrified by these amoral scientists. Pavlov was engaged then with his cruel experiments with dogs.

In *The White Guard*, in the midst of the random fighting and arbitrary tides of the Civil War, we find ourselves in a laboratory.

Nikolka took off his cap, noticing the gleaming black blinds drawn low over the windows and a beam of painfully bright light falling on to a desk, behind which was a black beard, a crumpled exhausted face ... he glanced nervously around the walls at the lines of shiny glass-fronted cabinets containing rows of monstrous things in bottles, brown and yellow, like hideous Chinese faces. Further away stood a tall man priest-like in a leather apron and black rubber gloves, who was bending over a long table ... he stared at the patch of bright light that streamed from the shiny strangely contorted lamps, and at the other things: at the nicotine-stained fingers and at the repulsive object lying in front of the professor . . .

It has to be said that this ugly little scene could be excised from the novel without making any difference to it. Then why is it here? Whatever was the experience or the information that inspired *The Fatal Eggs*, *The Heart of a Dog* and this laboratory scene, it went very deep, it must have.

They are protests about the unbearable. Because of the oppression and the censorship of the Soviet regime, nothing could be said openly. *The White Guard*, a realistic novel, had a stormy intermittent life. Fanciful writing had a better chance. *The Master and Margarita* was a protest in imaginative guise. I wonder if that great writer of realistic fiction would have used allegory and disguise at all, had it not been for the censorship? Someone not knowing about the nature of the Soviet regime would have read that book – and these days it is read – without seeing more than 'magic realism' or some such phrase that comforts people who need a tidy shelf with a label to sort out their fiction. But large tracts of it are fact, and it is painful reading, when you know even a little about Soviet reality – know that the book has a basis far from fantasy.

Mikhail Afanasievich Bulgakov was born in Kiev, in 1891. He trained for medicine, but instead became a writer – like Anton Chekhov. He began as a journalist, and this served him well with *The White Guard*, whose prose is taut, concise, but lyrical too. *The Heart of a Dog*, an early work, was not published in his lifetime in Russia, not until 1987. (He died in 1940.) There could not be a colder more contemptuous criticism of Soviet reality. A famous but evidently crazy professor adopts a stray dog and gives it a human heart and pituitary gland. But something goes wrong. The dog becomes the cruellest caricature of a boorish and stupid proletarian spouting revolutionary slogans he doesn't understand.

'A man with the heart of a dog,' say a colleague.

'Oh no, no, no,' says the experimenter, 'for heaven's sake don't insult the dog . . . no, the whole horror of the situation is that now he has a human heart. And about the rottenest heart in all creation.'

The White Guard was published, then suppressed; the play made from it, *The Days of the Turbins*, was produced in 1926 but then was suppressed. Meanwhile Stalin had seen it fifteen times.

In 1930, worn out with the effort to get his books published and his plays put on, Bulgakov petitioned Stalin to be allowed to emigrate. Stalin telephoned him personally, and arranged a job at the Moscow Arts Theatre. There exists a wonderfully persuasive imagined occasion, describing how Bulgakov was summoned to Stalin's presence in the Kremlin. There sits the renowned but hungry author in his Soviet rags and Stalin is summoning underlings, in the peremptory way of the autocrat, 'How is it our famous writer is in such a state? Somebody's head is going to roll . . . Bring him food . . . look at his boots – bring him boots. Bring food . . . bring champagne . . .' Bulgakov thinks, 'At last all my troubles are over. He must lift the censorship now.' It is fantasy: funny, painful, true.

A very odd life Stalin did lead with his writers. I have believed for a long time that Stalin wanted to write but had no talent. It would account for his obsession with literature. He personally oversaw everything published in the Soviet Union. He instructed song-writers how to write patriotic songs. Perhaps that famous little black book, such an enigma, really had in it synopses of plots, rhymes for an epic poem, for each stanza would have to end with some rousing thought: destroyed, killing, death sentence, obliterate, confess, assassinate . . .

Under Stalin, Osip Mandelstam, Pasternak, Solzhenitsyn,

Nadezhda Mandelstam, Akhmatova, Zoshchenko, Babel and many many others were murdered, exiled, tortured, tormented, but Bulgakov was not murdered or tortured or exiled, though he had a bad time of it. If he survived comparatively easily because his portrait of a gentle cultivated family fighting against the Bolsheviks was admired by Stalin whose efforts to exterminate any vestiges of the intelligentsia were so thorough, then that is the sort of irony that flourishes in mad paradoxical times.

Working at the Moscow Arts Theatre Bulgakov wrote plays, one about Molière who had to work, like him, under the eye of the censor, and a novel, *Black Snow*, which was dramatised and performed at the National Theatre in London not long ago: one of the funniest evenings at the theatre I remember. It is about Stanislavsky and his autocratic rule. Bulgakov was no gloomy satirist.

How did Stalin see himself, we may wonder, seeing him like a circus ring-master with a whip lashing at the constellation of writers Fate or the Logic of History had landed him with? Stalin did tend to go on about writers being the engineers of the human soul, but not one of his poets and wordmasters was interested in the kind of Soviet soul he hoped to forge in the fires of Revolution – forgive, but even the mention of Stalin brings on this kind of thing.

The Revolution did badly for Bulgakov in more ways than one. He adored Kiev, evoked so poetically in *The White Guard*, but he did not return to it. Civil war and the necessities of getting a roof over his head and enough to eat kept him in Moscow.

'Mist. Mist, and needle-sharp frost, claw-like frost flowers. Snow, dark and moonless, paling with the approach of dawn. In the distance beyond the City, blue onion-domes sprinkled with stars of gold leaf; and on its sheer eminence above the City the cross of St Vladimir, only extinguished when the dawn crept in across the Moscow bank of the Dnieper.'

Suppose he had stayed a doctor? There is a little book whose title translates as *The Notes of a Young Doctor*, or *A Country Doctor's Notebook*, about a doctor just out of medical school sent to the provinces to a country hospital. He is terrified, knowing his ignorance, but the experienced peasant nurses instruct him in how to do all these things for the first time – deliver a baby, perform dangerous operations. His patients are peasants, uneducated, superstitious, ignorant, 'dark' in mind, and our modern and scientific young doctor is shocked by them. This book has a freshness and liveliness which makes it some people's favourite. An interesting point: the First World War is going on, but its portentous events affect this rural backwater only when a soldier who has run away from the fighting comes home. The little book has an epic quality because of the background of Russia's vastness, the great distances, the weight of the ignorance, the need. You have to read it thinking of the Revolution and the Civil War, just ahead.

War ... Civil War ... Revolution ... Counter-Revolution ... murders and torture and interrogations, laagers and exile and forced labour – infinite suffering, these were the background to Bulgakov's life.

This is how *The White Guard* ends.

Above the bank of the Dnieper the midnight cross of St Vladimir thrust itself above the sinful, bloodstained, snowbound earth towards the grim, black sky. From far away it looked as if the cross-piece had vanished, had merged with the upright, turning the cross into a sharp and menacing sword.

But the sword is not fearful. Everything passes away – suffering, pain, blood, hunger and pestilence. The sword will pass away too, but the stars will remain when the shadows of our presence and our deeds have vanished from the earth. There is no man who does not know that. Why, then, will we not turn our eyes towards the stars. Why? Moscow 1923–1924.

'Now You See Her, Now You Don't'

In 1950 the *Observer* Short Story Competition was won by Muriel Spark's 'The Seraph and the Zambesi'.

The social atmosphere has changed so much that it is hard, from our perspective of heedless hedonism, to recall those surly and combative days at the height of the Cold War, which bred hatreds, suspicions, mendacity. War was believed to be imminent, and it would be started by the Soviet Union or the United States, depending on which camp you were in. The Korean War, whose nastiness has been forgotten, despite the television series *MASH* which compared to the realities seemed like anodyne tomfooleries, poisoned our days and our nights. Britain was still pervaded by a greyish postwar air. Food rationing was only just ending. It was a threadbare cold time.

The advocates of Socialist Realism, whose progenitor was the Soviet Union, sneered at their opponents' views, described as Art for Art's Sake. Unreal debates flourished, such as 'Graham Greene or Edith Sitwell?' and 'C. P. Snow, yes! William Gerhardi – no!', wasting time and the spirit.

These protagonists were shortly to be seen off by the arrival of what was inaccurately but economically called the Kitchen Sink. Disgruntled Osborne, snarling Lucky Jim, not to mention a galaxy of clever young men and a woman or two, mostly from the northern lower classes, were on the way, and here were arriving swallows from Africa, heralding an explosion of writing.

Two periodicals had about them the aura of rightness, of finger-on-the-pulse, the *New Statesman* under Kingsley Martin and the *Observer* under David Astor. Everyone read them. It must not be assumed that winning the stylish *Observer* short story competition meant then what it would now. It was a prodigious debut. This elegant little tale could not have been further from the temper of the time, and I remember reading it with the exhilaration that comes from the unexpected, from agreeable surprise.

Surprising, too, the experience it came out of. Everyone who goes to that part of Africa sees the Victoria Falls. It is not possible to remain unmarked by it. Muriel herself says she found it a spiritual impact. And she was no visitor, she knew the place well: Africa itself was in that tale.

She went out to Southern Rhodesia to marry, before the war.

While I was growing up there a certain brave figure would arrive in our land, the girl from Home who was going to marry a local lad. She was watched by a hundred cold and suspicious eyes: would she measure up or not? This meant, had she brought with her silly liberal ideas from Home that would spoil the kaffirs. Would she conform and become one of us? Most conformed. They had to, having already cast their bread upon the stormy waters of the Slump which was driving so many young people out of Britain, and besides the Second World War was already on the boil. Retreat was not easy. Conformity, even for an ordinary non-political person, wasn't easy either. It was an unpleasant society, for dissident whites, as well as for the blacks. If you were not dedicated to sport, and to conversations that nearly always centred on the Native Problem, seen as being the

fault of your black servants or labourers, if you were not prepared to see the white occupation of the country as 'civilisation'
you were much on your own. Now, I had been brought up with
all that, I knew how to dissemble, and the cost if you didn't. I
used to feel pity for the poor girls from Home, and even now
I feel a kind of retrospective protectiveness for Muriel Spark,
who couldn't have had any idea of what she was getting herself
into. The marriage did badly, but not too much should be made
of this. War marriages tend to fail.

But then there was Muriel on her own and stuck because of
the war. She did a variety of secretarial jobs. On Saturday nights
she danced with the RAF stationed in large numbers in various
parts of Africa, not to mention Canada and Australia. They
must have felt they were sharing exile with this fellow country-
woman. She tried to get a teaching job at the Dominican Convent in Salisbury, but found the nun who interviewed her
anti-Semitic and a bit of a Nazi. This was the same convent I
was in, a decade before. Hard to imagine sane and humorous
Muriel Spark anywhere near this unwholesome place. But she
was in some pretty surprising places, Gwelo, for instance. There
used to be a joke that Salisbury was a mix of a genteel English
country town and the Wild West, but Gwelo lacked any kind
of gentility, was a raw pioneer mining town. Most novelists do
tend to get about a good bit before settling down into the
narrowed life of a working writer. Or perhaps we could agree
that a novelist's talent may be allied to curiosity about other
lives, or at least an aptitude for the varied and the strange. I
cannot think of a better place to be than southern Africa in
wartime to encounter wide varieties of people and situations.
Muriel Spark was a good Scots girl from Edinburgh, and if she
had never left then we might have had different novels. Miss
Brodie commenting from a distance on wartime Africa – now,
that's a thought. But here I am uncomfortably close to sharing

Auden's thoughts on the subject: novelists doomed 'to suffer all the wrongs of man'. And I don't really. This is the belief that if you haven't committed murder or gone off with a handsome fisherman to the Mediterranean then you can't write about murder or handsome fishermen.

Muriel, in Bulawayo, did as many different things as I did in Salisbury. We did not meet then, but we have since compared notes. With so many men 'up north' – that is, fighting Rommel, and then going up into Europe with the Allied armies, women were easily getting jobs. Worth our weight in gold we were, I remember joking with female mates: intangible gold, of course, I can't imagine Muriel had much money to splash about any more than I had. If we had met then we would have had literature in common but perhaps not much else. I was much at home on soapboxes; some of them I now regret, others not, but that kind of thing was not her temperament. We found and treasured *New Writing*, John Lehman's wartime magazine, for it was in the bookshops. I was ordering books from London. They had to dodge the U-boats, in the precarious convoys. It would have been very nice indeed to have had someone like her to discuss them with. She was already on her road: winning a prize at the Eisteddfod for poetry.

Then the war was over and what we were both doing was waiting. Waiting was what millions (and millions) of people were doing during those interminable postwar years. Refugees waited to get back to their homes, if they ever did. Children waited for their fathers, wives for their men, airmen waited for boats to take them home at last, sometimes for years. People stranded like Muriel, waited: there was no air travel for ordinary people then, it was boats that took people between continents. People like me, who had longed for years to leave Rhodesia for London, and whose leaving the war had postponed, waited. Waiting is what our generation is good at: we have learned the hard way. And though this little memoir is not any kind of an attempt at literary criticism, I must mention the story 'Robinson', about a group of survivors on an island, waiting to be taken off, and the paranoias and fidgets and survival mechanisms that develop. There was Muriel in Bulawayo, waiting, and I in Salisbury, thinking it would never end, never; just as the war had seemed it must go on for ever so now this awful postwar time could, and in 'Robinson' they think like this too. It is always intriguing to watch writers sifting gold from muddy experience.

She returned to London and was working in the tight little world of magazines and poetry magazines, all underfunded, just emerged from the war where so many little magazines had gone under. Her life then is in *A Far Cry from Kensington* and *Girls of Slender Means*. What is interesting is how far that highminded, threadbare living is from the world of magazines now, so sleek and well fed.

I met her about then and it still seems improbable. Why I was in her flat in South London I don't know, but there she was, surrounded by heavy serious furniture and wearing clothes of the kind my mother would have described as 'good'. This description defines me as much as it does her. At that time I met mostly the Comrades, for everyone was pink or red or had been and was now violently opposed. No one had any money, and we were in the Bohemian life which I cannot recommend too highly for hard times. They might return, and so it is as well to remember that the rent for living in Bohemia is much less than for good furniture and clothes and a dependable roof. We all lived from hand to mouth. Colourful we were, if a bit gimcrack, and here was Muriel, the essence of good taste, and that made it harder to imagine her in raffish wartime Rhodesia.

The next glimpse I had was from newspapers and the posh magazines. Muriel Spark was living in Rome, living it up, her companions the rich and glittering. I liked that, particularly because at that time my life did not run to elegance, nor either, to much society. A small child kept me circumscribed. But was it true? We have all learned to disbelieve newspaper gossip about the famous. Muriel later told me a story about that time. The Media were anxious to fasten some eccentricity on her, I forget what. Television turned up, positioned their cameras, and the interviewer put a question designed to elicit from her remarks on that subject, which in fact did not interest her. While she protested her indifference, the camera had rested on the title of a book which could be seen as contradicting her, held it, and then panned fast down a shelf of books, too fast to let the viewer see the titles, to imply that all the books, like the first, were on that very subject. I have had the same trick played on me: the Media, that likes to present itself as fearless and perspicacious exposers of hypocrisy and wrongdoing, roots about until it finds evidence of some wrongthinking or doing. The interviewer asked me a question about – I think – the imminence of interplanetary tourist travel. I said no, I didn't believe it, but the camera had rested on a title and then rushed down a shelf of books, and so there I was, like Muriel, made out to be a liar. Do not imagine that the golden boys and girls of television are ashamed of their little deceits.

A simple question to Muriel would have sufficed. Did you in fact live in the fast set, dressed in designer frocks? But that would spoil the fun. It adds to the jests of life to read that such and such a person, whom you know to be a recluse, regularly attends international festivals where Japanese fighting fish engage in combat, or that a rigidly socialist friend who is uninterested in food will eat lunch only in the Ivy. Thus the journalists' bitter fantasy lives spread nets of wild fiction.

However long Muriel spent in the smart set, she soon was living, and still does, in a secluded village in Italy, far from the froth of London's literary life.

Her elegant, witty and shapely novels emerge from the dull plains of hard slog which alas are the proper terrain for novelists. When I meet Muriel I am reminded of the sensible Scotswomen on the farms around us when I was a girl – an area now terrorised by Mugabe's thugs. It is agreeable to accept a cup of tea from the hand of the author of, let's say, *Territorial Rights*, jealous wives, spies, criminals, terrorists in training, the terrible tensions between communism and the West, made into a witty tale – but what dark depths do lurk.

'Amid the chaos of war, when Russian liberators in Bulgaria followed upon German liberators, and in Italy the Allies finally liberated left, right and centre, the noble owner of the Villa Sofia in Venice died a natural death, while his friend Victor was killed.'

That young woman, sitting out the war in Southern Rhodesia, in a country seething with refugees, the bored RAF officers and Other Ranks, military staff coming and going, such movement, such restlessness, with the anguish of the battlefronts in our ears night and day from the radio – such a witness was well qualified to write such tales.

Writing about Muriel one has at least to mention that she is a Catholic, while if it were Graham Greene, the fact would have to be central. Hard not to think that he became a Catholic because it gave such productive room for his talent for the lugubrious satisfactions of guilt. Nothing of the kind, for Muriel.

'The churches were so much more cheerful than others, so full of colour, glitter, incense and images.' This is the sparkle of aesthetic enjoyment, to be shared by unbelievers, but surely what attracted her were the opportunities for ironic comment on our hypocrisies, or perhaps like was simply calling to like, for the wise intelligence in her work does put her in the company of writers who share the long perspectives of Rome.

She is no stranger to the dark nights, the depths and the deeps. It is now too much of a commonplace to say that literature cannot match the bizarre extremes of everyday life. Usually in our time the attempt is made in science fiction, or magic realism, but Muriel Spark's contribution is to convey them within the form we decide to call realism. In her latest book, *Aiding and Abetting*, let us take the scene where a woman decides to become a holy stigmatic, much to her profit, because she suffers profuse menstrual bleeding, and seizes her opportunities. 'Blood, once let loose, gets all over the place. It sticks. It flows. It garishly advertises itself or accumulates in thick dark puddles. Once it gets going, there is no stopping blood.' And there is her characteristic dry smile, that puts a stop to excess.

Muriel is not always hard at work in Italy. Sometimes she comes to England. One of the pleasantest days of my life was spent in the company of Muriel and other friends, at the Hay Literary Festival, from where we took off to lunch in the hills. England comes up more often than its detractors like to admit with days so perfect you have to forgive it on the spot for its extremes of gloom and dark. The country around Hay is, when the sun shines, paradisiacal. Birds, flowers, flowering trees; brooks babbling and streams sparkling. On a sandy spit in the middle of the Wye, that treacherous stream which can flood on an instant, two swans sat on their eggs with the sun shining on their backs. A delicious day. Such days cannot be planned for. They happen.

Stendhal's *Memoirs of an Egotist*

Opening a Stendhal after – you have to think – a far too long interval there is, at least for me, a rush of exhilaration, as if you have turned a corner and look! – there's an old friend you haven't seen for a time and you have forgotten what an extraordinary being he is. Stendhal said he didn't expect readers who would understand him until 1890; but this was a movable rendezvous with the future. At any rate they were still children or even unborn. This select few are now spread everywhere, but the nature of our fond addiction is perhaps not so simple, nor even entirely blamefree. A clue is in his remark that when he wrote this memoir he was not 38 but more like 20. And it is true that we may easily recognise our adolescent selves in his prickly self-regard. I was in my twenties when I found *The Red and the Black* – and a friend.

The ideal lover of Stendhal comes from a family of conventional people in a provincial town – in his case Grenoble – which is smug, complacent and reactionary both politically and socially. As he did. His family took their social obduracy to an extreme. His beloved mother died when he was seven, and he was brought up by three people he hated. One was a maiden aunt, who tormented him, one a despotic Jesuit, who tutored him, and taught him to loathe the church and all its works, and then there was his father, a lawyer, who 'had all the prejudices of religion and aristocracy and vehemently prevented me from learning music'. Without the interventions of his mother's father, a kindly and intelligent man, there would have been no softer influences on his young life. He was not allowed to play with children considered his social inferiors, was treated more like a recalcitrant animal than a child, was harried by injunctions and prohibitions he could never see the sense of. I do not think it irrelevant that at the end of *The Red and the Black*, when Julien Sorel is about to be put to death, the father visits him and complains that Julien has not repaid him the money spent on him for his food and his keep as a child. Monstrous parents and figures of authority abound in his work. Never can there have been anyone more thankful that he has finally grown up and is able to leave home.

He did not keep the snobbishness they tried to teach him, but he remained as sensitive to a different crudeness: the coarseness he hated was not social, but the bruising blunderings of the unkind heart.

'I have an almost hydrophobic horror of all coarse individuals. The conversation of a coarse fat merchant from the provinces stupefied me and left me unhappy all the rest of the day.'

Oh yes, the provinces – or, in my case, small town colonial society. '. . . the most tedious *despotism*. It is what is behind this nasty word that makes residence in small towns impossible for those who have lived in that great republic, Paris' (*The Red and the Black*).

This memoir is of a stay in Paris from 1821 to 1830. He wrote imagining it would be read by someone dear to him, 'such a being as Madame Roland or Monsieur Cros the geometrician'. Here in a few words are his passion for mathematics and his need for a sympathetic woman, but in this case she was dead, by the guillotine, whose shadow had to lie across his life and mind and those of his contemporaries, for good or for ill: it is hard to sympathise with his enthusiasm for some of its operations. Inevitable, I suppose that, brought up by tyrants, he applauded the instrument that had brought some tyrants low. The man was a mass of contradictions – and he knew it.

He writes to find out what kind of a being he is. 'What kind of man am I? Am I intelligent? Have I common sense as well as character? Have I a notable mind? Truly, I do not know.'

The lens of his intelligence is focused on himself with a concentration that amounts to ferocity. He lists his absurd characteristics as well as his good ones, and never spares himself the description of a moment of humiliation or silliness. He had Rousseau as an admired model, but I think that self-confessor did not come near Stendhal for honest clearsightedness, which quality is a compensatory gift to a child who has spent years observing with satirical and unforgiving eyes the hypocrisies and injustices of grownups; who has had in order to survive to learn watchfulness, which is the first qualification for a writer. The close observation of their enemies, mother, father, authority figures, teaches these unhappy children how to dissemble or keep silent and – see everything.

Stendhal left Milan – left his beloved Italy, because the Milanese police thought he was a spy. He left behind a love affair – no, a grand passion – that had made him very unhappy, and was unconsummated – though there are hints this might have been his fault. But if he had been happy we would not have had his book *On Love*, which he was to finish and get published in Paris, a cool dissection of the stages and processes of love, that is to say, romantic love. It is a little book which is a more useful guide to the follies of the heart than any I know. It has the wit that is the result of an absolute and unsentimental truthfulness. But this man who had such a talent for tender emotions reported as many failures as victories, and perhaps we should remember that his hero Fabrizio del Dongo (*The Charterhouse of Parma*) shared with other elect souls his belief that the condition of being in love was superior to the cruder pleasures of consummation.

What extremes this man did hold in balance. The extremest was his passion for Napoleon, which characteristic he bestowed on his dashing young heroes Julien Sorel and Fabrizio del Dongo. The idea of Napoleon stood for nobility of soul, courage to defy belittling circumstances (like Julien Sorel's misfortune of being born a peasant), loathing of the commonplace – like provincial life; it stood for gallantry, beauty, the vision of an eagle rather than the horizons of a titmouse.

We all have friends we must forgive for incomprehensible weaknesses, such as an insensate and uncritical admiration for – let's say – Rupert Murdoch. Interesting that searching for a contemporary comparison to that horizon-breaker Napoleon, it is financiers that come to mind, not leaders of nations. What present king, general or leader has the glamour of Napoleon? Perhaps we have become too wise to do anything but groan at the news of yet another Great Helmsman? What makes it more inexplicable is that Stendhal was on the Retreat from Moscow; he lived through that ignominious slaughter by disease and the elements. Yet he loved Napoleon, who he insisted was not to blame for the debacle. But if not him, then who? But we are in the presence of an uncritical passion. What could be compared to that Retreat now? The Iraqi soldiers who fled before the American and British troops in the Gulf War back to Baghdad, but retained a loyalty to Saddam? No, of course Napoleon was not a methodical butcher, like Saddam, he was merely an old-fashioned conventional conqueror who did not count the cost. But Stendhal's Napoleon had little to do with the real

Napoleon, was more of an idea of glory and magnificence to set against littleness.

Stendhal is one of those figures who provoke questions apparently far from a cause. I am thinking about an account, by a German soldier, as it happens in Hitler's army, in the Gross Deutschland, who describes unforgivable cruelties in the training of himself and his comrades, causing mutilations and some deaths. 'But we adored him,' cried the soldier of this sadistic general, 'we would have died for him.' Those soldiers who had not already died in Napoleon's armies adored him though he had ruined their lives. We are up against something dark and twisted here: something, it is certain, very ancient. But ambiguous too. Julien Sorel, adoring Napoleon, or rather that crystallisation of a hundred larger-than-life qualities that bore the name Napoleon, survived the destroying mediocrity of a provincial town, a brutal father, persecutions. As many a youngster since, stuck in some God-forsaken backwater, has survived by repeating some barb by a Stendhal character directed towards local stupidity. 'The Directory in Paris, putting on the airs of a well-established sovereign, revealed a total hatred of anything not mediocre.' (Insert your own government, council, helmsman.)

That was when women in their salons could make the fortunes of young men, whether their lovers or not. 'It is only by women we get on in this world,' counselled Stendhal's friendly mentors. Stendhal's heroes owed all the grace and charm in their lives to women and so did he. He did not only worship love, he loved friendship, both without limits, calculation, self-interest. Only generosity of spirit was permissible.

Arrived in Paris, he developed a friendship with a Baron de Lussinge, who shared his frugalities. But as he got rich, he became miserly and patronised Stendhal's poverty. Stendhal did a very French thing: he changed his café so as not to suffer the company of this man he saw as ruined by money. A painful sacrifice, he called it. But he never made things easy for himself. This memoir is full of opportunities for friendship, or for advantageous salons, missed. His excessive sensibility, his pride, the high standards of his demands on people, made him solitary. He was already known as a writer, having published works on music and art, but he was not well known. He suffered some savage reviews, which he cushioned by musing that 'one or other of us must be wrong'.

He missed possible love affairs, even when the memory of his Methilde had become 'a tender ghost, profoundly sad, and who by her apparition turned me with authority to ideas that were tender, good, just, indulgent'.

This ghost was not always beneficent. His tale of his failure to make it with a girl procured for him is very funny but mostly because he did not see that it was. He was unconcerned, the girl baffled, since she was young and had not experienced this before. His friends were scornful and unkind. For a short time he acquired a reputation for impotence, but as we know from literature and from life, this could – had he used it – have lured women to his bed, because of their instinct to repair the situation – like men's fascination with lesbians.

But he never did play his cards right. It wasn't in him.

It was painful for him to be in Paris which he had known 'as part of Napoleon's court'. He had made enemies, too. Offered in 1814 the post of the food controller of Paris, by the Chief of Police, he refused. The man who accepted became rich in four or five years 'without stealing'. This brevity is Stendhal's immediately recognisable characteristic, as a writer. He reports here on the financial morals of the time in two words.

'. . . an officer on half-pay decorated at Waterloo, with absolutely no wit, and if possible less imagination, stupid but immaculate in style, and *having had so many women he had grown sincere with them*' (my italics).

Or this, which could be the synopsis for a novel. 'This Madame Lavanelle is as dry as parchment and entirely witless also, and above all without *passion*, incapable of being moved otherwise than by the fine thighs of a company of grenadiers going through their evolutions in the Tuileries gardens in white cashmere breeches.' This time the italics are his. To be without passion: Stendhal could not say anything worse. He might laud Paris as an antidote to Grenoble, but he did not like the French, whom he saw as full of artifice, insincerity, and lacking in passion. 'They love money above all things and never sin out of love or hate.' Unlike the Italians, who are frank and natural and honest – with whom he felt at home.

'That government is good and does good which guarantees a citizen security on the highway, equality before a judge, and a judge who is enlightened, a safe currency, well-kept roads, and its protection abroad.'

We may imagine how this *mot* went down in the drawing rooms, under the rule of Bourbons, whom he despised, and under whom flourished every kind of jobbery, sleaze, corruption, just as happens today. This definition reaches heights of smiling insolence towards his peers and towards the regime. In Italy he had been suspected of being a spy; I don't see how he could have avoided being in the police files in Paris.

His trip to England was to defeat his low spirits, and to see the plays of Shakespeare, which he read, often, and which he had written about, together with Racine. The absolute contrast must have pleased him. He saw Kean in Othello, and was astonished that in France and in England they used different gestures to express the same emotions; he also was impressed that Kean spoke his words as if thinking of them for the first time.

He was charmed by Richmond. He disliked descriptions of nature, tried to keep his prose unadorned, like a military dispatch, but Richmond tempted him to forget his austerities.

There he was, wandering around London, going to the theatre, but he omitted to court that hostess who would have done him the most good. Instead he was taken to a little house where three poor shy girls with auburn hair, prostitutes, were kind, and had good hearts. 'What is amusing is that during my stay in London I was unhappy when I could not finish my evenings in that house.' What is more amusing – it charms – was his unworldliness.

Stendhal loved women, to use that word not as he did in *On Love* but as a sentiment of general empathy. He had learned understanding of women with his much loved sister Pauline, who was something of a madcap and rebel (perhaps inspired by her brother's contempt for the ways of society?). She wrote to him of an escapade where she had dressed as a man and gone out to see the sights one evening. He was horrified. His letter to her says everything about the situation of women then. He implored her never to do such a thing again. If she were caught, or even if there were rumours, then no one would marry her, and she would be doomed to a convent or to spinsterhood. Get yourself a husband at whatever cost, he told her, and then, once married, you can do as you like. Married women are free; unmarried girls slaves.

He was under no illusions about 'the cost'. The husband in *The Red and the Black*, the town mayor Monsieur de Rênal – has there ever been such a description of a boorish, stupid, rough-riding husband? Yet he is not a bad man, certainly desirable as a husband. Women's helplessness in the face of convention has never been written about more tenderly, but what could be more coldly sensible than that letter? In *The Charterhouse of Parma* he merely records, coldly, that a certain society lady had brought her husband as a dowry 800,000 francs, and was allowed by him 80 a month for expenses. No wonder women adored him, though he was not good-looking.

This memoir is incomplete because he was not writing about what was most on his mind, his time with Methilde. He did not want to sully his memories of her. But it could serve as an introduction to the great novels: here is the ore from which he fashioned *The Red and the Black* and *The Charterhouse of Parma*. There is also his autobiography *La Vie de Henri Brulard*. He used dozens of pseudonyms: his real name was Marie Henri Beyle. That book is less revealing than this little piece, written when he was raw and bleeding. He confesses he found it hard to keep it in chronological order, but that is good: more like what our memories really are, Napoleon and Methilde, Richmond and Racine and pale poor girls with auburn hair.

It is getting on for two hundred years since he was in Paris, and wrote this, which is like hearing his voice, perhaps speaking in some drawing room in his beloved Italy, in the company of charming women, one of whom is his mistress, or has been or will be, and their lovers. Husbands are curiously absent, but any there are his good friends. Stendhal's heaven, he dreamed of it: alas his fate took him to less kindly places.

Lost Civilisations of the Stone Age

Çatal Höyük, Lascaux, Huruk, Knossos, Avebury, Olduvai –
names like these make the pulses of many more people than
you would think likely dance and skip: Linear B, the Rosetta
Stone, hieroglyphs long ago stole our hearts away. These are
the natural readers of this book, but there will be many others,
for a start all those who have stood wondering with a chipped
pebble in their hands and the millennia whirling through their
brains.

People not experts in the field, mere amateurs wistful on its
edge, have noted how our pasts continually lengthen, disappearing into shadowy speculations, peopled perhaps from
William Golding's wonderful *The Inheritors*. There was a Victorian bishop who decided that the world was created all at
once, bang! (an eccentric version of the Big Bang theory) on a
certain day in, I think, 6000 BC. This is on the evidence of the
Bible. He could not be moved by argument. His descendants
flourish in the United States to this day, but it is not only there
that stubbornness persists: there has always been a tendency to
accept every new bit of evidence from the past as the last word.
The Olduvai Gorge was responsible for a good many definitive
pronouncements. But with every week there is another bone or

cave or corpse and a pronouncement like this one from Richard
Rudgley. 'Thus it cannot be ruled out that we may yet see the
origin of hieroglyphic writing, and therefore Egyptian civilisation itself being placed further back in time.' We have seen
generations of archaeologists refusing to grant certain qualities
to our ancestors, only having to eat their words as new evidence
comes to light. There is a great need in us, as Edward Thompson
pointed out, to patronise the past, though he was talking of a
more recent one. There are pessimists who think that our strongest need – it is certainly the most easily observable – is to have
inferiors to despise, and those old ape-men do nicely. And this
is what this book is about: a claim that civilisations and cultures
we have thought of as composed of grunting brutes with short
dangerous lives squabbling over marrow bones in freezing caves
were in fact complex, skilled, and with capacities that we like
to think of as our discoveries. Ancient humans had a global
trade network, clever accounting systems; they built skilfully,
understood medicine, practised dentistry and surgery, such as
trepanning and the excision of tumours; they made beautiful
artefacts and were often fine artists. In some ways they seemed
better at managing their lives than we are, but there were fewer
of them. Our general dissatisfaction with the way we live now
should not tempt us into thinking it must have been nicer in
the Palaeolithic, because every thought and action was governed
by the shamans and for that alone we should be happy with
now, with less shadowed minds. Less, only; our presidents may
consult soothsayers and businessmen their horoscopes. To me
the most frightening fact in history is that the Romans, so like
us, could not do anything without studying the entrails of birds.
Well, but that's 2,000 years ago – but what's that, as the past
unfolds behind us, a mere moment. Çatal Höyük, that ancient
town in Turkey where, it is claimed, farming began, has had
only its top levels excavated, and below them lie who knows

what surprises. Troy was felled and rebuilt, ten times. The Japanese for a long time ignored the Jomon culture as too primitive even to notice, but it turns out that it was complex, sophisticated. Recently we have been told that the Native Americans were not the earliest inhabitants of North America. If you travel to see the terracotta armies in Xian, you see too ancient mounds and hills that are cities waiting to be examined. And beneath them? – for desirable sites go on attracting settlement century after century. Under the Gobi Desert are cities, and what are they going to reveal?

As Rudgley says, 'The widely accepted view of the human story is wildly inaccurate.'

And yet it goes on, what seems like an instinctive refusal to allow past excellence. Interested in the origins of storytelling I asked an expert if the Neanderthals told stories, but the reply was, 'Certainly not, they did not have the brain for it.' So 140,000 years was not long enough to allow grunts to become speech, to develop from 'I visited my father's grave last night' – allowable, because fact, to '. . . and he said to me, My son . . .' Unallowable, a step into fantasy.

All our digging about in the past is confined to the last Ice Age and its warm intervals, but there have been many Ice Ages, and it is safe to say we don't know how many, know only that Ice is a more natural condition for our planet than the lushness of present times. Is it possible that in the warm intervals between those long past Ice Ages were civilisations whose traces we may one day come across, perhaps in the depths of an ocean where a glacier pushed them? This is a fertile and fecund planet. Species multiply, or at least they do between catastrophes. Wherever there is space for it an animal or a plant will insert itself and grow. It is hard to believe that this process began only with the last Ice Age.

There is another recent book, which with this one will transform our view of BC. The Rhône Poulenc prize for scientific writing designed to inform amateurs went to Jared Diamond, for a book called *Guns, Germs and Steel*, and it challenges all notions of inferior and superior races, explains the uneven development of cultures. It is geography that accounts for it all, and as you read you think, of *course*, how was it we didn't see that. Two wonderful books. I recommend them.

Henry Handel Richardson

Ethel Richardson decided to test the contention that it is easy to see when a book is written by a woman. She wrote *Maurice Guest* as a man, as Henry Handel Richardson, and proved her point. She has often been claimed as a great writer, and I think she is. For years I was asking Australians here what they thought of her, but they said 'Who?' When I went to Australia and asked reading people, they sometimes had heard of her. She is caught sight of in literary departments. The trouble is, her three major books are so unlike each other, and the same set of phrases will not do to describe them all. Each asks for a different kind of approach.

The easiest to come at is *The Getting of Wisdom*, about a girls' boarding school in Melbourne. She described it as a 'little book', written as a relief after the eleven years' slog of *Maurice Guest*, but surely her tongue was in her cheek. It is a coldly angry, contemptuous novel. She knew her compatriots do not forgive criticism, and cut excelling people down to size – their own. I think she was doing what she had learned at school. 'Laura grew very sly . . . a regular little tactician.' 'She pocketed injuries . . . played the spaniel to people she despised . . .' 'Laura began to model herself more and more on those around her; to grasp that the unpardonable sin was to vary from the common mould.' This was the wisdom that had to be got at boarding school, in order to survive. She had the disadvantage of being a poor girl from a poor country place, competing with richer girls. This and the violently emotional life of these schools is her subject. There is a small but unforgettable scene of the poor women teachers for whom to teach in this sixth-rate place at all was probably a defeat, reading Ouida and joking feebly about marrying the first man who asks them, but they know they will soon be old and alone and poor. H. G. Wells and others called this novel a masterpiece. It belongs on the shelf with the classic school novels.

Her first novel, *Maurice Guest*, was a bold book then for man or woman writer. It is about erotic obsession. Reviewers were quite upset. It is set among music students in Leipzig in the 1890s. Most will be music teachers, but many are there because of the freedoms of bohemian life, an escape from the tedious proprieties of the time. Maurice is an ordinary young man, but he falls in love with Louise Dufrayer, an archetypal sex woman, lazy, sluttish, dishonest and unscrupulous, from moral inertia. She is a slave to the one real talent in the town, a 'genius' in the nineteenth-century manner. Women – naturally – do not see her fascination, but a man describes her like this:

> Believe me, there is more thought, more eloquence, in the corners of a beautiful mouth – the upward look of two dark eyes – than in all women have said and done since Sappho.
>
> Do you really think man asks soul of a woman – with such eyes and hands as those? There is only one place for him and that is on his knees before her.

This is said to Madeleine Wade, an Englishwoman who is all admirable qualities, a daylit woman, to whom everything Louise stands for is contemptible. Comedy; high comedy. And social comedy too: there is a landscape thick with subsidiary characters: landladies, warring prima-donna music teachers, tavern keepers, Americans 'doing' Europe, girls wanting husbands, people who love the aromas of 'art' and who think the life of cafés and salons is what art is. And embedded in this, the relentless tale of self-destructive passion. Louise could easily be one of Dostoevsky's masochistic women. This novel has been claimed by many for the gallery of the great, and it belongs there. It is unputdownable, unforgettable, but if it is a good read no one could say it is an easy one, for it is too painful.

And now the three volumes of the *Fortunes of Richard Mahoney*. If tragedy is a great character brought down by inner weakness, then this is not a tragedy, yet it has the effect of one, because if the hero is not up to the role, he nevertheless stands in for England, Europe, the Old Country's values. This is Europe on trial and Richard Mahoney makes a poor showing. He is clever, book-loving, full of touchy pride and prickliness, and takes his stand on being a gentleman, not a claim to make Australians like him. Yet many do, and admire him too. What he yearns for is to be well-off and respected, to have cultivated friends and properly brought-up children. Twice he succeeds, starting from nothing, but an inner enemy, invisible to him if not to others, forces him to depth-charge his own success. He ends up very poor, mad, and dependent on a wife whom he has always patronised for being too earthy and practical.

Lucky for him that she is. Mary Mahoney is one of literature's great women, though her qualities are not likely to be admired by feminists. She married her Richard, moth to star, aged sixteen, and for ever after subdued her needs and wishes to his. She loved him. That this author could create the awful Louise Dufrayer, and then Mary Mahoney, shows her range; and, too, the simple-minded Maurice Guest and the contradictory complexities of Richard Mahoney. This is another novel dense as a plum pudding, nineteenth-century in feel, slow-moving, contemplative, while we watch fates and destinies reveal themselves. People who enjoy Trollope would find themselves at home here: the same sense of quiet and patient irony, the same understanding of weakness.

If one may read *Maurice Guest* to know what it was like to be part of the musical life of Germany in the 1890s, then *The Fortunes of Richard Mahoney* is as much a history of the early days of Victoria: the gold fields of Ballarat, the infancy of Melbourne, the small towns and villages just holding their own in the bush. And if we read Patrick White at least partly to find out what Australia is like now, then Richardson provides the same service for the past. They have a good deal in common, for in both there is the same feeling, as if a hand were stretching out to encompass more than is possible for it. Australia the continent, the deep alienness of it, the difference of it, seems to mock Patrick White's people, and so it does the people of Ethel Richardson.

A reissue of *The Golden Notebook*

This novel's progress continues to surprise me, because it keeps putting its head up in new places, and often not where one would expect. The most recent was China, where I was on a trip at the invitation of the Chinese writers. They published an edition of 80,000, not a large number in that vast country, a small edition for them. The edition sold out in three days. It had been published once before, and had done well. 'Everyone has read it,' they say, meaning, as this usually does these days, mostly people in universities. The universities I visited in Beijing, Shanghai, Xian and Canton (Guangjou) have a most lively and informed interest in British and American literature. Only now has it occurred to me that universities are more and more our equivalent of the medieval monasteries, keeping things of the mind alive and well in poor countries where people cannot afford to buy books. (Not that China can any longer be described as a poor country.) Recently I got a letter from a waitress in a hotel in Rio saying, 'I can't afford to buy books. My husband works in the university and he is allowed to use the library and he got *The Golden Notebook* for me and I feel I must tell you . . .'

I hear that the book is being set in history classes and politics classes in schools and universities. This pleases me, since one of the reasons I wrote the novel was that I felt there are blank spaces where novels ought to be particularly in nineteenth-century literature. I still would like to read novels that gave the flavour and taste of let's say the Chartists, and their personal lives, their discussions, their conflicts, or perhaps the small revolutionary groups that flourished in London, most of them fomenting revolution in Europe. I think *The Golden Notebook* is a useful testament to its time, particularly now that communism is dead or dying everywhere, or changing its nature. Nothing seems more improbable than what people believed when this belief has gone with the wind. Novels give you the matrix of emotions, give you the flavour of a time in a way formal history cannot.

A Yugoslav woman student said to me (this dates the reminiscence). 'How interesting to read about all those old politics.' Old and exotic in communist Yugoslavia, but you may hear too, 'It describes what happened in my political group in the seventies' or '*The Golden Notebook* describes my life as a woman.'

When it first came out it was considered quite an advanced book, but recently it was given to girls of fifteen in a school in North London and they took it in their stride. This year it is being read in a class in the University of Zimbabwe, at the request of black and white students, male and female. They were surprised, so said the teacher, a friend, that the talk of the young communists was idealistic and optimistic in those ancient days before there was a communist regime in Zimbabwe. They associated communism and communists with self-seeking and opportunism. It had not occurred to them that communism had begun as a genuine dream for a better world.

I continue to get letters from men about *The Golden Notebook* – as many as from women. They may say that it opened their eyes to the feelings and experiences of women, or that what interests them is the politics, or the 'style' of the main American character, who now seems to them quite ridiculously macho. Or a woman writes to say – and this has happened often – that her boyfriend or husband gave her the book, saying it influenced him. I also hear the other side of this when a man says he has just read one of my books and liked it. He was at a university where Doris Lessing was the property of the women's movement, and so he did not bother to read my books and now he was sorry he didn't and was writing to tell me so.

Yes, I do get a lot of feedback, and I am always interested, particularly when it is unexpected. In Vermont there is a bookstore called The Golden Notebook . . .

I reread the novel the other day and remembered the fury of energy that went into it. Probably that is why the book goes on and on as it does – because of its 'charge'. It does have a remarkable vitality. Some of it is the energy of conflict. I was writing my way out of one set of ideas, even out of a way of life, but that is not what I thought while I was doing it. Inside that tight framework is an effervescence. Sometimes the energy in a book contradicts its apparent message. The first time I thought about this was when I read Dostoevsky's *The Devils* and found myself invigorated and optimistic when in fact a more pessimistic story can hardly be imagined. The other of my books written with the same intensity could not on the face of it be more different than *The Golden Notebook*. It is *The Making of the Representative for Planet 8*. Both books mark limits.

I meet women in their fifties who say, 'I was influenced by this book and I gave it to my daughter and she loves it.' Or a young woman says, 'My mother gave me this book because she said it was important to her and now I understand her much better.' I used to hear, 'My mother read it and now I do' –

so that's two generations, but the other day I was told of a grandmother who gave it to her son who gave it to his daughter. Three generations. Yes, I am indeed flattered.

Currently I am writing Volume I of my autobiography, and thinking about some of the people and events that went into *The Golden Notebook*, I have to conclude that fiction is better at 'the truth' than a factual record. Why this should be so is a very large subject and one I don't begin to understand.

Anna Kavan

Anna Kavan wrote quite a few novels, some under her own real name. She is better known in Europe, but if her reputation here is still small it is secure and growing. The nets of mystification she wove about herself have frayed a little, but her intention that her life should not be known frustrates biographers. Some facts are certain. She was coldly treated as a child, saw her mother for ten minutes every day before dinner, was neglected, found herself aged six in a boarding school. She suffered mental breakdowns, took heroin and finally died of it.

Change the Name was an early work, and there cannot be a better novel about the fate then of a middle-class girl denied training. Celia Henzell's course was determined when her father would not let her go to university. She at once got herself a husband to escape from a home like a cold hell. Soon she was a colonial wife in the East, where her husband died leaving her with an unloved baby. Unwelcome in her parents' home, she again used a man to escape. People who tried to help her were exploited and hurt. She became a writer. Her neglected daughter killed herself. A first-class bitch, but she is pitiful too, for there is something stunned and blind about her, as if she has been stung by a spider. I met women like this when I was a child, cynical, scheming, using sex, for men were their meat and without them they could have no decent future. This is a conventional novel, short, bleak and shocking because of its honesty.

My Soul in China begins 'Once there was a house somewhere, a small house on a hill, and it had an innocent look . . .' This novel's intensity compresses it into a sort of poetry. 'Wandering lost and aimless without even a name to connect me to life I begin to add up dismal accounts of loss . . .' Kay is well-married, lives in an atmosphere of cocktail shakers and hearty parties. She attempts suicide, is in a mental hospital, but has to go home to good times. She drifts off with an Australian to a paradise of Pacific coasts, Californian poppies and sea zephyrs. Love, too. But she does not enjoy love. This idyll is to last six months, when the lover must return to his wife. No use offering a short-term idyll for a little girl who is longing for Daddy's strong arms to enfold her and never, ever, let her go. He thinks she should enjoy what there is while they have it, he thinks she is neurotic. But her soul is in 'China', and 'No mirror will reflect the face of a person whose soul is in China.' A miscarriage. Breakdown . . . Yes, we are in Jean Rhys country, women doomed by their natures. This very short novel is kept company by nine fine short stories.

Ice, a late book, is a phantasmagoria, and was claimed by Brian Aldiss as the best science fiction of 1967. 'She is De Quincey's heir and Kafka's sister,' he said. However we class the book, there is nothing else like it. The narrator is forever pursuing and missing, then finding but losing, a girl, 'the girl' with her glittering falls of hair. She is the property of someone else but at last she becomes his. Too late, for the world is freezing up. Later, in one of my novels, the earth was swallowed by ice, but I had not read Anna Kavan's. Is this half-conscious terror of another Ice Age deep in all of us? We may glimpse perspectives of ice all over the place, in scientific predictions, let alone science fiction and in dreams.

The human race has every reason to fear ice. But this *Ice* is not psychological ice, or metaphysical ice, here the loneliness of childhood has been magicked into a physical reality as hallucinatory as the Ancient Mariner's. Anna Kavan, an ageing woman – it is easy to fancy – peers back down the years to a girl, 'the girl', trying to find the young creature she so thoroughly cocooned in fantasy, for even her diaries, she exults, are a fake. When she does find the girl there are only minutes left to the terrible cold world of ice and death. In an interview just before she died Anna Kavan said, 'I haven't felt anything for 20 years.'

Novelists are always being asked if their work is autobiographical. Exasperated, they reply that it is or it isn't, but the question is off the point. One might offer these three novels to such an enquirer, together with David Callard's *The Case of Anna Kavan*, the biography where the girl, the woman, and their images of herself are like the smiles of the Cheshire cat. 'My *mind* is quite honest; it is my foul imagination that destroys me.' Discuss.

Philip Glass

Seven years of 'music lessons' did I undergo as a girl, and by the time I said, 'Enough, I have no talent', I could play easy piano pieces but knew nothing of the history of music, nor how an orchestra works, nor could I read music. This experience used to be common. I was left with a feeling about the world of music that I must for ever stand at its edge with that particular wistfulness due to a promised land from which you are too long excluded. When I came to England, I went to the opera and was charmed out of my wits. Perhaps the day-in, day-out grind of getting an opera on sometimes prevents the makers from remembering that those people out there are in a kind of wonderland.

And then, with an invitation from Philip Glass to do an opera with him I was plunged into active participation. I had not heard his music then. He sent me a tape of *Satyagraha*; I'll not forget how my ears balked and sulked, expecting resolutions they were not getting, but they soon understood they must listen differently, and then this 'new' music was as accessible as any other kind. That was his 'minimalist' period (he did not use the word himself, it was a label) before he wrote so extensively and variously for film and theatre. Recently I heard an old-style opera-goer protest, 'Why Glass if you can have Verdi?' But why not both? Besides, if Glass were not the Verdi of our times, why is his music used (without acknowledgement) for every second television and radio programme, and so many advertisements, just as Verdi's would have been.

While final rehearsals for *Akhnaten* went on at the English National Opera Philip Glass and I were working on the libretto for *The Making of the Representative for Planet 8*, tucked away in a back room. So I was involved, at a remove, with David Freeman's production. What we were working on was a cold world: snow, blizzards, a planet freezing up, but *Akhnaten* was sand and heat and the alienness of Ancient Egypt, which I am sure it is no good trying to domesticate in our imaginations: it was the counter tenor in *Akhnaten* that set the piece where that distant world should be – well beyond our grasp of it. That unhuman voice, the naked heads, the cruel gods, an unhuman religion of pure love – and then the moment when the tiny city lay before us in its desert of sands, a dream city, where the big people moved like children among sandcastles. Meanwhile our minds were full of gigantic geometric snowflakes. And that is theatre and that is why I love it.

The first night of *Akhnaten* was electric. Glass fans were noisily present, determined their hero was not going to be done down by philistines. Some of the audience were dismayed, others delighted. Critics were observed leaving with ostentatious contempt and angry glances all around, a scene wittily described by Proust. I was there with my cousin Diana Morley, who has always been at the heart of the music Establishment, and she told me I must understand that people with her kind of music training would find it hard to accept Glass's music. I was at the last night of *Akhnaten*, and behold! it had become just another opera, with a calm appreciative audience: I had again witnessed that process which is so often repeated, how something new and gritty becomes absorbed.

Audiences liked *Akhnaten*, and so did some critics. Other critics violently and bad-temperedly did not. This sums up reactions to his music everywhere. When *The Making of the Representative for Planet 8* went on in Houston, Amsterdam, Germany the audiences were enthusiastic, not to say sometimes ecstatic, but the critics were half and half, except in London, where except for some fringe papers not a good word was said. I have never read anything so venomous, so poisonous. Philip said this was going to happen, and that I would come in for the flak. 'They're going to say *Representative* is terrible but they were wrong about *Akhnaten*.' And this came to pass. His experience with opera has been that critics damn a first showing of a piece, but when the next one appears they damn that saying what a pity it is not as good as the last. Used as I am to the sporadic and comparatively mild spites of the literary world, the malice of music criticism is amazing. Also, the wrong-headedness. I am often surprised, when an opera has been rubbished, to the point where I nearly don't go, but then I do, remembering how often this has happened before, to find something wonderful. Successive Benjamin Britten operas were described as so difficult and obscure; when I went, there was nothing difficult about them. I remember a marvellous *Eugene Onegin*: not a good word from the critics. Is it possible that the emotionality of music provokes violent responses? The history of music is full of unhappy and noisy scenes, to the point of riot and mayhem. Or is it that some critics have in them a well of malice they need to empty from time to time?

I certainly am not saying I love everything the ENO does. More than one production I have sat through with my eyes closed, unable to bear it. But when I think of the pleasures, what matters an occasional over-raked floor, while you sit, terrified the singers are going to slide down towards you like kittens on a tray, or that extraordinary bedstead, presumably meant to suggest unbridled sensuality, which turns you into a housewife, wanting to put a mattress and sheets on it, or a queen wearing a gown that looks as if it were bought for 50p in a street market? For every evening of indignation – and that can be a pleasure in its own right – there are twenty of delight. I immediately think of *Lady Macbeth of Mtsensk*, *Wozzeck*, some *Così Fan Tutte*s, various Handels, the Benjamin Brittens – I could go on, and go on again, but above all, the unforgettable *Khovanshchina*, and I wish ENO would bring it back, what a splendid and sonorous evening. But I see we are going to have *Boris Godunov*.

Trail of Feathers

The complaint goes that this planet, like an overused adventure playground, no longer provides the thrills of the unknown, and that from Kamchatka to Cape Horn there is no more to be said or done. Luckily original travellers continually appear. Those who have read Tahir Shah's previous books, *Beyond the Devil's Teeth* and *The Sorcerer's Apprentice*, know that he has a talent for inventive and outrageous travelling. He uses a natural candour to confront villains, mountebanks, lunatics and murderers, allowing situations to develop which would have most of us running and screaming.

Always interested in rumours that some people have flown, fly now, he noticed that often where feathered men and serpents appear so do shrunken heads. At an auction for these apparently covetable items – semi-clandestine, since shrunken heads could hardly be more politically incorrect – he met amiable lunatics, for instance, the man who knows a flying machine was found in Tutankhamen's tomb, that the Valley of the Kings should be called the Valley of the Dead Pilots, that it was the Egyptians who taught the Incas how to fly.

Well, why not! Anything is possible!

London's libraries and salesrooms, myths and legends, all

pointed to Peru and the Birdmen. The Wright Brothers and Leonardo da Vinci are as far as many of us get, but hundreds of attempts at flight have been made, everywhere in the world. What is odd is not that we flew when we did but that it took so long. Surely some of the wings made of feathers, silk, bits of this and that flew far enough to be called flight? But our author's interest was in long, fabled flights over jungles and desert. When he asked shamans and the initiated, did these people *really* fly? the answers were tantalising. Soon he knew that the hallucinogen ayahuasco was a clue.

The author's love of comic excess is such that even the list of provisions for the journey, inspired by his friend Wilfred Thesiger's Victorian standards, are good for a laugh. Among them were 22 family-sized sachets of Lancashire hotpot, and off he set on the Inca Trail from Cusco to Machu Picchu, described as worse than Everest. He noted that Machu Picchu looks from above like a condor.

Peru never had African slaves, and, therefore, no Macombo, so strong in other parts of South America. The systems of belief are native shamanism, and very weird they are. Festivals throughout southern Peru honour their beloved condor by capturing one, feeding it stimulants, and sewing it on to a band tied around a young bull. The frantic bird tears the bull with its beak, striving with its great wings to escape, bird and animal like a mythological beast providing the intoxicated populace with what is called a bull fight.

Outsize characters abound. Sven from Bratislava who had done seven years in a high security prison was walking around the world in the name of peace and poetry, pursued by a Parisienne in search of a father for her children. She was armed with a smelly llama foetus, which was an aphrodisiac and also good for hangovers.

Nasca of the famous desert patterns that make sense only

from the air is a nasty little town, but flourishing because crammed with initiates, every one of them claiming to know the Secret. More important still are the thousands of mummies being excavated for whatever will sell to museums and tourists. We have forgotten that powdered mummy from Egypt was the snake oil of the Middle Ages. The last mummy dust was sold in Germany in 1908 at seventeen marks a kilogram.

Near a cemetery high in the Andes Tahir was told by a sha-man that he was filled with evil spirits. He undertook the cure, which began by him being stroked all over, naked, with a hypno-tised guinea pig, whose entrails were later examined for marks confirming the possession.

In the poshest hotel in Lima he was the only guest: it was empty because a murderous she-ghost with a cleaver had taken possession. Tahir survived, with a bad headache.

A traditional storyteller in a market told him a tale 'in my family for fifteen generations' which is known all over the Middle East, and appears in the *Arabian Nights*. But she did point him onwards on the trail. By now he knew he had to find the Birdmen, far away in the jungles, safe from civilisation. They are the Shuar tribe, dreaded by everyone as murderers, torturers and sorcerers. Naturally this did not deter our author. In a town called Iquitos, described as the Saigon of the Amazon, apparently filled only with crooks and bar girls and beauty queens, whose best talent is to pick up white tree grubs with their teeth, standing, from the floor, Tahir was fleeced of his last money.

Now what was he going to do?

Enter Richard Fowler, a Texan ex-Vietnam vet. 'The Tet Offensive, Battle of Hue, Hamburger Hill, and all that shit.' The Amazon jungle was now his turf, and he undertook to keep Tahir alive. He began by hiring a rotting boat, already holed, full of rats and wolf spiders. Into this piled Tahir, Richard, a shaman and his relatives along for the ride, and some hitchhikers, and they

embarked on a vast tributary of the Amazon, flooded and dangerous, to reach Shuar country. The food was disgusting, and the
Lancashire hotpot came into its own.

After days of what sounds like hell, though the Vietnam vet
was enjoying every minute, they reached the Shuars, but they
had become Christian and had given up killing. Not ayahuasco,
which the missionaries had known better than to forbid.

Now they set off into the depths of the jungle, together with
a sloth whose severed head would be needed for some magic-
making. If to ingest revolting substances with a smile is a necessary talent for this kind of travelling then so is the ability not
to show shock at the cruelty to animals. The author's tender
heart was clearly under strain. After days of walking, during
which he decided he preferred to experience the jungle on television, they reached the big man, the great sorcerer Ramon,
and there at last Tahir flew, on ayahuasco. His shoulders and
arms grew powerful muscles and white feathers burst forth. He
was on the far side of a wall in a no man's land of illusion, but
Ramon told him ordinary life was an illusion and this was real.
Witches in Europe told the Inquisition they had flown and seen
marvels. Mushrooms, probably, or datura.

Tahir Shah's relish in storytelling is such that it would be
easy to forget this is a serious, well-researched quest.

There are two useful appendices, one about ayahuasco, the
latest fashionable fix. The author is worried because it is being
taken wrongly and dangerously prepared and out of its cultural
context. The other is about shrunken heads and other items of
magic and mystery. It seems we have got shrunken heads all wrong.
They are of no interest to their makers once made. Their use is to
imprison the vengeful spirits of the killed so that they do not get
out and attack their killers. Just imagine, all those little heads with
sewn-up mouths containing murderous spirits looking for a crack
or cranny to wriggle out of so they can do their worst.

William Philips, who died in 2002

In the late fifties and well into the sixties visitors came from everywhere to London because of what was being seen as a renaissance of democratic socialism. The collapse of communism everywhere, given impetus by the Twentieth Congress and the Soviet invasion of Hungary, not to mention the foul odours that increasingly came from behind the Iron Curtain, meant that everywhere the Left was in trouble. But westward – look! – the land was bright: over there in Britain was a new dawn, partly because of the Aldermaston Marches, which attracted people with horizons and ideas much wider than the simple Ban the Bomb! and partly because of the New Left, which already had its periodical, the *New Left Review*, was young, noisy, energetic, irreverent about the schisms of the past.

William Philips came partly from curiosity and I think too because of a hope that at last there would be a genuinely democratic socialist party. People were asking if the New Left could develop into a political party of a sane, wholesome non-dogmatic kind. I met William at Wayland Young's house in Bayswater, invited there so he could meet a representative of the new thinking – me. Wayland at that stage in his life was a romantic socialist, a generous soul far from the viperish or peevish intrigues of the Left. To see me as a representative showed how innocent he was. But more than once I was summoned to Bayswater or recommended to some visitor hungry for political enlightenment whom I was bound to disappoint, because I had been so relieved to throw off the whole murky bundle of tricks which was communism that I had perhaps gone to an extreme of reaction: a plague on all your houses, leave me alone.

That Wayland had become this focus was ironical enough. He was so visible because the newspapers loved to photograph him marching from Aldermaston, with his lovely wife and at least some of his children. It is not only Brits who dearly love a Lord: Wayland would be Lord Kennet. Foreigners have always been intrigued by the way aristocrats in England so easily espouse the extreme left wing. There used to be a joke on the Left that the Communist Party could never get one of its own into the House of Commons, but there were always CP members in the House of Lords.

On that first evening, sauntering back into central London along Bayswater, I was struck by the detailed and well-informed cross-questioning I was getting, by a man who knew the history of socialist Britain as well as he did the story of the labour movement in America. Here was a real politico, as I had known them for years now, and the best did their homework, as William was doing. There were ironies. The old jokes about the difference between a Catholic and a Protestant atheist applied by analogy: William had been a Trot, and I a Stalinist. For years I had been impatient with all this, believing that if Trotsky had won the battle for power he would have been as ruthless as Stalin: that pickaxe, with a slight turn of history, could well have landed in Stalin's brain. But the New Left youngsters were all Trots, in an inspirational warm-hearted way. I was able to tell William that their hearts were in the right place, but I doubt whether he could have approved of what must have seemed to him amateurishness: the rigorous analytical phases of the *New Left Review* were still ahead.

Years later, in New York, when the Soviet Union was no more, I asked William if he had never thought like this: Suppose the Left everywhere had never paid allegiance to the Soviet Union, had said 'That struggle has nothing to do with us' – then certain things could not have happened. The Left's support of the Soviet Union meant concentration – that above all – on failure; on lying, on the defence of mass murder; meant, inevitably the corruption of itself, because of always having to swear that bad was good, lies the truth, failure success. A left wing independent of all that would have meant a healthy Left, instead of one mortally wounded and corrupted. Yes, said William, he had indeed pursued these ideas, but surely I must agree with him that this was unhistorical thinking? Yes, yes, I admitted, true, but just suppose ... The fact that we could have that conversation at all shows how far we had travelled from those days when William came to London, telephoned me, and we met for a meal, or I took him to a meeting he thought might be interesting, or I invited some real representative of the New Left who could satisfy William's expert questioning.

I was also in a false position because I had read and admired the *Partisan Review* for years, but for its stories, poems and criticism, not for its politics, which struck me as sound and fury in a teacup. Over there in the United States there was this minute Communist Party and an even smaller Trotskyist Party. And so what? The vast power of America would absorb these like little fleabites. How wrong I was – both had influences far beyond their formal boundaries. But what I wanted to talk about was literature; and I questioned William about the writers and poets. So there we were, agreeably strolling about London, mildly at cross purposes, and mostly I was listening to this urbane, clever, well-informed man, the editor of a magazine as influential in the arts as in politics. I have often been told by this or that writer how much he owed to William's advice and help. And it is my belief that this is how William will be remembered. The politics, as happens so often, will seem increasingly like noisy sophistries, but the writers and poets he published and helped will be his real monument.

There aren't many people like William now, so well read, well informed, with such a range of interests. These days savants don't come so well-rounded, many sided.

When I took to visiting New York, meeting William and Edith Kurtzweil was always a high point: conversations were an antidote to whatever enthusiasm or fad was sweeping America. This was particularly true through the effluvias of Political Correctness. William was all his life at an acute angle to current conventional thinking, was in minority positions, always the acerbic and level-headed critic, but never was he more at odds with his time than during Political Correctness.

I visited William in hospital in and found him in a room so stuffy, noisy and hot you'd think it was impossible to retain a clear thought in your head, but he was alert and wanted to know what was going on in southern Africa, in the Labour Party in Britain; who were the new writers? Was it true the young were not interested in politics? How about feminism? What did I think about . . . ?

Books

It is an astonishing fact that Zimbabwe, after twenty years of a rule which has starved libraries and schools of books, is full of people who yearn for books, who see them as a key to a better life, and whose attitude is similar to that of people in Europe and America up to 50 years ago who read because they agreed with Carlyle's dictum 'the real education is a good library' – and they aspired to be educated.

There are libraries and libraries. Some I am involved with would not be recognised as such in more fortunate parts of the world. A certain trust sends boxes of books out to villages which might seem to the ill-informed no more that clusters of poor thatched mud huts, but in them may be retired teachers, teachers on holiday, people with three or four years of education who yearn for better. These villages may have no electricity, telephone, running water, but they beg for books from every visitor. Perhaps a hut may be set aside for books, with a couple of shelves in it, or shelves or a trestle may be put under a tree. In a bush village far from any big town, or even a little one, such a trestle with 40 books on it has transformed the life of the area. Instantly study groups appeared, literary classes – people who can read teaching those who can't – civil classes, and groups of aspirant writers. A letter from there reads 'People cannot live without water. Books are our water and we drink and we drink from this spring.'

An enterprising council official in Bulawayo sends out books by donkey cart – 'our travelling library' – to places where ordinary transport cannot go, because there are no roads, or roads that succumb to dust or mud.

A friend of mine, known to be involved with organisations that supply books, was approached by two youths in a bush village near Lake Kariba, who said, 'We have built a library, now please give us the books.' The library was a shelf in a little lean-to, of grass and poles, but the books would never succumb to white ants or the book-devouring fish-moth, because they would always be out on loan.

A survey was made in the villages, and it turned out that what these book-starved people yearn for are romances, detective stories, poetry, adventures, biography, novels of all kinds, short stories. Exactly what a survey in this country would reveal . . . that is, among people who still read.

One problem is that these people do not know what is available that they might like if they tried. *The Mayor of Casterbridge* was a school set book one year: it was read by the adults, and so people asked for books by Hardy.

The most popular book everywhere is *Animal Farm*. Another that has queues waiting for it is *World Tales*, by Idries Shah, and it is not only the tales themselves, but the scholarly footnotes attached to them which they enjoy. They say of a story perhaps from the Sudan, or America, 'But we have a story just like that.'

One problem is that people, hearing of this book hunger, at once offer to donate their cast-off books. These are not always suitable. Donations would be better. Book Aid International, based in London, sends books out to book-starved countries.

Niccolò Tucci's *Before My Time*

Through tumults of swirling snow and wind, a blizzard of Russian intensity, struggles a family group, adults with small children, appearing in glimpses to the reader's view during momentary weakenings of the storm, all huddled indomitably together against Fate and the weather like exiles off on their long walk to Siberia ... but wait, this is not Russia, this is Switzerland, though the family is Russian, and they are taking a walk for their health but above all because, as Russians, they understand snow, its subtleties, and its beauties – its essential qualities – as no one else in the world can do. If Switzerland is bourgeois and soulless, a mere spittoon of a country, then at least its snow is not. Like all Russians away from their *rodina*, their homeland, they are exiles from their best selves. Yet they live abroad, from choice, and continue to do so, while forever deciding to leave at once for Moscow, or for almost anywhere, '... for she had dragged her unhappiness from town to town, from hotel to hotel, taking time from her major sorrows to note in passing that the cooking was horrible and none of the guests had enough wit to cheer her'.

Niccolò Tucci is Italian; his father was the poor and idealistic doctor who fell in love instantly and fatally, a marriage of souls, with a daughter of this rich Russian family, and who spent his life thereafter captive to their whims and lunacies knowing that somewhere along this destiny-ruled road he had sold out his best self. A contradiction, you are thinking: it doesn't add up? Not at all, nothing less than a total impossibility rooted in the very nature of life would do in this family. *Before My Time* is a portrait of the family, but it has the quality of a novel, and as soon as you begin to read you forget it is a memoir, for the imagination of an artist has transformed memory into a work like Proust's; for *À La Recherche du Temps Perdu* should be called *Autobiography*, if this book is; both are full of characters observed through a magnifying glass, the enormity of family life as a child experiences it, but distanced by the necessity to put oneself as far and fast as possible from its quicksand seductions. For ever and ever will the boy Marcel lie awake weeping till morning because his mother has forgotten to come and kiss him goodnight, and it is tolerable because the author Proust has shut the pain safely into his pages, and for ever will this family of stupendous Russians, all adepts in sadomasochistic emotional torture, torment each other, but safely, in this memoir transmuted by the intensity of experience into a novel.

Often young writers write a certain kind of novel which is an act of self-definition, for their idea of themselves has been knocked askew or eroded by whatever it is they have suffered – and endured by observing, learning the cool ironical eye. In this case the author has defined himself not by insisting on his own life, but that of his parents, and above all, the monstrous matriarch who stamped her image on them all.

She is of the same literary provenance as Chekhov's Lyuba Ranevskaya and Irina Arkadina, but most of all Dostoevsky's prodigious grande dame in *The Gambler*, who tyrannises and bullies everyone, and then loses her entire fortune at the gambling tables in one night's play and says Forgive me, Forgive me, as if she has mislaid a purse with a few roubles in it. (How did these terrible women, who drive themselves and everyone else crazy, ruin themselves and everyone around them, come into existence? What permitted them?)

Mamachen, Grossgrandmutter, Grossgrandmamachen, or – seldom, just Madame, manipulates her children like puppets in orgies of emotional blackmail and self-flagellation, while she corresponds with Tolstoy, sharing with him her lofty thoughts (she knows he has got some of his best ideas from her) and allows her vast fortune to be stolen from her by a whole army of servants. Her particular victim, her alter ego, is Mary, the author's mother, she who was the other partner of the destined love. 'She woke up and as she knew her husband detested tears in the morning (how uncivilised of him, how Italian, how peasantlike) she left her bed and in a great hurry took her tearful face like a *soufflé de fromage* right from the oven, to the exacting gourmet who liked tears hot and rich, made to order and plentiful; and in her mother's arms she cried and cried and cried ... The doctor found them together in tears and he was very angry. 'Cry as much as you like,' he said, 'since that seems to be a Russian sport ... But if you must, close the window at least, it is freezing outside.'

This is a comedy with the abundant inventiveness – each climax of mad improbability topped by another – of Gogol's *Dead Souls*, which is its nearest literary relation. Gogol (on Pushkin's generous suggestion) sent his hero travelling around Russia in search of his gallery of grotesques, but why travel if what you need is at home, in your house, in your own memory?

Each member of this family is as wondrously distorted as the mysteriously suggestive shadows in a shadow puppet play, or the wildly leaping shadows thrown by a draught-tormented candle: not only Mamachen, but Mary, her captive and jailer; and the 'immoral' daughter Ludmilla who finally turns her family against her at that moment when she crosses her legs and lights a cigarette, proof of the ultimate depravity, loss of virginity; and Pierre, the superior son in Moscow who appears only at the end, at the matriarch's death. This is a scene of wonderful lunacy, each member of the family plotting how to cheat the others out of what is left of the mother's inheritance, while each hints the others are mad, and broods secretly about the possibility of having them locked up. There is, in fact, a locked-up daughter, that common figure of the time, and not exactly unknown in ours, the girl who was never mad, but found too 'difficult' to be allowed to remain at large.

The servants who sponge off the family are the progenitors of scenes as richly comic, close to farce, as any in Russian fiction. They manage with superb impertinence to make anyone who remonstrates with them feel guilty. This is usually the unfortunate doctor, who finds himself scolding them for wasting a few loaves of bread while whole fortunes stream past his face into their sticky fingers. (Thus are they enabled to complain they are forced to eat stale bread out of the wastebin while ordering in meals cooked by a local gourmet chef – that is, for themselves, not for their masters.) So unpleasant do they make it for their employers when they protest their depredations are not only forgiven or glossed over, but their salaries are doubled and trebled. (I keep thinking of Ostrovsky's play, *Too Clever by Half*, that crescendo of comic impertinences that recently at the Old Vic in London had whole audiences weeping with laughter.)

How is it possible such a superb book has been so overlooked? It is true that there have been, ever since it appeared, a few who have admired it, who have spoken of it to each other and to friends, but mostly it has been ignored. This is because it does not fit a category. Autobiography it may be: for the author insists it was all true; but we do not read *David Copperfield* because it was all 'true'. It may have an Italian author, brought up in Italy, but it is a Russian novel if there ever was one. The Russians could claim it, and I believe they will. It is a modern novel, that is, set in the first part of the twentieth century, yet it has the atmosphere of the nineteenth – or of timelessness.

There are many readers who mourn the nineteenth-century novel, its capaciousness, its pace, its scope, its ironies, the firmness of characterisation that is rooted in a world with neater moral boundaries. Those readers will find food and delight here.

I think this is one of the books, unjustly ignored, which come into their own when their time comes at last. This, I hope, is the time for this one. It is a great book, which will, I am sure, continue to gather lustre until it is set firmly on that special shelf side by side with the classics of world literature.

The Wrong Way Home

This book first appeared when David Koresh at Waco, and Jim Jones at Jonestown, were recent events and of illustrative value. Research had been, and since has been, going on into cults and cultish behaviour, and how we are all influenced by peer pressure. It is fair to say that few people who think at all have not given thought to cults, those they have been in, are in, or might join. Arthur Deikman's prime and particular contribution, apart from drawing attention to the problem, was to point out how much cultish behaviour goes on unrecognised, in, for instance, business life or in apparently harmless organisations, religious or philanthropic. It is useful to ask oneself the question: do I feel superior because I belong to – whatever it is? Do I look down on people outside? Perhaps the most easily seen feature of a cult is that: *we* are better than *them*. It is salutary to recognise how often in a day we feel disapproval or superiority, matching ourselves with 'outsiders', who are black, white, fat, old, young, men, women, Muslims, Jews, Palestinians. Some of Arthur Deikman's conclusions provoked anger. It is not pleasant to be told that one's dear, reputable, ethical club or church or party sometimes behaves like the most intolerant cult.

The perspective has shifted, and since September 2001 the talk is all of terrorism. A new chapter discusses al-Qaeda, as a cult. With such a wide lens an attempt at definitions must surely be made. The accepted criterion used to define a cult also describes a nation at war or under threat. What, then, is the immediate usefulness of being on the look-out for cult behaviour, thinking of groups or a religion like Jim Jones's People's Temple, when your country has embraced that basic, not to say most primitive of stances, My country, right or wrong. Or, but this usually the cry of extreme political parties: He who is not with us is against us.

We are now using the word terrorist as once, and not long ago, we talked of 'communists', as an all-purpose all-embracing evil. Or, in some parts of the world, hard to understand in others, the word 'liberal'. In South Africa, under apartheid, that was not an epithet you would want to attract.

One kind of terrorist may be dismissed from this study at once: summed up by the immortal lines of Sir John Harington (sixteenth century).

> Treason doth never prosper: what's the reason?
> For if it do prosper, none dare call it treason.

Not a few of today's leaders, Israel's for one, have been called terrorists. It doesn't do to be too hasty with one's definitions.

Another kind, a minority, but notable, is the young man – usually male but not always – of good family, or even rich, who becomes violently opposed to what has made him. This has been called the Younger Son Syndrome. The Red Brigades of Italy, the Bader Meinhof Gang of Germany, were of this type. In my belief it was the brutal anarchy of wartime Germany and Italy that created them, but that is another question. Lenin was an example: from a cultured family, that verged on the nobility, he turned against his origins, was a true terrorist – that is, advocating terrorism as a policy – and evolved into a revered leader. For a time. Bin Laden comes from a very rich family: he is no representative of the poor and the downtrodden railing against the rich: typically, while execrating the indulgences of the Great Satan, a good many of his followers, if not himself, have become addicted to the fleshpots. These types of mal-content, or revolutionary, or reformer, are easily spotted and understood.

The movements now often called 'terrorist' are sometimes vast, may comprise whole populations. They have little in common with the true terrorists, like Bin Laden's specially trained terrorist groups.

In 1986 I went to Pakistan with a group involved with the plight of Afghan refugees from the Russian invasion. Around the towns, but particularly around Peshawar, on the border, were refugee camps full of women and girls: the men were inside Afghanistan fighting. The women and girls were prisoners in the camps, monitored by the mullahs, who are ignorant men without education. The girls got no education at all. The boys, however, did: they were taught, day in, day out, to recite the Koran, by these same mullahs. And that is all they were taught. Visitors to the camps or to the streets of Peshawar were sur-rounded by flocks of lively, if undernourished, boys of all ages, clamouring for a book 'please give me a book', or a biro, or a piece of paper. They wanted to learn. They knew that beyond the confines of the tents or hovels that made up the camps was a world they could aspire to, with education. But an education for the modern world was not what they were getting. Delightful boys, funny, clever – and heartbreaking. Soon they became the Taliban. Ignorant, obsessive, fanatical, often cruel, these fright-ening young men had been those attractive children. And there they still are, set aside, and they have no place or function in the modern world. Educated as the poor have been in Islam for centuries, by no more than a ritual chanting of the Koran, they might just as well be fourteenth-century people. These young men, soon to be middle-aged, are described as terrorists. They were the direct product of the Russian invasion, which the Afghans well named the Catastrophe. They are still a danger. Given the opportunity they might rise up on some mindless surge of destruction, like blowing up the great statues of the Buddhas. They would go back to persecuting women. But that is what they were taught: were never given an alternative.

How can one equate these with the dedicated, specialist operatives of al-Qaeda?

In parts of Africa where Islam is merely a rumour are children, including girls, who are the result of murderous genocidal wars. Like the Taliban they will find no role in the modern world because they have no education.

They yearn to learn. Anyone visiting Africa knows how they beg for books, paper, biros, anything, please send us to school, please send us a teacher. There they are, potential armies ready for the first demagogue who will give them identity and self-respect by enrolling them in a party, an army. Anywhere in the poor world, the Third World, if you look close, there they are, the uneducated children for whom the modern world will always be a dream.

You cannot legislate against terrorist groups once they come into being, but you can prevent terrorists from coming into being. A good modern education is the solution. Some of the billions we spend on weapons and war would do it. But I doubt if the people who wield the weapons, and who make money out of them, would listen to the argument.

I saw this. I was by chance in Ireland on that shore across the bay from where Lord Mountbatten was murdered. The murder of a political opponent may be described as a gallant act of war. I looked down from my hotel bedroom and saw thirty or so street kids, poor kids, marching around under banners and posters – home-made, bits of cardboard – exulting in the murder of the English enemy. The point is, this was before the European Community poured money into Ireland: those kids now would not be fodder for the IRA recruiting officers. Then, they would have to grow up to join the IRA. They had no other role model, for brave heroes. And once inside the IRA they were stuck. One does not say to a fanatical organisation, 'Sorry, I made a mistake, I want to take my exams and become an engineer.'

Why is it so hard to solve and soothe the hurts of Ireland? A member of the IRA or Protestant action squads is a hero. They have earned respect from their fellows for the murders they have committed and the kneecaps they have blown off. Disband these organisations and what are they? Untrained, uneducated, they are fit to become clerks or street cleaners. It is a mistake to forget that when a youngster joins a cause, an army, a cult, follows a leader, he is given an identity. A kid on a street corner in LA or Rio or Lagos is a social nuisance, given as much respect as a stray dog, but then he puts on a uniform and becomes somebody. A badge will do. A T-shirt. The most common cry of our street kids in Britain is for respect. 'I beat him up because he gave me Dis.' Disrespect.

Any of the kinds of people I have mentioned may be called terrorists. What they have in common is the need for an enemy.

And now the worst of peace's enemies, anathematised every time President Bush or Prime Minister Blair makes a speech. Everywhere we are told are the groups of Muslim hardliners, biding their time in hiding, waiting to attack. These men – and some women – have had a religious upbringing, but it is striking how often the relatives of friends of some discovered fanatic will say: 'He was quite normal, a delightful fellow until suddenly . . .'

What was sudden was religious conversion: from ordinary congregational religion, religion shared with your community, to the membership of an elite group.

Some extremists, of any persuasion, are obviously psychopaths. It seems to me an insufficiently noticed fact that a person may be quite mad, but if he or she is in a political or religious context, then no one sees it.

Instructive now to read Dostoevsky's *The Devils* (sometimes translated as *The Possessed*), a story set in provincial Russia about a terrorist cult. This group existed for destruction, the creation of anarchy, of fear. Why? Just for the hell of it. Since then we have become familiar with killings or mayhem for its own sake. The enjoyment of destruction is deep in the human psyche, and of evidence there is plenty. The Red Guards in China: accounts record the relish in destroying everything from productive orchards, to temples, to art treasures. Cromwell's men in Britain relished destroying religious art. King Henry the Eighth's men thoroughly enjoyed wrecking monasteries. My question is, how often is this deep and sick need to destroy being led under the guise of ideology? When a cult calls itself Cleansers of the Pure Flame (an invented name) and then kills, tortures and burns, blows up buildings and burns crops, it is surely time we asked, not 'Are they sincere in their beliefs?' but 'How much of it is for kicks, for fun, for pleasure?' I do not doubt that the al-Qaeda groups are sincere in their abhorrence of the West, but if there were not martyrdom, murder and the infliction of pain as part of their agenda, would they have so many recruits? And we must remember the pleasure people take in secrecy, the taking of oaths, knowing themselves to be part of an invisible brotherhood, being 'in the know'. The belief that you are one of a powerful minority and *in the right* – in the eyes of God or of History or your revered leader – is seductive, like a drug. The memoirs of some spy – there have been so many – tell what a thrill he got out of knowing he was seen as an ordinary not very interesting person 'but what I knew could destroy them all'.

The leaders of al-Qaeda are not mad; they have a different world-view, so different it is hard not to despair of the two sides coming to an understanding.

Outside our chief mosque, in London, at the time of the 11 September attack a Muslim youth was filmed saying, 'Did you see all those yuppies flying out of the windows? It was so funny.' He meant the people jumping to their deaths. One's blood freezes at what is revealed here. First, the language of the dispossessed: the word 'yuppies'. Envy, powerfully part of the hatred of the Great Satan. And then, those people working in the Twin Towers, and they included Muslims, were enemies, not human, their deaths were 'funny'. The youth was rebuked by religious superiors, but the chilling evidence is there, on record, and to be learned from.

'We' and 'They'. 'Us' and 'Them'. 'He who is not with us is against us.'

The main plank of cultish behaviour is that the outsider, the person not on your side, is demonised. Cultish? It goes back thousands of years to our origins in the tribe, the clan: cults, nations, warring armies. 'My country right or wrong.'

And now, in a world as threatening, as full of hatreds as ours, what is to be done?

As always, there must be an appeal to the moderates on all sides. There are moderates and peace lovers and people of goodwill and it is essential to remember that when leaders posture and threaten: the voices of common sense are always softer than the noisy rhetorics of extremism.

In Britain there are organisations of moderate Muslims who dislike and disown the Muslim extremists. They are informed, educated, intelligent, and have solutions to problems that are as much theirs as ours. The edifice of Muslim civilisation which is old, and has given the West so much of its mathematics and science and medicine and art and literature, is threatened by the fanatics, the terrorists.

In this country, we do not see our rulers consulting moderate Muslims, or if they do, they keep it quiet. And there must equivalent people in the United States.

Meanwhile it would be a help to stop using the word 'terrorist' like a witch's spell, and restrict it to the real terrorists.

'Ignorant armies' like the Taliban are not terrorists. Saddam Hussein is not a terrorist, he is a brutal dictator, on a model we are familiar with: Stalin, Hitler, Pol Pot. Iran is not a terrorist regime, though it may be sheltering terrorists. It is another brutal regime whose human rights record, according to the United Nations, is among the worst.

Terrorists are those highly trained ruthless groups waiting in the United States and in the countries of Europe to murder, poison and destroy. Let us catch them, if we can. In order to understand them we must learn the laws that govern cults, and brainwashing.

Biography

A letter arrives from a young woman who says she has a contract to write your biography; she will shortly be with you and looks forward to your co-operation. It is evident from the letter's tone, which is that of a happy chipmunk who has just found a stash of hallucinogenic mushrooms, that it has not crossed her mind her victim might not welcome spending what is bound to be weeks if not months in the company of someone she has never met and certainly would not have chosen, sharing intimate details of her past and deep thoughts about life in general. *Of course* everyone must be delighted at such news. I wrote refusing, saying that I believe biographies should be written after the favoured one's death. At once indignation and letters that verged on the threatening. My friends, invited by her to talk, asked me what to do and I said, Ignore her. So they too refused but some got back letters: It would be in your interest to co-operate. To no one did she say that I and my friends were not involved.

It is not that I dislike biography, on the contrary. Once I planned to write one about Olive Schreiner, a remarkable woman born out of her time, but when I got from the library extant biographies, found that there must once have been an

Ur or prototype biography from which the others had been derived. Applying for guidance to an expert friend, his reply was that 'This kind of thing is not unknown.' Original research was called for, but that would have to take me to South Africa, where I was then a Prohibited Immigrant. Besides, it would use up four or five years of my writing life. Since then I have had biographers as friends and marvel at their diligence and dedication, creating their labour of love. Which is what a good biography is.

The chipmunk's biography of me is to hand. It might be argued that a writer who has not co-operated with a biographer should not complain about inaccuracies and untruths. We are in the public domain, so the saying goes: but I would argue that our works may be, but we are not, more than we choose to be. In the present charming climate it is assumed that if a writer does not want to be done, it is evidence of dark concealed secrets, but perhaps it could be evidence of an inclination towards privacy? And surely it is forgotten that a writer's life includes friends and family: why should they be exposed? Isn't this a simple matter? There are people who like being bio-graphied. But the ones who refuse, may we not be excused? After all, we will be dead soon enough.

It seems to me that novelists need biographies less than any other kind of person. An ounce of nous can tell from a novel, let alone two or several, most things about a writer. Not what date he or she went here or did that, but the essence of the matter. I have just reread *Villette* – bought from the trestles outside the National Theatre (and with copious and indignant black notes on the lines of *Wrong*!!!!! This kind of storm???????? Not at the ascribed time of the year!!!!!!) and I maintain that anyone over the age of twenty can understand anything of importance about Charlotte Brontë from that book.

This biography includes errors by the dozen that could have

been avoided by consulting published factual material and my autobiography. Which I wrote naively imagining it would protect me against misinformation. All the facts about my family are wrong, including my daughter's name. You'd think that even an unambitious biographer would get that right.

A bad biography has its uses: it is easy to examine the myths that accumulate around every public person. My favourite here is that damned farm I am supposed to own in Zimbabwe. *The Times* wrote an article where I and Ian Smith were enterprisingly juxtaposed as both owning farms which were being compulsorily purchased. My refutation, that I had never owned anything, let alone a farm, in either Southern Rhodesia or Zimbabwe, was duly printed. Then our dear *Guardian*, ever devoted to accuracy, repeated the interesting news, and they too printed a denial. Does it make any difference? I may not want to own a farm in Africa or anywhere close but clearly other people want me to. The mantra, 'I had a farm in Africa, at the foot of the Ngong hills . . .' is as powerful as 'Last night I dreamt I went to Manderley again.'

Should I leave this phantom farm to someone in my will?

Phantom friends populate a poor biography. Because my own friends are not there, people are trawled up and described as friends who were acquaintances or those names I don't remember. They know all about me. Which reminds me of when I went to Harare, spoke at a British Council meeting, and a woman came up who said her fondest memory was of how we sat together at the same desk to do our matric exams. (Equivalent: A level.) I said I had never taken an exam in Southern Rhodesia, but she calmly replied that she remembered it. There is nothing to be done about this kind of thing.

Not unless driven to extremes. A friend *in the public domain* driven out of his wits by phantoms, once patiently corrected the myth-makers: 'No, I was not born in Benares, but in Brooklyn

. . . I was only married twice . . . I do not own a Lear jet.' Now he agrees enthusiastically to everything. 'Let them sort it out.' Mind you, playing this game it does not do to invent: 'My three-legged dwarf wife who left me for an impotent steeplejack who plays in a Tibetan brass band . . .' That would be below the belt.

Are writers a kind of Rorschach test? We are certainly confessors, but what can one say about a nineteen-page letter as detailed as an obsessive diary by someone on the point of suicide? 'Help me! Help me!' But there is no return address.

'That black blotch there, what does it make you think of?'

'A kind friend who will listen to me and my troubles day and night and only say, Poor Thing.' 'That bitch my Aunt Bessie who used to steal my pantyhose.'

It appears I had a deep relationship with Ronald Laing who claimed that I was his patient and he gave me six doses of LSD. Isn't this kind of thing a slander? Libellous? No? But it is a lie. I met him half a dozen times and he came to my home, but only once, because he made my friends play the Truth Game, which ended as disagreeably as one might expect.

If I know the market – and I do, I do – my relationship with Ronald is now engraved in stone.

But, one must have a sense of proportion. One must rise above the petty and stick to the important things. Never mind about the phantom farm, my poor family, Ronald Laing, the places I am supposed to have visited, the things I am supposed to have said. This woman says that my (naturally) curly hair was achieved with the aid of *a home perm kit*. Now that's fighting talk.

There is an additional hazard with American biographers. They over there across the pond, we over here, we laugh at different things. My jest, when asked by an interviewer if I prefer people to cats, that cats are better because people don't purr, was analysed solemnly as a symptom of misanthropy.

About Cats

The most often heard remark about cats is that they are 'independent' and then, that they don't care about people, only about places; and these from people who knew their cat will sit waiting for them looking out of a window, every day.

It was Kipling who did the damage with 'The Cat Who Walked by Himself'.

Studies of communities of feral cats – house cats gone wild – reveal that the females form nurseries and creches, guarding and feeding their own and each other's kittens, while one or two of their number go hunting to feed them all. Young males of many species have a hard time, on the edge of the secure female group. The young toms hang about, hoping to nip in for a quick mating when the boss cats are indulgent or not looking, and often trying to be kittens again, crawling into nests they have grown out of. The mature males, finished with mating and fighting, or perhaps defeated by their offspring, go wandering. It is they who walk by themselves, solitary in hedgerows or wild places, but they do not live long, succumbing to diseases, fight wounds, and in built-up areas, traffic.

People who do not observe their cats, but only rely on 'received' wisdom, miss out. A cat gives back what you put into it, returning affection and attention, but withdrawing in dignified silence if ignored. No creature is more sensitive to slights and taunts and even teasing. Too much, and they will take themselves off in search of a more sympathetic home. And yet one may not generalise: people who have had more than one child know that every baby is born different, and similarly, in a litter of kittens each one will be an individual. Like humans they are coarse-grained and sensitive, stupid and clever, clinging and standoffish. They may be talkative and silent, show-offs and modest introverts.

They are more observant than sometimes we like – know more about us than we think. There are moments when our 'pet' will surprise us by some little act or attention, showing that we have been understood. You are sad, anxious, apprehensive – and your cat will come and show sympathy with a lick or a purr. You are busy and have forgotten her – but you will be reminded by a gentle nip or a tap of the paw. You have slept too late and open your eyes to see the cat, its face six inches from yours: you have been woken by its purr.

We share our emotional apparatus with them, though there are those who angrily deny it: but some people like to inflate themselves with superior feelings about other species. Observing cats you see the whole gamut of human emotions – love, affection, antipathies as apparently irrational as some of ours; you see hurt feelings, and jealousy, and that is very strong in cats, they like to come first.

And they can think, as we do. An intelligent cat may go in for long-term planning. One, who was a stray, conducted a campaign to live with us, a slow, deliberate, thought-out plan. For days he waited outside the back door till we softened. Then he was offered a chair in the kitchen, where he stayed for a while. Then he achieved an intermediate place under a bath. Finally he challenged us to eject him from the living room: but we gave him a bean bag in a lowly place that would not offend the other cats. And then he chose a moment to leave that and claim a good place, thus throwing down the gauntlet to the boss cat.

And does a cat have a 'sixth sense'? There is a radio programme going on as I write, discussing this. I think they do. I believe they know what you are thinking, and sometimes behaviour that seems inexplicable can be explained by remembering what you were thinking at the time.

The Maimie Papers

A remarkable document has had a number of godparents.
Maimie's letters, kept for half a century by the recipient Fanny
Howe, were handed on to her daughter Helen, who donated
them to the Schlesinger Library at Radcliffe College. They were
found by a researcher, Ruth Rosen, and all kinds of scholars
and historians, and then the National Endowment for the
Humanities, worked for their publication. At once the questions
have to start. *Why* was so much effort needed to get into print
material you'd think any publisher anywhere, male or female
or of any political complexion, would clamour for? It doesn't
make sense. Is it conceivable that ordinary publishers turned it
down? It is not that the Feminist Press, who did the book first
in the United States, shouldn't have done it if ordinary publishers were available, though one does have to hope that a
book with such a wide appeal won't lose readers by being seen
as a 'woman's book', but that the way it is presented, as if
daunting problems at last have been solved, is surprising. For
Maimie is as immediately likeable as Moll Flanders. Contemplating all this, one has to wonder if the striving and difficulty
that was in everything Maimie did has to be part even now of
what survives of her? Sometimes a person or book seems to be

on a wavelength or to give off a note, and nothing can change that. Nothing so simple could possibly happen to Maimie as a publisher saying, 'What a find! We'll put an editor on to it, and here is an advance.'

I've read it three times, carefully, because of the way it springs speculation and fresh associations. This is partly because so much is between the lines. I am reminded of the fascination I felt first reading *Clarissa*. Life has done almost as well as art. Yes, *The Maimie Papers* does have the quality of a novel, for Maimie was able to bring a person or a scene to life with a word. It is also social history.

In mentioning prostitution first, I am giving the emphasis everyone does; how lucky we are to have information from that class of woman who through history has been inarticulate, the working-class prostitute. True. But the first thing you think is that Maimie would not now be classed as one. Or not so relent-lessly. Then, she had to accept the label and be defined by it, though she saw herself as superior to the lower classes of prostitutes, and was fiercely proud about the things she could not allow herself to do. Yet this did not mean she despised those who did what she would not. Nor did she despise herself. She had a common-sense way of judgement, and that kept her self-respect even under the dreadful pressures of the hypocrisies of the time.

Maimie was born May Pinzer in Philadelphia in 1885, to Julia and Morris Pinzer, Polish-Russian Jews. They were comfortable. The father was a pillar of the little community, was known as generous and kindly. The mother seems never to have been up to much, characterised by Maimie as 'that woman is the nearest thing to nothing I ever knew'.

Morris Pinzer was brutally murdered – and that is all we are told. Julia was left with five children, and in poverty. Maimie was twelve. A clever girl, longing for education, which all her life she saw, as children do now in poor countries, as the only door to a decent life, she had to leave school. She went to work in a department store, then often the way in to prostitution for poor girls, who were surrounded by pretty things they could not buy, and besieged by men who hung around the shop waiting to supply them. The wages were not enough for the girls to live on, so they had to be at home, and what they earned was given to the parents. Often they were allowed nothing to spend on themselves. On one side, then, the poverty of their homes and long hours on bad wages, and on the other, easy pleasures. The girls would come home late, be told never to do it again, but of course did it again and found themselves outside a door locked against them. But the good-time flats were always open, and brothels, and bars. To us, now, there is this quality of melodrama, Maria and the Red Baron, good and bad, vice and virtue, choices that have dramatic and indeed eternal consequences. A quality bred of the desperation of poverty, the real, grimy, just-above-the-abyss poverty full of drunken despairing men and easily dying children and exhausted women? We do not have this kind of poverty now, not in our part of the world, not at this time, 1979. (Though we are all of us secretly afraid of what might happen again.) So, you find yourself thinking, was it the poverty of *then* that made such an either/or, knife-edge of life? But no, it was not only poverty, but poverty plus religion, the religion of the north, so damning and condemning and dour. After all, a Maimie in let's say Puerto Rico would not be hounded all her life, not be damned and disgraced and cast out. What we are reading about is something of the north. Yet that isn't true either: we can find exactly this savagery of judgement about women at this moment in Muslim countries ... But there *is* a black cold dirty ugliness of poverty that is northern and of industrial cities, and it breeds a grim rigidity of outlook.

Maimie loved elegance and pretty things, had natural taste and discrimination. She went out with the young men, quarrelled with Julia, and found herself in a prison with common criminals, put there by her mother. The prison had a library of Hebrew books donated by her father for Jewish prisoners, but this did not help her.

The mother was abetted by an uncle who had sexually assaulted Julia as a small girl. 'Your honour, take her into care, I can't do anything with her.' But now, or so one hopes, there would be some kindness for the child. For Maimie was classed as a prostitute, and she was thirteen years old. Her mother would not respond to her pleas to take her home. And, like Maimie, you find yourself unable to condemn this blancmange of a woman, or even to expect anything. She was always, all her life, the property of the nearest person who wanted to manipulate her.

Maimie was for a year in a Magdalen Home for bad girls, where she was cold, frightened, abandoned. She was so hungry she ate banana peel from the rubbish bin. But she was also able to teach girls older than herself to read and write.

At home again, she and Julia fought. For instance, she bought a toothbrush and mouthwash. These, she knew, were what refined people used but they were seen by Julia as evidence of wickedness. What infections was she concealing? All the neighbours were told, and they condemned Maimie. She left home at fourteen and went to Boston where she was for four years with a lover of whom she never said much more than that they lived as man and wife. She did nude modelling for artists, and a little acting. And earned money, or at least presents, through sex, when she had to.

Not yet twenty, she was in a charity hospital where she had 31 operations on her left eye, which was removed. The suggestion is that she had syphilis. Did she? Now it seems almost not to matter, put in the context of everything else – she had, for instance, to be cured of morphine addiction. But if she did, for this most straightforward of women to lie about it says everything about the experience. And, too, there was the way she fought, later, so passionately, for girls who had syphilis and who could not easily get treatment. She said that she felt she was fighting for herself as a girl.

She had hit bottom. Alone, disowned by her family, uneducated, believing she had lost her attraction for men because she was so thin and so sick, she coldly thought out her position. And married. For security.

The alternatives for an unqualified woman were three. Marriage, prostitution, or the sort of work she refused to do, scrubbing, washing, kitchen work.

I wonder how a girl reading now of Maimie's choices sees it all? (Reading this book I've had an imaginary companion, of about twenty, and I ask: What do you think of this? Of this?) It must seem like another planet. Yet it was such a short time ago. Now Maimie would get work on a newspaper, write a novel, find all kinds of openings, because she was so resourceful and clever. Again, one has to think of a poor girl in the slums of a South American city, in Africa, in Algeria . . .

That was the epoch of 'The Twelve Pound Look'. Nora had slammed the door not long before. Anna Karenina had gone through her unnecessary, socially imposed, agonies. The 'Woman Question' was being debated everywhere.

Maimie did not find security in her marriage. Mostly, she had to keep her husband. It was not his fault. He, too, was unskilled, and work was scarce.

This was the poverty, not of the lowest depths, but when you are struggling not to fall in. Everything you do and think and strive for is to keep up the appearances that will enable you to stay out of the abyss. And this is a most real and palpable abyss: all around you can see people falling in and disappearing. Cleanliness costs money: you wear your clothes more times than you would like, and suffer if you are fastidious. If you are given a white dress, you hand it on to someone better off, for you cannot afford to wear white. (I put being clean first, because Maimie did. Cleanliness was so expensive a commodity then, and so hard to keep.) Your soles have holes, but you keep the uppers polished. You catch cold because it is very hot and you have only winter clothes and you get overheated. You pawn everything but what you are wearing. You live for weeks on a pint of milk a day and dry bread, and often there isn't that. You walk because you can't pay fares. You are thrown out of your room because you are a few hours late with the rent.

> In all that time, I dug up the money, never asking any favours of these people from whom we rented, until last Monday, when I asked them to wait until Saturday for their money. As we paid in advance, we owed them nothing; but they would not hear of waiting until Saturday, as I had nothing else to pawn and could not without humbling myself ask of anyone and we had to get out. They told us at six o'clock that the room had to be vacated that night. I thought I should go frantic. It was so hard for me, as we didn't have a nickel. But there was 50 cents coming to us that we had deposited for our night keys; and I thought we should use that to procure a place of some sort to stay Monday night and . . .

Always, there was the cold. In southern countries poverty has one threatening face the less. For the poor of the north, winter is the greatest enemy, dreaded, outwitted in a hundred threadbare ways, survived with such a long drag of effort.

Maimie was surviving . . . and into her life had entered Mr Welsh the philanthropist.

There was a class of Americans then described by Helen Howe in *The Gentle Americans*. Did it have its counterpart in our country? They could not talk about money, nor make it, for trade and earning were vulgar. But, they had money, plentifully, and devoted themselves to artistic, literary and humanistic pursuits. Mr Welsh was one. His friend Fanny Quincy Howe was another. He asked Fanny Howe to write to Maimie. Thus began the correspondence that was Maimie's support for twelve years. 'You see, when I write you, I write everything, and mostly the things that trouble me, and that is because I love you and don't stop to think whether it would be better to write this or that – but just keep on writing what is in my mind – things that I have always had to keep to myself, for I never trusted any other woman.'

Of all the people whose personalities come through so strongly between these lines, Mr Welsh is the most vivid – and the most unlikeable. He was patronising, weak, dishonest, vacillating; the same kind of saintly man as the one in *Rain*. Clearly, he was attracted to Maimie, perhaps did not know it himself, and then did, and panicked, setting bounds of an insulting kind. Maimie knew it all of course, and so did Fanny. Maimie's letters to Fanny are masterpieces of tactful implication. One can imagine, if there had not been letters, the two women sitting together, and no more than a look being needed. Luckily for us the women only met twice, and everything is in print. Mr Welsh, having sharply withdrawn, told Maimie that 'his people' did not want him to do 'this work'. Maimie wrote to Fanny how she was humiliated at being 'work', an 'exhibit', after being treated as a person. Mr Welsh has handed around the letters she wrote to him among fellow philanthropists. She could not have believed he could do such a thing. But Mr Welsh was all emotional reaction. Meeting Maimie, obviously with reluctance, he complained that her hat, made by herself out of bits and pieces, was too bright, and that she was wearing rouge. Maimie writes to Fanny that she has never worn rouge, her own complexion has always been too high, her efforts have been to tone it down. She describes the exact construction of the offending hat. Fanny talks to Mr Welsh, explaining about how Maimie feels, and he resumes a friendship. But with limitations. Thereafter she calls him her father. Nothing he does for her, money given, or aid of any sort, is done without ifs and buts and conditions. Maimie says to Fanny that Mr Welsh is altogether too good to be true, a saint, and if he were to be described, in the idea he had of himself, to people hearing of him, they would never believe that such a being could exist.

Disliking him so much, one tells oneself to be fair: that was *then* and Mr Welsh was a child of his time and could not help it. But Fanny Howe was a child of *then* too, and she was incapable of patronage or of being humiliating. Maimie withheld nothing from her, told the most painful truths. But with Mr Welsh there is a frantic striving and effort to adjust herself against her own honest standards. This was not only because of her own need. She was always asking aid for others.

How was it possible that two women so different could be real and mutually respecting friends? Who was this gentle lady, Fanny Howe, with her wealth and her position and her talents? She wrote books, though under men's names, as women then so often did. She had 'wit and heart and warmth', and was a hostess, and had a husband as nice as herself, and children. But Fanny's daughter says she was, too, melancholy and reserved, known for her acerbity and warmth, aloofness and passion, 'sensitive to the sufferings of others, and with an icy barrier of reserve around her own'. She was 'a deeply ingrained agnostic'. She experienced a 'general distrust of life and tended to perceive the only reality in life as unhappiness, the stretches of happiness being only parentheses'.

One imagines these burningly plain-speaking letters arriving, sometimes in batches, in that home where money and sex could not be mentioned.

Her letters to Maimie were long and generous and described her daily life, which Maimie needed to know about. Fanny represented that ideal to which Maimie always aspired. Not the least of the useful reminders here is that a passion for respectability does not have to be only a need to be exactly like everyone else, because of the discomfort of not being so – but it can be, too, what keeps a person trying for something better against the odds. Maimie was all the time refining herself in ways sometimes painful to read about. For example, nagging her family over table manners. But this was an aspect of her wanting them not to be just 'phlegmatic' and ordinary and satisfied with earning money and eating and sleeping. She wanted them to be like 'people of your sort'. To be 'gentle people, your kind'. There were scenes of Maimie, the prostitute, the bad girl, for she was always treated as such by her relatives, lecturing them that it is not correct to take bites out of a whole piece of bread, but one should break off bits and butter them separately, and then one should . . . and should . . . and should . . . And they listened to her, sullenly, attempted reform, and hated her. Who was she to act superior to them, with her fancy ways and fancy friends? All of them used her as an unpaid servant, and never once helped her, even when she was destitute and sank her pride to beg from them.

Here again we meet the ambiguous results of the virtue of Mr Welsh. He insisted – making it a condition of the charity which he so slenderly provided – that she should be prepared to suffer, for the good of her soul, all the indignities heaped on her by her mother and her brothers. She most healthily rebelled, and often; but he never ceased these pressures, again and again returning her to every sort of servitude and insult. She resented her submission. 'There is something so empty in their relationship with me that I think it would be folly to force it any longer. This condition exists not only with me but between themselves. Their love for each other, if it could be called that, is absolutely hollow.'

Yet she was prepared to go to them when they were in need, and did her best to find a mother in Julia, and then, when she could not, a friend. Julia was always demanding from her, being given, and then turning on her. Maimie was the only one of the children to help the mother, providing little holidays and comforts.

> ... and I force myself to keep in mind that I was born of her, that I lay in her arms as a baby, nursed of her breast and was at one time her chief interest, I listen for a cry in my heart for her and there isn't any. I look at her and feel toward her only coldness. This I am sure is unnatural and I feel sure I am to blame. Don't think that I bear her any ill will for wrongs, fancied or real – I don't. I want so hard to love her – or even like her and I can't.

Maimie had decided to leave her husband. Mr Welsh opposed this. But she made attempts to live on her own, earning a pittance addressing envelopes by the thousand, or other unskilled work. It is interesting that this unqualified woman who always found it so hard to get work knew Russian, German, Yiddish, French. The excuse was always her appearance, her patched eye. She could never be used 'out front' where she could be seen, or as a saleswoman. Again and again she was refused because of her appearance. And people took advantage of her. She wondered to Fanny if perhaps she was not like that little dog who has had its rump kicked so often that it backs towards its oppressor to save both of them trouble.

Now a good thing happened, but it had to be seen as 'a

temptation'. There was a childhood sweetheart, Ira. He had married badly, as she had. There was a baby, and he set up his mother and sisters on a farm with this child and undertook to support them all. Then he searched for Maimie, for he loved her, and thought her a wonder, which of course she was. During this period, when she had left her husband and was being tempted back into 'the life', Ira wanted her to live with him in New York. Her own attitude was:

I consider them (divorces) a lot of foolishness and a marriage ceremony the worst lot of cant I ever heard. That is my honest opinion and why bother about it: I could go on deep into that subject to show how I have arrived at such an unusual conclusion but I will simply say because of my observation of the various marriage contracts I know intimately about, my own, my sister's, my mother's, and a host of others.

She did go for a short time to New York, and her letters about the cleanliness, the prettiness of her suite in the hotel, new clothes, theatres, the pleasures of it all, are wonderful, and you catch a glimpse of a Maimie who had been smothered almost to death. But she was married to another, and so was Ira, and this was sin and it was adultery, and Mr Welsh could see an affectionate mutually comforting relationship only as another aspect of Maimie's weakness towards 'the life'.

But it is not so simple. Blaming Mr Welsh for his bigotry, for, quite simply, his lack of common sense or ordinary gumption, a built-in and perennial silliness – when reading through and around and between these lines, you have to see that while Maimie valued Ira, his devotion, his desire to provide for her, he was not good enough for her. Not judged by the standards set by 'your kind of people'. And not by lower standards either: there is a letter to Maimie from him which is that of a child.

There followed another period of difficulty and striving. Maimie was helped through it by Fanny with clothes, money and best of all the long letters. She had decided to learn stenography, and Fanny and Mr Welsh helped. She had to live with her brother, the one who disliked and used her worst. When she got a job of the better kind at last, her cleverness was at once exploited. Recasting form letters for commercial firms, for instance, the credit and pay were taken by her employer. Her one eye was again being used as an excuse for making a favour of employing her at all. And she continually suffered attitudes towards women which now, in some places at least, are obsolete or kept at bay.

There is an account of her stranded at four in the morning, on a cold night, in a strange city, where she had travelled, typically, to help someone. She went to the only place open, a bar, and her handbag was stolen when she was in the lavatory. In it were little items of 'luxury' she had treasured and was going to find it so hard to replace: gloves, a comb, soap, ribbon. And her money. She complained, and the barman said it was her fault, she had been drunk. But this was not true. The police backed the barman. Reading this even now is to feel her imprisonment in circumstance.

She was at last being recognised in the firm she worked for, and was sent up to Montreal. After ups and downs, each one described to Fanny in the smallest of details to do with prices, rents, food, keeping clean, she started a sort of copying agency. This was together with some girls she was befriending. During all her vicissitudes, we find her again and again when just on survival's edge herself, risking everything to stake others. The opposition to a group of girls setting up this business was strong. Maimie explains that the attitudes towards working women which had seemed bad enough in the United States were very much better than those in Canada.

Yet she was on the verge of succeeding. She would have made a living for herself, and for the others . . . but it was 1914, the war started, and everywhere was bankruptcy and failure. Again, she was destitute, and would probably have gone under without Ira, who had come to Montreal to be near her. His family demanded every cent he could make, but he did what he could for Maimie. The war increasingly dominated everything. Maimie chronicles it all for us, the struggling of so many people to keep alive, when there is no work, and it is so cold, and then the food shortages, and everything going to the army.

Maimie wants to help girls who are drifting into 'the life', and knows exactly how to do it. She has no money, and is set up in rooms with the aid of Mr Welsh and Fanny Howe and some of Mr Welsh's philanthropists, where she can provide what would have saved her when she was a young girl, a place where they can drop in any time and have a cup of tea, and listen to the gramophone and look at magazines and – above all – find affection. 'Many girls before they give themselves over to the sinful life have the love of their parents, but people of the sort they spring from – as were my people – are singularly undemonstrative and often it isn't for lack of love, that the girls go astray, as much as for some evidence of it, which in the sinful life they get in abundance – of a sort, of course.' But she has no intention of making what she provides an accompaniment of 'preaching and long faces'. An argument ensues between Maimie and Mr Welsh, because he, typically, wants to call it the Montreal Christian Mission for Friendless Girls. He insists. And does call it this. So do the spies he sends up to see what is going on. But Maimie will not, and writes to Fanny Howe: 'I thank God you are not friendless, but if you were – and were 18 years old – you could no more admit it than any girl does. The kind of girl – the human jelly fish – that is willing to be classed as "friendless" I haven't much time for, and I'd like to see the place I'd have walked into when I was a young girl that was known to be a haven for friendless girls.'

Maimie is standing firm in a way which she has not been able to do earlier. She is not the flimsy self-doubting person she has sometimes been. Now she has learned that if there had not been a war, she would have been running her own business, and Montreal will always be for her the promise that independence for a woman is possible. Maimie is standing up not only to Mr Welsh, but to doctors, hospitals, social workers, Charity Boards, enemies of all kinds, who will only help the girls for whom she is trying to get cures for venereal disease, and food, and shelter, and proper jobs, at the price of their protégées' putting up with contempt, dislike, patronage, preaching. But not all of them are like this; and sometimes Maimie records that he, or she, is *really* kind, a real human being.

In the flu epidemic after the war, Maimie was nursing her family, all down with it, and burying the dead: there was no one else to do this.

And now, at last, she is ready to marry Ira. The divorce, which she thinks is a lot of cant, has been got, but at the price of such travelling about and waiting and difficulties, and the money that neither of them can afford. But she is virtuous, that is the main thing. The last we see of her is with Ira and a crowd of prostitutes and some girls who have been rescued in a house by the sea rented to give them a holiday and some decent food and clean air. They are being harassed by the police and they have no funds. Maimie married, it is clear, is seen by her protectors as one in no need of further financial aid. She writes that Ira is supporting his large family and cannot afford to fund so many needy girls.

And there the letters end. Fanny Howe's to Maimie have not survived, though we may be sure that Maimie treasured them. Mr Welsh had long ago demanded, making a big thing of it, the return of his to Maimie. What can possibly have been in them?

We do not know what happened to Maimie. It is surely a statement that the letters *did* end here. Is it possible that Maimie and her protégées have become too much not only for Mr Welsh but also Fanny Howe? No, we cannot believe that Fanny would let Maimie drop out of sight. Was it that Maimie did not want to go on with it? For the second time, she had married security. Of a kind. The fight had become too much for her, though she does not say it. But she had turned her back for ever on becoming like 'you people'. Was it some sort of shame? Did she feel let down? Was it that she felt she had failed, and as can happen, drew a black line across her page and wanted to start again?

Did Ira and she go on giving up any sort of personal comfort, a personal life, for the sake of the girls? The twenties had started, plushy for the rich, bad for the poor; the hungry thirties were close! What of that appalling family of hers? Did they cease to treat her so badly now that she was a properly married woman again?

She had not given up her aspirations for more education:

'I want to go to school – i.e., I want to take up the study of something. I am fearful lest my equipment is inadequate. I haven't any idea of what I should aim for, and above it all, I am so afraid that I overestimate the worthwhileness of it. I haven't discussed this with Ira, mainly because in his estimation I know now more than anyone alive! However, I know what I have yet to know. My love to you all.'

That is the last letter.

Fanny Howe, the writer, always urged Maimie to try her hand at autobiography. But Maimie said, 'There seem so many reasons why I could not do it. For instance, the little time, even if it only took 15 minutes a day is so hard to spare. There are so many tasks – stockings always to be darned, letters to write, sometimes work for the office – that I don't feel I could accomplish much if I did start. I really feel I could write it, if I could write it a bit at a time, and maybe I will try it and . . .'

She never did. Yet the letters got themselves written, out of her love for Fanny Howe, in the few odd minutes she could find in a day, sometimes going without meals to do it. And here is the book she doubted she had the equipment to write.

Olive Schreiner

She was thinking about what the nineteenth century called the Woman Question when still a little girl, as her first novel, *The Story of an African Farm*, shows. At eighteen she had an experience which changed her: a conversation with a black woman

> still in her untouched primitive condition ... she was a woman whom I cannot think of otherwise than as a person of genius. In language more eloquent and intense than I have ever heard from the lips of any other woman, she painted the condition of the women of her race; the labour of women, the anguish of woman as she grew older, and the limitations of her life closed in about her, her sufferings under polygamy and subjection; all this she painted with a passion and intensity I have not known equalled ...

But in all her bitterness, there was not one word directed against any individual man, for men were, with her, part of a process – life, and the conditions of her race being what they were ... and so Olive Schreiner, too, for she saw things as a working-out, a conspiracy with the creative principle, and always in the service of the evolution of the human race. This incident

195

contributed to a key concept, that 'women of no race or class will ever rise in revolt or attempt to bring about a revolutionary readjustment of their relation to their society however intense their suffering and however clear their perception of it, while the welfare and persistence of their society requires their sub-mission'. Here we can see the defensiveness of women then, who had to prove their right to rebel, and to make new defin-itions; also Olive's persistent deference to the great imperative. As for us, we may profitably be prodded to think about why people may sometimes rebel, but sometimes not, not even when it seems inconceivable to outsiders that they do not. South Africa now; Rhodesia until recently – why do people put up with it?

Olive thought about women and men, women and sex, women and children, all her life, but particularly women and work; and for a good part of it she was writing a vast book called *Musings on Women and Labour*. Her relationship with Havelock Ellis supported her where she needed support, but the questions she wrestled with were broader-framed than he ever could share with her, though she called him her soul bother, and they were friends all their lives. The bond was intellectual. Because of its strength – and it was forged first when she came to England full of the need for intellectual companionship that had been starved in South Africa, that 'country of lower-middle-class philistines' – she tried for years to make their relationship more than it could be. None of us is easily able, when a match is made in one area of ourselves, to relinquish hope for more. We do not easily say: I had an intellectual bond with that one, but emotionally we were uneasy, and physically awful. Or: physically perfect, but emotionally a disaster and intellectually a non-starter. No, a strong attraction in one area makes us gloss over lacks in the others. Besides, we are not taught to think in this way: 'cold', we judge it – but then, we are a sentimental lot. Poor Olive floundered in this 'soul friendship' for years, and the correspondence between her and Ellis is full of strain, showing as mawkishness, whenever they left the area where they were at ease: discussions on intellectual problems. Olive was very neurotic, and knew it, and understood why. The 'liberated woman' of that time paid a heavy price in invalidism. Look at Florence Nightingale, at Elizabeth Browning, many others. How about Isabella Bird, always ill, in fact at death's door in England, but as soon as she could get away from awful British conventions, in bouncing health, usually on a horse in a blizzard in the Rockies or Mongolia or anywhere really difficult. Olive knew her neurasthenia was because she was always pitting her naturally reserved person (full of 'modesty', in fact) against public opinion; but conflict was ever a begetter of insight. She was making volumes of notes on sex, sexuality, for her big book, and kept at it even when it made her ill, because she was learning so much about the damage done by prudishness, by ignorance.

Later she married Samuel Cronwright, an ex-member of the South African legislature, and they got on wonderfully out of bed as well as in it. They began together a life of energetic campaigning on many issues, feminism being only one. But she was always at work on her great manuscript. The Boer War found her and Cronwright-Schreiner (he was able to add her name to his) campaigning here and in South Africa to persuade the English into an understanding of the Boer point of view. She was judged anti-British, and a risk. The manuscript was left in her Johannesburg home when the war forced her away from it, and it was destroyed when the house was sacked and burned. Nothing was left of the book she had cherished so long and which she believed would contain her best work. She was imprisoned in a little shack alone with her dog, not allowed books and newspapers, kept under guard by 36 armed soldiers, day and night. She had no light once the sun went down. In these conditions she rewrote from memory part of her book on women. This, then, is the result: a much shortened reconstruction. The book has been out of print a long time, hard to find out of libraries: but it is a classic of the Labour movement, and has had a large influence. It is strong, large in scope, generous, bold. Olive's subject is humanity, and woman as she can contribute to the development of humanity. I do not think she would recognise as 'sisters' those women who make 'Women's Lib' a means to the narrowing of their sympathies.

This book, and *The Story of an African Farm*, show her at her best. She did write other novels, but they didn't jell. One, *Trooper Peter Halket of Mashonaland*, protested against the barbarous conquest of what was Rhodesia. Brilliant agit-prop, this is, but no more. (Raising questions about what makes a work of art, for this is not one). It caused much heart-searching, but did not stop Rhodes from subjugating Mashonaland and destroying a culture that will come (and this is already happening) to be understood as being every bit as valuable as the 'progress' that supplanted it. On the subject of South Africa, read Olive Schreiner: her polemical writing is still valid, full of insights useful now.

Originals like Olive provoke questions . . . many of the rights she demanded for women are here: it is the fate of originators that they may fight so well their descendants wonder what all the fuss was about. But none of the basic problems she spent her life thinking about are anywhere near settled.

The essence of what she wanted was satisfying and meaningful work for women – and men. But men and women had been stripped by the Industrial Revolution of what had made them human. Women for most of the human story had been able to say: I grow and prepare the food, make the clothes, keep the home that shelters the family: women had a function, were irreplaceable. But now, like men, they had brutish ugly work, or none at all. Three sections of this work are on parasitism, defined by her thus: '. . . parasitism is not connected with any definite amount of wealth. Any sum supplied to an individual which will so far satisfy him or her as to enable them to live without exertion may absolutely parasitise them.'

Well, how about that, then?

She is fierce about fashion, both in dress and taste and in thought, seeing it as slavery. She is right, but anyone saying so now would earn at best a tolerant smile.

'It is this consciousness of large impersonal ends to be attained, and to the attainment of which each individual is bound to play her part, however small, which removes from the domain of the unnecessary, and raises to importance, the action of each woman who resists the tyranny of fashions in dress or bearing or custom which impedes her stride towards the new adjustment.'

In only one sphere did she claim for women more than for men: women know the cost of human flesh in ways that men do not. Here perhaps one may juxtapose Kurt Vonnegut's (brave) remark that the real motive for Women's Lib, though an unconscious one, is that women are refusing to spend their lives nurturing people who they know will fry or frizzle, be poisoned, blasted, pulverised, obliterated . . . Or words to that effect.

I can't be alone in using a certain device to highlight present situations: which is to bring back in imagination people from the past, and let them stand in comment on . . . let us for instance imagine Olive Schreiner, a dumpy, shabby, most uncool little figure, standing in on this our charming scene, where pleasure and comfort and gain are first principles. How about a room full of children watching television, incited day after day, year after year, by the advertising – that most efficient conditioning system yet devised by man – to guzzle, gobble, grab and get, to believe that we are all entitled to absolutely anything we want the moment we want it . . .

'But these are your children! Your future! The best part of you! Why is it allowed? Does no one object?'

'Well, there are some who object to children seeing sexy scenes . . .'

'No, no, I mean all this gluttony, the emphasis on the material things, the animal things . . .'

'But our economy would collapse if we didn't sell goods!'

'. . . so that each child we bring to life, not one potentiality shall be lost nor squandered on a lesser when it might have been extended on a higher and more beneficent task. So that not one desirable faculty of the marvellous creatures we suffer to bring into existence be left uncultivated . . .'

'Oh come on now, Olive! Don't be so earnest! Don't be so boring!'

When I was young . . .

When I was a young woman an old woman said to a group of us that the greatest difficulty confronting young people is that they feel powerless, small and insignificant people in a world full of great power machines. She told us to remember that it is the efforts of individuals that move the world, and that nobody must think themselves small and unimportant.

When I looked around the world then, I saw the Soviet Empire, Hitler's Germany, Mussolini's Italy, the British Empire, the White Supremacy of South Africa and Southern Rhodesia, Salazar in Portugal and Franco in Spain. All these people and powers seemed so strong they must be permanent, impossible to imagine them overthrown. And now they have all disappeared, and soon people won't remember them at all, or they will be a line or two in history books.

What I do remember is the individuals, some of them apparently insignificant, who in fact did change things. (And of course an individual may be an influence for bad, so one has to be able to choose right.) But I want to pass on what this old woman said to us: 'Remember that it is the efforts and courage of individuals that count, in the long run.'

Preface for the *Writers' and Artists' Yearbook 2003*

Since I began writing seventy or so years ago everything has changed for writers. Then 'I want to be a writer' meant you were in apprenticeship to a hard craft taught by extensive reading of the best that has been written. It might take years to get your first book published. You were probably going to be poor, at least at first. There was room in this design for respect for those writers who could never command big sales, might never be known to more than a discriminating minority. Stendhal said he expected to be read and understood in a 100 years' time by the happy few. He was wrong about his prospects but his stoic stance on solitary excellence was a banner that some of us, at least in our better moments, were happy to march under. Writing was a vocation, a dedication. To write for money was to sell out – never mind about Dr Johnson. Too much socialising and celebrity must be death to integrity. This was then understood by publishers: when my first book did well, they apologised for asking me to do an interview.

Dear dead days. Now, 'I want to be a writer' usually means, I want the bright lights, a big advance, prizes, and the bigger the promotional tour the better.

This is true for a good many aspiring writers. There remains, and always will, a minority who know that what makes a real writer is the solitary hard slog. There are exceptions. Balzac thrived on society, and Victor Hugo was not averse to notice. Salman Rushdie can party all night and write the next day. But on the whole it is better for writers to shun the razzmatazz. Not much chance of that these days; the publishers see to that. Yet it is bad for a young writer to be exposed suddenly to a glare of attention. Not a few have written a good or promising first novel but then the second, written in time snatched from journalists and interviewers, might not be so good, or there might be a long wait for it. But it is no use saying what ought to be, what one might prefer: one has to work inside the limits of what is.

Until recently, asked if I always intended to be a writer, I would say no, not until my twenties. So much for lying, twisty memory: I met a woman who remembered me from school, when we were eleven, sitting on our beds in the dorm, and I said I was going to be a writer. I had been writing bits of this and that always, the first when I was seven. I wrote two novels when I was seventeen, but I was too raw to match up to my ambitions. One of them was social satire, about the bright young things of Salisbury, Southern Rhodesia (I was shortly to become one of them), and the other was . . . but I have no idea. Written in a kind of trance of delight at the easy way it all poured out. I could not read a word of it back. That taught me a lesson. If you have even mildly dodgy handwriting, do not use a pen.

I am glad to say I destroyed those two early novels and much else. I went on writing when I could, even when I had two small children and no sustained work was possible. I have always had to write in short concentrated bursts, because of pressures. All this time I was saying I was going to be a writer and other people said it of me, on the strength of some cocky early stories in South African magazines. Young writers brought me their work to judge and I had not had much published myself. I look back on this with surprise. I had reached my mid-twenties, always saying I was a writer – and where was the evidence? I gave up my job in a lawyer's office and began on *The Grass is Singing*. I earned my living part time, and better than in a full-time office job, doing typing for Parliament and Select Committees. I was pregnant then and had a small child, luckily an easygoing one.

I finished *The Grass is Singing*. Now what to do? This was wartime. It took six weeks to get letters and packages to London. No airmail then, it had to be by sea, by convoy through the submarine-haunted oceans. When you launched your precious offspring into the mails you knew it might find a watery grave. I sent *The Grass is Singing* and some short stories to publishers and magazines, notably *New Writing*. Six weeks there, the usual delays, six weeks back. I am reading a book now about Matteo Ricci, a traveller to China in the sixteenth century, and when he wrote a letter home to Italy he knew it would take seven years for a reply.

Always keep a copy of what you send out. And do not believe the promises of friends, agents, impresarios when you trust them with a precious only copy. They will lose it and not know how it happened.

I got encouraging letters and began that collection of rejection slips which is essential discipline for every writer. It is not a bad thing to learn patience. The novel was rejected and by the time it had got back to me, I knew why. It was too long, three times the final length. Two-thirds was social satire, but I had been too ambitious again, I did not have the lightness of touch. I threw away two-thirds, and the rest became *The Grass is Singing*. It found a Johannesburg publisher who turned out to be a crook. He would take 50 per cent of the proceeds, but he didn't publish it anyway: too politically risky.

Having at last reached London I sent short stories to Juliet O'Hea of Curtis Brown, who asked: did I have a novel? I said yes, but it was bespoke. She asked to see the contract, then said she had never seen such a shocking contract. She sent a telegram to the Johannesburg publisher threatening him with exposure, and sold the novel over the weekend to Michael Joseph. It was reprinted twice before publication, but I was green, and thought this happened to every writer. The book did well. But this success was preceded by years of writing, tearing up, rewriting. When I am asked for advice by young writers I say that what makes the difference between amateur writers and professionals is that the latter work hard, tear up, rewrite, and are always ready to let something go that doesn't match up. A ruthlessness towards one's dear progeny, that's the thing.

They ask, What is your routine? How do you write? Do you use a processor, a fountain pen, a quill? Do you write in the mornings or perhaps at night? Do you . . . ? Hidden in this kind of questioning is the belief that there is some trick or secret recipe; this is because all one needs to write is a biro and an exercise book, a provisioning that gives an illusion of ease. Alas, no, the trick, the recipe, is hard work.

Simone de Beauvoir

Even before *The Mandarins* arrived in this country it was being discussed with the lubricious excitement used for fashionable gossip. Everyone knew the novel was about the political and sexual lives of Jean-Paul Sartre and Simone de Beauvoir and their friends, a glamorous group for several reasons. First, they were associated with the French Resistance, and of all the heroic myths of the Second World War the Resistance was the most potent. Then, they were French, and it is hard now to explain the degree of attractiveness France had for the British after the war. It was only partly that we knew our cooking and our clothes to be inferior, that they had a style and a panache we lacked. The British had been locked up in their island for the long years of the war, could not refresh themselves outside it, and France wore the features of some forbidden Paradise. And, too, intellectual communism, intellectuals generally, were glamorous in a way they never have been here, not least because what the mandarins were debating along the Left Bank were questions about the Soviet Union scarcely acknowledged in socialist circles here, or, if so, only in lowered voices. There was another reason why *The Mandarins* was expected to read like a primer to better living, and that was the relationship between Sartre and de Beauvoir, presented by them, or at least by Sartre, as exemplary. It was close and matey, like a marriage, but without the legalities and obligations of one, while both partners had absolute freedom to pursue sexual adventures they fancied. This arrangement, needless to say, appealed particularly to men, and innumerable sceptical women were lectured by actual or possible mates on how they should take a lesson from Simone, a woman above the petty jealousies that disfigure our sex. As it turned out, women were right to be sceptical, but there was for us too an attraction in that comradely relationship over there in Les Deux Magots and the Flore, where Jean-Paul and his long-term woman Simone together with all his *petites amies*, where Simone and her steady, Jean-Paul, and her other little loves, male and female, all foregathered daily to partake of lofty intellectual fare, watched by hundreds of reverential disciples. But it turned out there was nothing of this ideal relationship in the novel, and the Simone figure, Anne, was presented as a dry and lonely woman, in a companionable marriage, resigned to early middle age.

Sartre then stood for an adventurous optimism about science. There was a film about him, showing him stepping out of a helicopter, then the newest of our toys, hailing the brave new world of technology, the key to unlimited progress. We needed this kind of re-evaluation, after watching for the years of the war how war used our inventions and discoveries for destruction.

And then, there was Existentialism. Just as most communists had never read more of Marx than *The Communist Manifesto*, most people attracted by Existentialism had read Sartre's plays and novels. Thus diluted, it was agreeable latter-day stoicism that steadily confronted the terrors of the Universe while refusing the weak-minded consolations of religion; courageous, solitary, clear-minded.

The Left Bank was, quite simply, the intellectual centre of

the world, no less, and here was *The Mandarins*, a guide to it written by one of its most glittering citizens.

But Paris was only the half of it. Simone de Beauvoir had had a much publicised affair with Nelson Algren, and the novel describes it. Algren, then, was famous for *The Man with the Golden Arm* and *A Walk on the Wild Side*, cult novels romanticising the drug and crime cultures of big American cities. Drugs, crime and poverty were as glamorous as, earlier, had been La Vie Bohème and its TB, its drunkenness, the misery of poverty. The bourgeoisie have always loved squalor – in fiction. (In those days the words bourgeoisie, bourgeois, petit-bourgeois tripped off all our tongues a dozen times a day, but now it is hard to use them without being overcome by staleness, by boredom.) To be bourgeois was bad, middle-class values so disgusting that people dying of drugs, or in prison for selling drugs, or with lives wasted by poverty were in every way preferable, full of poetry and adventure that cocked a snook at capitalism and the middle class. When Simone de Beauvoir loved and was loved by Nelson Algren it was the symbolical mating of worlds apparently opposite but linked by a contempt for the established order, and a need to destroy it.

All that has gone, no glamour left, and to read *The Mandarins* without those flattering veils has to be a sobering experience. What remains? For one, the politics of that time. Young people are always asking, but how was it possible that people could support the Soviet Union at all? Here it all is, the debates, the agonisings, the betrayals, the hair-splittings, the compromises and the self-deceptions. What it was all based on, what was never questioned, was the belief that no matter how terrible the Soviet Union was, it had to be better than capitalism, bound to be the future of the whole world once the infant communism was over its teething troubles. Another never-questioned pillar was that whatever decisions one made, whatever stance one took, were of importance to the whole world: the future of the world was at stake, dependent on the 'correct' or otherwise decisions of those people who – as the phrase then went – knew the score. Initiates – that was what they were, or how they saw themselves.

These politics already have something of the flavour of ancient religious squabbles, but the novel will continue to be read, I think, for an ironical reason: its brilliant portraits of women.

There is Josette, the sweet, passive beauty who was a collaborator with the Germans because of a rapacious and brutal mother, quite one of the nastiest women in fiction. There is Paula who will not admit that her great love is in fact ditching her, and lives in a state of delusion, claiming him for herself. Above all, there is Nadine, daughter as it were of this group of mandarins, sullen, angry, always resentful because of past but unspecified wrongs, unscrupulous, manipulative, unlovable and unloving, and finally getting her man by the oldest trick in the book. She is a psychological black hole, absorbing into itself all life, joy, pleasure, love. Never has there been a more unlikeable character, nor a more memorable one, for she dominates the book, even when she is off-stage. And finally, there is Anne Dubreuilh herself, the psychiatrist, whose kindness, patience and common sense on behalf of others does not seem to do much for her own happiness.

The Mandarins is a novel that chronicles its time, but with all the advantages and disadvantages of immediacy, for large parts of it are like the hot, quick impatience of reporting.

My Room

This room is a converted roof space at the very top of the house and it looks south-east. I have my bed along the French window, which fills the wall, so that I can lie in it and look at the sky where the sun gets up in a variety of dusky, pink-streaked, red-flaring or plain skies, and travels past all day, and then the moon follows soon after in all its many sizes, colours and shapes. The moon is sometimes high, sometimes low down, and may disappear for a while into the branches of the great ash tree at the bottom of the garden, which is a long London garden the width of the house.

From the balcony outside the French window I look down at gardens stretching the length of the street, some neglected, a bird-inhabited confusion, some designed and formal, some the crammed delicious tangle amateurs like me may achieve, roses, irises, lilies, clematis, all out together, but then a kind of jungle, because I am too busy to keep it tamed. In these gardens wander cats of all kinds, designer cats and moggies, and the trees are noisy with birds. I and others feed them. Last week a wood-pecker and two jays visited my lower veranda to find nuts that might have been rolled into spaces between pots, overlooked by squirrels and pigeons.

A big birch tree is as tall as the roof and the ash behind it is gigantic. There are cherries, apples, pears, a blackthorn, planes, and around a great green space the size of a small airfield are trees and bushes. This green field is a reservoir – the Victorians put their water under lids of earth. Across it, if it is fine, you see over roofs to the Houses of Parliament, and down to Canary Wharf, and, looking left up a hill it is Hampstead, and if you didn't know, you'd think it was a hill of trees with an occasional roof dotted about.

From my high window I might as well be in the country. It is quiet up here in the day and at night silent, not a sound.

Down on the pavement you could think this was a London street with houses packed up behind it. Beyond the other face of houses are playing fields and an old cemetery, so in fact this conventional city street runs between green fields and trees. No one driving along it could possibly guess the truth.

It is not on the top of a hill, but almost: the reservoir is the top. The street running up to ours is so steep that when there is snow the cars slip and slide, so it is better to drive around another way. Not long ago this was a wild green hill that people might ascend going north-west, then, after resting on a flattish place, start climbing again to the heights of Hampstead. This knot of streets was built in 1890, all at once, as one of the first commuter suburbs. In the area below the reservoir, to the south, until the First World War were fields, cows, little streams. I knew an old woman whose used to take a penny bus ride on Sundays from Marble Arch to where the mill was that gave Mill Lane its name – soon to be replaced by boring flats – so she could put her feet into the streams and watch cows.

As I write leaves are spinning off the trees and the gardens seem drowned in gold and orange and green, and the grass on the reservoir is emerald green in watery sunlight.

A book that changed me

I do not believe that one can be changed by a book (or by a person) unless there is already something present, latent or in embryo, ready to be changed. Books have influenced me all my life. I could say as an autodidact – a condition that has advantages and disadvantages – that books have made me what I am. But it is hard to say of this book or that one: it changed me. How about *War and Peace*? *Fathers and Sons*? *The Idiot*? *The Scarlet and the Black*? *Remembrance of Things Past*? But now they all seem dazzling stages in a long voyage of discovery, which continues.

So I have settled for *The Sufis* by Idries Shah, as the book that had an immediate impact. I had been looking about for a way of thinking, of looking at life, that mirrored certain conclusions and discoveries I had made for myself. But I could not find anything appropriate. It could not possibly be, I decided, that I was the only person with these thoughts in her (or his) head.

Then someone told me that there was a man called Idries Shah, representative of a very ancient way of approaching life – which, however, had always to be presented in contemporary terms, suitable for the society in which it found itself.

Shah was at that moment writing a book to present this philosophy to Western readers. I ordered it from the United States, had to wait, and when it at last came I found what I had been looking for. Robert Graves, who wrote the preface to that edition, described this scene of recognition: 'At last, this is what I have been waiting for . . . so I am not crazy after all . . . many people before me have made exactly this journey and come to the same conclusions . . .'

The Sufis has taken its place as a key book for our time, transforming what used to be called 'Eastern Studies' and often ill-informed writings about 'mysticism'. Idries Shah has pointed out that very little in the book quoted from scholarly sources did not come from Western writers, though their research had often been overlooked by specialists in the field.

The Sufis is quoted now as source material in a dozen different disciplines and in countries East and West. But this is not my personal concern. I continue to find the book full of information, revelation, a mine of thoughts and ideas. I reread it from time to time and always find something new, which can only be said about 'real' books.

The Autobiography of an Unknown Indian, Nirad C. Chaudhuri

A book may live quietly, half-visible, for decades, admired and talked about by a few, and then there is a new generation of readers, a change in the prevailing wind, and there it is, towering over its contemporaries and clearly seen for what it is. Reading this book is to be immersed in India, you feel you are living that life, such is the power of this acute, stubbornly honest, capaciously minded writer to recreate his times. He is a product of the period when Indians were nourished by English literature, law, thought. The contrast between the vivid details of village and family life and the slow growth towards the grandeur of his moral and literary vision provides the tension of these vivid pages. This is one of the great books of the twentieth century.

Old

The approach to old age, that Via Dolorosa, is presented to us as a long descent after the golden age of youth. Yet it would be hard to find someone who wouldn't shudder at the idea of living through their teens again, or even their twenties. You have to grow slowly into a competence with your emotions and I have heard plenty say their thirties or forties were the best time. Not so clean cut, living, classified by Shakespeare as one stage after another, particularly when the first signs of physical old age start pretty young, with your first white hairs, snow in summer.

Yet, that at some point along the way certain events will take place, we know: we have been warned, they never stop going on about it. Teeth, eyes, ears, skin: you'd think there could be no surprises. But I don't remember anyone saying, you are going to shrink. My skirts, comfortable at calf or ankle length one day, are sweeping the ground the next. What has happened? Have they stretched? No, I am four inches shorter, and from thinking of myself as a well-set-up woman I begin to wonder what height qualifies me to be called a dwarf.

It is not a surprise to look in the mirrors and think: Who's that old woman?

Not unexpected to see yourself in old family photographs as your mother, or grandfather.

To find the years start skipping by: that acceleration began early.

But now start the delightful surprises. Time becomes fluid. It is entertaining to look at an old face, on a bus perhaps, and imagine how it must have been young, or to smudge a young face into what it will be in 30 years, or 40. A little girl, dancing about: you see her as a young woman, middle-aged, old. Computers have taught us to do it.

And inside this fluidity a permanence, for the person who looks at the old face in the mirror is the same as the one who shares your earliest memories, when you were two, perhaps less: that child's core is the same as the old woman's. 'Here I still am: I haven't changed at all.'

Best of all, not ever predicted nor, I think, described, a fresh liveliness in experiencing. It is as if some gauze or screen has been dissolved away from life, that was dulling it, and like Miranda you want to say, What a brave new world! You don't remember feeling like this, because, younger, habit or the press of necessity prevented. You are taken, shaken, by moments when the improbability of our lives comes over you like a fever. Everything is remarkable, people, living, events present themselves to you with the immediacy of players in some barbarous and splendid drama that it seems we are part of. You have been given new eyes. This must be what a very small child feels, looking out at the world for the first time: everything a wonder. Old age is a great reviver of memories, in more ways than one.

Professor Martens' Departure

Jaan Kross was born in Tallin, Estonia, studied law, taught children, was arrested in 1946 and spent nine hard years in Siberia, with innumerable other exiled Estonians. The two books we have of his, *The Czar's Madman*, published last year, and this one, were written under Soviet domination.

There is a class of novel we do not have because of our more fortunate history, written to outwit censorship, using past events to inform the present. When in this novel (as in *The Czar's Madman*) you find whole passages like. 'Where nations in their internal lives do not grant citizens inalienable rights, we shall find neither judicial order nor respect for the law in international affairs', or remarks like, 'I really couldn't afford to sulk in a world ruled by princes', you know that the writer is confronting present oppression and expecting his readers to understand him. Many such books, written plentifully in the Soviet Union and in Eastern Europe, are of only local interest, but this author's scope and depth make him a world writer, and his work is translated into every major language.

The frame of this tale is a long leisurely train journey from the rural Estonia of his childhood to St Petersburg where the professor is Your Excellency and a Privy Councillor, and it can be seen as a representation of an ascent from poverty and humble beginnings to his achievements as an internationally acknowledged expert on international affairs. The professor is assessing his life, his successes, his loves, and is proud of himself, but fretting (though with the dry humour of old age) at the fact that his lowly birth has always made it impossible for him to be accepted as an equal by the aristocrats with whom he has spent his life: he may secretly call the czar 'Nicky' as much as he likes.

He is evoking not only his personal past, but Russia's, for he has had to think like a Russian – with the aid of imaginary appearances in the compartment of his wife, to whom he mentally proposes an open and candid telling of the truth, dissolving the lies – or the tact – that have sustained a long and successful marriage. This is one source of the irony that infuses the novel, because the lady would not tolerate the truth, as we know – and so does he. She is a senator's daughter, irreproachably conventional, whom an ambitious young plebeian married to further his career.

Slowly the professor's picture of his Kati, which is affectionate and even loving enough, yields to the reader's understanding that he does not know as much about her as he thinks, just as his telling of the story of a rapturous love affair with a poor student artist, remembered as 'I lost the woman I loved', tells us of his egotism, unrecognised by him in old age, for he still does not seem to see how badly he let her down.

Yet this complex and contradictory man is far from lacking the sympathies you would think out of reach of the Privy Councillor. Because of his origins, a man conservative by nature and made more so by a lifetime spent at the top levels of government, does retain an understanding of the poor people he came from, and attempts sympathy with the revolutionaries of that explosive Russia. His memories present us with a panorama of the times, and not merely a view from the top.

And of former times too, for he is privately convinced he is the reincarnation or at least a repetition of an earlier very high official of the same name, who also spoke six languages, and who wrote a history of the treaties and conventions between Russia and foreign countries, just as he, the present Martens, has done, twenty volumes of it.

The professor, his memory thus extended, is enabled to brood about Czars Alexander and Nicholas, and an assortment of Bonapartes, about events from the time of the French Revolution by way of a host of international crises, taking in, notably, the Russian-Japanese War and Bloody Sunday, and the First World War, because Africa and the European scramble for it is on his agenda.

As with *The Czar's Madman*, where it slowly becomes evident that the narrator is describing people more intelligent, brave and idealistic than he is, so here the professor's view of himself erodes, for the reader, and for the professor too, if not quite as much. The journey concludes with a truly comic encounter – if by comic is understood the clash of irreconcilable substances – when to the professor's compartment comes what was then still described as a New Woman, young, attractive, clever, educated.

He has believed, and believes now, that his long and complex life enables him to put everyone he meets into their social and geographic context, for is he himself not at times and places Estonian, German, Russian, with affinities to all the peoples of the Baltic? Has he not himself been poor and insignificant, and then powerful? Yet he understands nothing about this young woman, his assessments of her are wrong, and as he understands how wrong, all his judgements must be called into question, and he knows it.

This is a dense and many-layered novel. To borrow Virginia Woolf's remark about *Middlemarch*, Jaan Kross is a novelist for grown-ups.

How Things Were

My mother was a nurse in the old Royal Free Hospital when it was in the East End of London, long before it moved to the heights of Hampstead. It was one of the first charity hospitals, financed by Royalty and the rich. Hospitals then had long wards with high ceilings and tall windows and acres of polished floor. No curtains, hygiene forbade them. The ghost of Florence Nightingale still ruled.

The nursing staff was as structured as the army. The lowest were the probationers, then the first, second, third year and staff nurses, then the ward sisters and over all matron, whose martinet eye did not miss a grain of dust or a bed whose corners were half an inch out.

My mother fought with her father to be a nurse: he could not agree; middle-class girls did not become nurses. Defying him she left home and without any support from him worked her way up that jealous hierarchy. Pay was bad, and the food poor. Most nurses had help from their families. It was hard for her, but she did it, and became Sister in time for the First World War. For the four years of that war she nursed the wounded soldiers sent back to the hospital in Britain from the casualty stations and makeshift hospitals in France and Belgium. The

Royal Free was overfull with soldiers, one of them my father who always considered himself lucky to have got shrapnel in his leg in time to get him sent home before the Battle of Passchendaele where every man in his company was killed. When the war ended she was offered the job of matron in the old St George's Hospital on Hyde Park Corner, now a prestigious hotel, nothing left of the tall hall-like wards, the tall austere windows. She was 32, and young for that coveted position. It must have been hard to turn down something so suited to her talents and her temperament, but she did, and in due course found herself on a farm in the old Rhodesia, in a house that was an elongated mud hut, rooms one, two, three, four under thatch. In a trunk was her Sister McVeagh's uniform, and the nursing manual from her student days, which I devoured, aged eight, nine, ten, with incredulity.

There, on that hill, around and through the house dust blew in the dry season, or bits of burned grass from the bush fires; straws, loosened by borers, fell from the thatch where mice and, more than once, little monkeys scurried and played. Over whitewashed walls white ants made ingenious tunnels of red earth which had to be brushed off when they dried, leaving faint pink stains. I liked to keep the door open, though frogs did hop in and out of the room, mosquitoes hunted for their blood feasts, and mosquito nets bundled over the beds could easily have dust in them or a blown leaf.

Thus surrounded, I read about the day and night vigilance to preserve hygiene, in the old Royal Free Hospital.

Every bed frame, locker, bed table, light bracket, chair, had to be wiped with disinfectant every day. The walls and ceilings were wiped over with disinfectant once a week. Floors were scoured daily. Bedding was changed every day. Patients were washed or washed themselves, face and hands, twice a day and all over once a day. Every time a patient was moved from one room to another, or left, and a new one brought in, each surface had to be scrubbed with disinfectant, floors, walls, ceilings, bed, locker, table, light, chair.

Bedpans had a room to themselves and were continually being sluiced with boiling water and disinfectant. Nowhere more than here lingered memories of the typhoid and cholera of past wars where more soldiers died from them than they ever did from bullets.

Each ward had a kitchenette where tea, beef tea, hot drinks, jellies, and special delicacies like arrowroot jelly and calfsfoot jelly could be prepared, to tempt sick appetites.

On a wall in the staffroom a notice exhorted: 'Never forget! The cleanliness of the nurses is of equal importance to that of the patients!'

Nurses' hands, forearms, nails and hair were examined by the sisters, and everyone was monitored by Matron.

Doctors were on a parallel ladder of achievement, and had nothing to do with this ferocious structure of cleanliness and discipline. Matron, I think, would not dare to examine their nails and hands and hair for dirt, though it is hard to imagine a doctor, no matter how senior, withstanding Matron's cold stare at fingernails or hands.

All this I read about, lying in bed, in the middle of southern Africa, while the many winds of heaven wafted what they willed into and around the house, and in the dry season my bathwater might be red with the day's dust. My mother, Sister McVeagh, countered my incredulity with, 'You see, if you are nursing people, there are all those germs about, so *of course* it is important to have *absolute* hygiene.'

Last year I sat by a bed in the new Royal Free, in Intensive Care. What expertise, skill, dedication, devotion; how moving it was to see. What wonderful care my sick relative was getting. But the hours passed, and then a day, and another, and I entertained myself with imagining that Sister McVeagh walked in, a tall and commanding figure, with her full crisp white veil, her little cape, not a hair out of its place. There is a photograph of her in this outfit.

She is bewildered.

'Who are all these people?' she demands.

'They are the doctors and nurses.'

'Why are they wearing pyjamas?'

'Don't you see? These cotton tops and pants, they are all so practical, they don't get in the way when they work, and then into the washing machine they go . . .'

She sighs. 'Washing machines . . . now, if we'd had those . . . keeping those mountains of sheets and pillowcases clean, it was a nightmare. The laundry, it was the most important place in the hospital. But when you went in – you had to sometimes – you'd think it was an inferno, it was so hot, and the clouds of steam . . . the washing women always had coughs, it was not a place anyone would work in unless they had to.'

Now she is looking at the beds, and at the patients in them, each one with two or three or sometimes up to five lines attached to them, and the equipment: she is listening to the clicks and calls and chattering of the machines.

Eighty years or so of evolving hospital techniques means that Sister McVeagh, who in her time was as skilled as anyone in her profession, doesn't know what she is looking at, and would hardly dare to try to read a dial or adjust a tube.

A nurse – a little girl – so it would seem – goes to a patient with a thermometer, and lifts the wrist to check the pulse. This at least is the same.

'She is so small', my mother whispers, but she is overheard, and the nurse – she is from Taiwan – says smartly, 'But I'm strong.' She is eyeing Sister McVeagh, wondering what part of the hospital she can be from. She has never seen anything like the full veil, the starched cuffs, and cufflinks, the gleaming starched collar.

'Will you explain these machines to me?' My mother realises she sounds commanding, and though this is hardly correct, from a sister to a mere nurse, adds, humbly, 'Please.'

The nurse is busy, and she is tired, being in the eleventh hour of a twelve-hour shift: this at least she shares with Sister McVeagh – being overworked – but she says politely, 'This one here, it monitors the heart beat: it calls us if the heart gets out of phase. This tube – it's for rehydration: this patient is badly dehydrated. This is blood. This dial monitors blood pressure. This is for intravenal feeding. This is oxygen. This is for antibiotics . . .'

'Well, we did have oxygen,' my mother says and I can tell she is ready to cry. 'If we had these things, if we had had them, then those poor boys wouldn't have died so often, my poor boys wouldn't have died, and they were so young, some of them, it was dreadful, sometimes it didn't matter what we did, we couldn't save them. Those poor tommies, if we had these things then . . .'

The nurse is being called from a near bed, where colleagues have arrived to deal with a crisis. She wants to leave, but Sister McVeagh is going on, she has to, she needs so badly that this young woman should understand her, acknowledge her.

'After big battles like the Somme, like Passchendaele, the stretcher bearers were bringing in the wounded off the lorries and the carts for hours. The men lay on their stretchers all along the corridors, calling and crying for help. Dreadfully wounded men. Sometimes they died before we could get to them. All the hospitals in London were the same. And we got them into the beds, those poor tommies . . . if we had then what you have now . . . antibiotics, you say . . . is that disinfectant?'

The nurse has to go. She gives a last puzzled look at this

extraordinary figure and she is thinking, Did they call patients tommies then? Her boys, she says . . . which war was that? – But it is all too difficult and she is already with the other nurses and doctors by the crisis bed.

Sister McVeagh stands watching. The concentration, the dedication, is familiar, yes, once she herself . . . but she understands nothing of what they are doing with this patient.

I hear her sigh. I hear her murmur: 'If we had had these things, don't you see? – they needn't have died, at least not so much, the poor boys . . .'

I watch her walk away out of Intensive Care and back into the past.

A Nazi Childhood

With this book we are on familiar territory. Winfried Weiss's father was a small-town sergeant in the SS. Everyone knew Hitler was a great man, Germany's saviour. Jews were inhuman.

Nazism at the grass roots was an evil-smelling compost of fervent patriotism and self-righteousness, cruelty, greed. Mind you, reading how the family might pour another cup of tea and remark: 'he is getting his arse beaten', while listening to the screams, I remembered a friend who, living next to a police station near Notting Hill, moved because he got fed up listening to the yells of suspects being beaten. I also remembered white Southern Rhodesia. This book is shocking, not because it disturbs set mental images, but because it makes it all worse. The Nazis were perverts we say, and here it all is, perversity as the ordinary, a stench coming off everyday life. The child was taught to admire male strength and beauty, power, bullying, uniforms, blood. Wholeheartedly did they all loathe the Allies, who callously bombed them, and totally did they despise degenerate democracy. Then the Americans came in, and overnight it was as if Hitler had never been. The parcel of violent emotions was transferred to the Amis,[3]

---

3 The Germans called the occupying Americans 'the Amis'.

to America and democracy; and with these handsome, swaggering, male conquerors who dispensed food and comfort and sadomasochistic pleasures the child fell in love, and remained so, for as soon as he could he went to the United States.

What price indoctrination? Well, the Nazis lasted only thirteen years.

Incidentally I have never read such an excremental book. Is it possible that the author, who celebrates his Nazi childhood in a rich prose, suffers from an uncompleted psychoanalysis?

It goes without saying that when the Americans told the former Nazis about the camps they said indignantly that it was all a pack of lies, because 'we Germans could not possibly do such things'.

Knowing How to Know: A Practical Philosophy in the Sufi Tradition

During that hallucinatory decade, the sixties, there appeared a thousand cults, gurus, holy men, all promising spiritual delights. Among these noisy voices was a different one, quiet, unexcitable, not using the traditional terms of religion and mysticism because, it was claimed, these were worn out, debased. The voice was that of Idries Shah whose book, *The Sufis*, was felt by people all over the world to be what we had been waiting for – to explain obstinately non-conforming thoughts and intuitions that had puzzled us all our lives.

There followed a succession of books by Shah, a Sufi teacher, of an astonishing variety, any one of which could be read for pleasure, or instruction, yet was part of a pattern of books designed to make a whole, offering, *for our time*, the Sufi message. For it is claimed that this teaching, which has always been in the world, in this guise or that, under different names or with no name at all, must always be reintroduced to fit the time, the place and the culture. That is to say, a Sufi school in one part of the world might not resemble one in another.

Idries Shah died in 1996, but left books to be published posthumously, to round out the instruction for students, or to attract new readers. All Shah's books, whether an anthropological view of magic, collections of metaphysical jokes, or of tales, or of comments on our contemporary scene, are fresh, unexpected and full of surprises. They are full of unique insights into our psychology, our society, and the human condition.

Together, they form the most remarkable literary and instructional phenomenon of our time, with material to be found nowhere else, from a hundred different times and cultures, most of it never seen in the West before, much of it revolutionary in its implications. For instance, the Sufi use of literature is of a sophistication – and antiquity – that makes ours seem clodhopping.

There is nothing secret about this or other aspects of Sufism: at least there isn't now. Facts, history, plans for the future which in the past were confined to the few, mostly because of repressive politico-religious regimes, are in the open for anybody prepared to spend time and trouble.

In Sufi study, questions in one book may be answered in another; a train of thought begun in one may be taken a stage further in a second and concluded in a third: the aim is to provoke thought in people attracted to this 'message', so that what many at once demand (being children of the 'I want it now' culture) – a thesis of the academic kind – is simply impossible. *Knowing How to Know*, like the other books, needs attentive reading, if only because some of its contentions are startling and need time to think about.

Sufism is not a religion, but claims to be the truth that lives in the heart of all religions. It is not a cult: Shah points out that those who have described what he has introduced as a cult are ignorant of the definition of a cult which our society has accepted. And this brings us to one of his perennial complaints: that we ignore information about ourselves that comes from our own serious research, and which we should be using to change our societies.

Real Sufism is evolutionary: the Sufi view of us at our present stage is not necessarily flattering. 'A caterpillar was told it would one day be a butterfly. "Show me, now, while I am crawling up this tree."'

Sufis think we value emotion to the point that we are crippled by it: this is not a diagnosis that is always welcomed. There are few of our sacred cows that they value.

I have been studying this material for 30 years: one of the satisfactions is to see how traditional religious texts look when put into this cool, apparently non-religious, context. 'The only thing that should be hated is hatred': because all destructive behaviour is the result of ignorance.

This would not be a book by Shah if it were not often very funny. In short, those who know Shah's work will not need to be told it is a cornucopia of very various delights; those who do not may find it a fascinating introduction to the Sufi view of life.

The tragedy of Zimbabwe

'You have the jewel of Africa in your hands,' said President Samora Machel of Mozambique, and President Julius Nyere of Tanzania, to Robert Mugabe, at the moment of Independence, in 1980. 'Now look after it.'

Twenty-three years later and the 'jewel' is ruined, dishonoured, disgraced.

Southern Rhodesia had fine and functioning railways, good roads, its towns were policed and clean. It could grow anything, tropical fruit like pineapples, mangoes, bananas, plantains, pawpaws, passion fruit; temperate fruits like apples, peaches, plums. The staple food, maize, grew like a weed and fed surrounding countries as well. Peanuts, sunflowers, cotton, the millets and small grains that used to be staple foods before maize, flourished. Minerals: gold, chromium, asbestos, platinum, and rich coalfields. The dammed Zambesi created the Kariba lake which fed electricity north and south. A paradise, and not only for the whites, the blacks did well too, at least physically. Not politically: it was a police state and a harsh one. When the blacks rebelled and won their war they looked forward to a plenty and competence that existed nowhere else in Africa, not even in South Africa which was bedevilled by its many mutually hostile tribes and its vast shanty towns. But paradise has to have a superstructure, an infrastructure, and by now it is going, going – almost gone.

One man is associated with the calamity, Robert Mugabe. For a while I wondered if the word tragedy could be applied here, greatness brought low, but Mugabe, despite his early reputation, was never that, was always a frightened little man. There is a tragedy all right, but it is Zimbabwe's.

Mugabe is now execrated, and rightly, but blame for him began late. Nothing is more astonishing than the silence for so many years of the liberals, the well-wishers – the politically correct. What crimes have been committed in its name – Political Correctness. A man may get away with murder, if he is black: he did, for many years.

Early in his regime, we might have seen what he was when the infamous Fifth Brigade, thugs from North Korea, hated by blacks and whites alike, became Mugabe's bodyguard, and did his dirty work, notably when he attempted what was virtually genocide in Matabeleland. Hindsight gives us a clear picture of his depredations: at the time mendacity ruled, all was confusion, but the fact was, we knew the Fifth Brigade: it had already murdered and raped.

It was confusion, too, because Mugabe seemed to begin well. He was a Marxist, true, but like other politicians before and since he said the right things, for instance, that blacks and whites must flourish together. And he passed a law against corruption, forbidding the top echelons of officials from owning more than one property. When his officials only laughed, and bought farm after farm, hotels, businesses, anything they could grab, he did nothing. It was at that point when everyone should have said, This is no strong man, he is a weakling.

From the start Mugabe has been afraid to show his face out of doors without outriders, guards, motorcades, all the defences of paranoia. When the Queen visited and refused to be in an armoured car, insisted on an open one, people jeered as the frightened man clung to the sides of the car while the insouciant sovereign smiled and waved.

Here is the heart of the tragedy. Never has a ruler come to power with more goodwill. Everybody, the people who voted for him and the ones who did not, forgot their differences and expected from him the fulfilment of their dreams – and of his promises. He could have done anything, in those early years. When you travelled around the villages in the early eighties you heard from everyone 'Mugabe will do this . . . Comrade Mugabe will do that . . .' Will see the value of this or that plan, build this shop, or clinic or road, help us with our school, check that bullying official. If Mugabe had had sense to trust them, he could have transformed the country. But he did not know how much he was trusted, because he was too afraid to leave his self-created prison, meeting only sycophants and cronies, and governing through inflexible Marxist rules got out of textbooks. Someone allowed into the presence looking for evidence of Mugabe's reputation as a well-read man found only Marxist tracts. He had come to Marxism late, converted by Samora Machel, who was a sensible large-minded man, undiminished by Marxism. (Machel was murdered by the South African secret police.) There are those who blame Mugabe's wife Sally from Ghana for what seemed like a change in his personality. She was, this Mother of the Nation, corrupt and unashamed of it. Departing the country for a trip home and stopped at customs with the equivalent of a million pounds' worth of Zimbabwean money, she protested it was her money, and only laughed, when she had to leave it and travel on without. But that was when legality still remained.

Mugabe gave refuge to the brutal dictator Mengistu from Ethiopia – he is still there, safe from the people who would try him as a war criminal.

And excuses were being made, as always. He had been in a brutal prison under Smith, who refused him permission to attend his son's funeral. He had experienced nothing soft and kind from the whites: why should he now show kindness? As for Mengistu, well it was in the finest tradition of chivalrous hospitality to shelter refugees from justice.

Mugabe became a close friend of Mahathir bin Mohamad, the infamous Prime Minister of Malaysia and attempted to sell him a controlling interest in Zimbabwe's electricity, but the *quid pro quo* was not enough and the deal fell through.

In the early nineties there was a savage drought. When members of Mugabe's government sold the grain from the silos and pocketed the money, by then the popular contempt for these ministers was such that the crime was seen as just another little item of the indictment. The United Nations was saying as early as the mid-eighties that Mugabe's government was the most rapacious bunch of thieves in Africa.

Well! said his defenders, corruption was not unknown in Europe.

The Secret Police were arbitrary and bullying? 'But you can't expect democracy of the European type in Africa!'

And now the paradox. If you visited Zimbabwe and met only that type of white, or black, who never leaves Harare or Bulawayo, you heard only laments for the corruption, the incompetence, the general collapse of services, but if you took the trouble to visit the villages then it was impossible not to be inspired by the people. The Shona are a sane, humorous enterprising lot, but they have a fault: they are too patient. I have heard a famous Zimbabwean writer complain: What is wrong with us? We put up with you whites far too long and now we are putting up with this gang of crooks.

The villagers joked about their oppressors, and continued to dream about better times, which they were only too ready to help bring into being by their own efforts. In the early years, promised free primary and secondary and university education, they were helping to build schools, unpaid, though soon free education, or, in some places, any education at all, would be a memory. For education, they did much better under the whites.

Denied proper education, or any, they hungered for books. Surveys said that what they wanted was novels, particularly classics, science fiction, poetry, historical fiction, fairy stories, and while at the beginning these were books that were supplied, soon rocketing inflation made it impossible to buy anything but the cheapest and locally published instruction books. How to Run a Shop. How to Keep Poultry. Car Repairs. That kind of thing. A box of even elementary books may transform a village. A box of books may be, often is, greeted with tears. One man complained, 'They taught us how to read, but now there are no books.' Three years ago a Penguin classic cost more than a month's wages. But even with books that were so far from what was originally dreamed of in no time study classes began, literacy classes, maths lessons, citizenship classes. The appearance of a box of books released (will release again?) astonishing energies. A village sunk in apathy will come to life overnight. This is not a people who wait for handouts; a little encouragement, help, sets them off on all kinds of project. This week (January 2003) I heard from one of the Book Team. 'I was out this week. I was talking about books to people who haven't eaten for three days.'

And there it is, the tragedy: one that could not have happened if Mugabe had been even half the man people took him for.

People say, 'Get rid of Mugabe and we will get back on course.' But he has created a whole caste of greedy people like himself. Get rid of him and there will be others as bad. If this is the merest pessimism and the crooks can be got rid of, then there will remain the damage that has been done.

Sometimes an adage dulled with age comes startlingly to life. 'There is a tide in the affairs of men . . .' Had Mugabe ridden that tide that was running at Independence, Zimbabwe could have been an example to all of Africa. But he didn't, and the shallows and the miseries are there as evidence. Nothing now can recover that opportunity. Those of us who are old enough can only mourn lost possibilities. Words as familiar as a Christmas cracker motto carry a history lesson as sharp as the bitterest experience. There are indeed tides that will never repeat themselves.

The racial hatred that Mugabe has fomented will not die. Throughout the period from Independence anti-white rhetoric went alongside the Marxist slogans which were as primitive as if Marxism had been invented in Zimbabwe. Yet what everyone remarked on was the amiable race relations, friendliness between whites and blacks, compared to South Africa, where apartheid created such a bitter legacy. Fiery articles in the government press were read in the same way as were the public pronouncements of the Soviet government, or any communist government. The rhetoric in Zimbabwe was worse than anywhere in Africa – so said the United Nations: 'Never has rhetoric had so little to do with what actually went on.' This anti-white rhetoric was generally directed, but particularly at the white farmers, who were growing most of the food and earning the foreign currency. They were well aware of their anomalous position and the organisation representing white farmers and some black ones, the Commercial Farmers Union, was putting forward proposals for the redistribution of land which would not disrupt the economy. Not one of these proposals was ever even acknowledged by Mugabe. Meanwhile farms that had already been acquired by the government were not being developed for the poor blacks: that happened only at the beginning. They were being acquired by Mugabe's greedy cronies.

Why then did Mugabe unexpectedly launch an attack on the white farmers, when there was no need for confrontation?

Mugabe had enjoyed seeing himself as the senior black leader in southern Africa: this at a time when he was increasingly seen as an embarrassment. When Mandela appeared and became the world's sweetheart Mugabe was furious. There were ridiculous scenes where Mugabe imagined he was establishing himself as first in importance. At a certain conference at lunchtime Mandela queued with everyone else, at the buffet, while Mugabe sat at a table rearranged to be prominent, and had followers bring dishes to him where he sat. This made everyone laugh at him, but surrounded by flatterers, he never understood why people were laughing.

He became desperate to establish himself as the Great Leader. The land issue had always rankled, not least because during the War of Liberation he had promised land to 'every man, woman and child'. Why had he made such foolish and impossible promises? Ah, but then it was by no means certain he would come first in the race to be Leader. But now he, Mugabe, the Great Statesman, the Father of his people, would throw out the white farmers and Mandela that paltry figure would be forgotten. And here and there, in more backward places he has acquired fame. He did it at the price of ruining his country, already so misgoverned it was on the edge of collapse. And here there is an unanswered question. Mugabe isn't stupid. His cunning as he established his position showed a scheming guileful man: for instance the war in the Congo, which impoverished Zimbabwe when it was already on its knees, enriched him with the loot he got from its mines, in return for his sending troops. And it enabled him to buy off his greatest threat, the army officers who are the only force that can dislodge him.

Many people said he was mad: I among them. But perhaps one has to be a sentimental liberal to doubt that a leader, particularly one so prolific with resounding upwards-and-onwards rhetoric, can be prepared to ruin his people. Did he really not foresee what his campaign of forcible acquisition of land would achieve?

A friend of mine, meeting a former friend, black, a Mugabe crony, in the street, heard, 'We never meant things to get out of hand like this' – spoken casually as if about some unimportant failure. 'The trouble is that Robert can think of nothing but Tony Blair. He is convinced Blair wants to ruin him, even kill him.' My friend said, 'I doubt whether Tony Blair thinks of Mugabe for as much as half a minute a week.' 'Ah, but Robert would not like to believe that' was the answer.

Now, putting on the spectacles of hindsight, it is easy to see scenes and events that spelled danger. First, and above all, the masses of unemployed black youths. Anywhere in Zimbabwe, along the roads, in distant villages, outside schools and colleges and missions, were the very young black men just standing about, or more often with pitiful carvings of wooden beasts – elephants and giraffes and so forth. Also, some sculptures. Zimbabwe has fine black sculptors. Typical of the magical thinking that has always bedevilled Zimbabwe was 'If he can make all that money from carving stone figures, then so can I.' There are places in Zimbabwe where the sculptures cover acres. Most of it is rubbish. And there was the future, to be seen: youths who had no future because Mugabe's promises had come to nothing, hungry, forever idle, hanging about everywhere in their thousands. It was these youths that Mugabe paid to go around the white farms (and the richer black farms too) in the name of the War Veterans. And they are still hanging around, brutalised, drunk and futureless, because if they have acquired a little plot of land, they have no equipment, or seed, nor, above all, skills. Many have already drifted back to town. They are heard to complain, 'We did all these bad things for Comrade Mugabe but now he has forgotten us.'

Another little scene: it is 1982, two years after Independence, and there is still a sullen, raw, bitter postwar mood. But in an inn, formerly a white drinking hole, in the mountains above Mutare stand a group of young black people, dressed for a night out. The men are in dinner jackets, the girls in dance dresses. They look like a thirties advertisement for cocktails. Nothing could be more incongruous in this homely rural setting which has probably never before seen a dinner jacket or a décolleté. But they are thinking that this is what the long war was about: here they are in this hotel, formerly a white enclave, dressed to the nines – just like the whites, drinking fancy drinks, and above all, waited on, like the whites, by black menials.

For the 90 years of white occupation the blacks, most of them roughly torn from their village life, had watched – unreachably far above them – rich whites with their cars and their black servants. The rich whites had included many poor ones, but most blacks were so far below an apparently cohesive white layer that they could see only riches. Effortless riches. A white youth, who had left Home in Britain because of unemployment during the Slump, working as an assistant to an established farmer, before he tried for a loan to make the gamble on his own account, a man without more than his clothes, and the family in Britain who were probably only too pleased to get rid of him, while they battled with the Slump, seemed to the black waiter who served him beer at the district sports day like some rich apparition to whom everything was possible. The white were all rich. And the most enticing of the dreams, the unobtainable dreams, was the life of the white farmer, the life of the verandas. When they thought of Mugabe's promises during the War of Liberation, that everyone would have land, this is what they wanted. A house like a white farmer's, the spreading acres, the black menials – effortless ease.

A fact about the white farmers that must be recorded is that most were very good farmers, inventive, industrious, with their ability to make do and mend even when Mugabe would not allow the import of spare parts, supplies, sufficient petrol. To visit a white farm was to be taken around by people proud of their resourcefulness. 'I invented this . . .' a process in the curing of tobacco, a bit of machinery. 'Look at this . . .' The farmer's wife has made a cottage industry out of delicious crystallised preserves from the gourds the cattle eat. Many built up their farms from nothing – from raw bush. Their attitude towards their black employees – by the nineties it was changing. I was brought up with the unregenerate white farmers of the early times. At best they were maternal, paternal, running basic clinics, or elementary schools. At worst they were brutal. Attempts are being made now because of the enforced exodus of the white farmers to soften their history. This is not possible: too much has been written and recorded. But visiting them in the late eighties or the nineties, they were, most of them, making attempts to change. Few, however, as the collapse of the country worsens, can resist: 'We told you so. We always said they couldn't run a bicycle shop, let alone a country.' This from people who had made sure there was not merely a glass ceiling, but a steel one, preventing blacks from rising, from getting experience. In old Southern Rhodesia, when there were too many blacks on the voters' roll for the whites' comfort the qualifications for voters were adjusted upwards, to exclude them. In Zambia, at their Independence Celebrations, I saw a District Commissioner radiant with malicious delight because the newcoming blacks had mismanaged a minor aspect of the festivities. Not very nice people, some of them. But changing. Alan Paton, in *Cry The Beloved Country*, '. . . by the time they have come to loving, we will have come to hating'.

The reporting of this transfer of land has been biased. All the emphasis has been on the white farmers. That hundreds of thousands of black farm workers lost their work, their homes, were beaten up (are still being beaten up), their wives raped, and their daughters too – not nearly enough has been said. Well-off black farmers – some assisted by their white neighbours – and more modest black farmers have had their land taken from them. A key fact, hardly mentioned, is that since Liberation 80 per cent of the farms have changed hands, and under the law they must have been offered to the government, which refused them. Mugabe's rhetoric about white farmers grabbing land from the blacks is contradicted by this fact. His campaign of misinformation means that you meet people who will tell you 'the whites threw my grandparents off their farm and took their house.' At the time of the whites' arrival in the area now called Zimbabwe there were a quarter of a million blacks in it, and they lived in villages of mud-walled grass-roofed huts. The women grew pumpkins and the maize brought from South America, and gathered plants from the bush. The men hunted. When I was a girl you met the men walking through the bush, dressed in animal skins, carrying assegais, people a step or two up from hunter gatherers. On a BBC programme you hear a young woman, in all sincerity, saying that the playing of the *mbira* (what the whites called the handpiano – strips of metal on a gourd) was forbidden under the whites. Yet when I was growing up the tinkling of the handpiano could be heard every-where. It will take a long time for Mugabe's version of history to be corrected, if it ever is.

He has recently set up compulsory indoctrination classes in villages throughout the country, mostly for teachers, but for other officials too, where they are taught that they should worship Mugabe and be totally obedient to ZANU, the ruling party. All the ills of Zimbabwe are said to be caused by machina-tions of Tony Blair in cahoots with the opposition parties. The students learn useful skills like how to murder opponents with a blow to sensitive parts of the body, and how to strangle them with bootlaces. This type of sadistic cruelty is not part of their own traditions and history, to which lip service is continually paid.

Many blacks I've talked to and heard about do not like their own history, although they talk about 'our customs'. In fact, many I have seen and known cannot wait to wear dance dresses, behave like whites, live the white life, put the bush far behind them. A group of sophisticated, urban blacks will make sentimental remarks about photographs of a traditional village, but they haven't been near their villages for years.

If you want to see just how much 'our customs' really mean, then visit the park in Harare on Saturday or Sunday, where dozens of wedding groups arrive, the brides in flouncy white, and veils, with bridesmaids and pages. The woman may be very pregnant, or with several small children. But this rite of passage into the modern world, the white man's wedding, they must have, and the photographers are there to preserve the beautiful sight for posterity. (It should perhaps be asked why a ritual invented by middle-class Victorians should have conquered the world from Japan to the Virgin Islands.)

The only time 'our customs' are valued is when it has to do with the subjection of women. The law of the land may say one thing – Zimbabwe's early Marxist days, as in other communist countries, ensured all kinds of equality – on paper. But 'our customs' still make sure that a woman has no right to the money she has earned, or to her children. She is her husband's vassal. When Mugabe was met at the airport by handclapping and kowtowing maidens, and he was criticised (in the early days) for this backwardness, the reply was 'It is our custom.'

A man in a three-piece suit, in a government job, will still beat his wife – or try to: the women are fighting back. And he will consult the soothsayers and shamans. Superstition rules. It is 'our custom' when a family member gets sick or a cow falls lame to look for the evil eye, and then pay the witchdoctor to exact revenge. It is becoming 'our custom' to seek for a virgin if you are HIV positive, for to have sex with these will cure you of Aids. The use of human parts in medicine goes on: it is the custom. The politically correct response to this kind of thing is 'But how can we criticise the blacks for being superstitious when we had President Reagan who consulted fortune-tellers.'

And now the expulsion of the white farmers is nearly complete. It is evident that what we have been seeing has nothing to do with race: it is a transfer of property.

Many of the poor people who settled on white land have been thrown off again by the powerful blacks. Those still there may grow maize and pumpkins and rape on their patches – when it rains, that is. There is a bad drought again. The poor settlers are farming without machinery or even sometimes implements. The irrigation systems have broken down. Another prophetic scene from the eighties: a water tank at a certain school is not working. A valve had gone. No one replaced it. The women went back to getting water from the river which was infested with bilharzia. Two years later the water tank had not been mended.

The recent settlers who had depended on Mugabe ('Comrade Mugabe will look after us.' 'Comrade Mugabe will . . .') have no chance of getting their children into school because school (unlike under the whites) costs a lot of money, and how will they get money for clothes, even if they survive this terrible time when there is nothing to eat and people are dying of hunger.

If they manage to stay on the land they will be as poor as subsistence peasants anywhere in the world.

Every telephone conversation with Zimbabwe, every visitor from there provides tales as bizarre as anything out of Africa.

The black elite drive around the white farms and say, 'I'll

have that one.' 'No, I want that one.' Mugabe's wife had herself driven round, picking through farms like fruit on a stall. She chose a really nice one.

A white farmer's wife watched a black woman arrive in her smart car. She was pushed out of the way, while the interloper began measuring for curtains. 'Are you going to live here?' enquired the dispossessed one. 'Me? I wouldn't live in this dump,' scorns the black woman. 'I'm going to let it. I've already got three houses in Borrowdale.' (The most fashionable suburb in Harare.)

Around Harare and Bulawayo at weekends on the farms taken by the blacks, cars arrive and out pile the city dwellers enjoying this rural excursion. They set up the barbecue, music blares across the veld, they sing and dance and eat, spread themselves for the night through the empty house, and depart next morning back to Harare.

A farmer from Matabeleland, third generation, whose boreholes supplied not only his labourers but those on nearby farms, now black owned, saw a car driving up, and out got some drunk black men. 'We are taking your farm,' said they. 'I shall take you to court,' he said. 'But we are the law now.' They had parked the car just outside his gate. He asked them to move it: That's where the cattle come across to the dam.

'We know why you want us to move. You don't like to look at black people.'

'But I look at black people every day of my life from sunup to sundown.'

They drove off, returned, drunk and took over a wing of his house, where they drank and caroused, day and night. After months the farmer snapped: all this this time he had been maintaining the water machinery, but now, when he had tried to show the interlopers how to look after it, and failed, he simply left. 'Why are you taking away those ladders?'

'They are my ladders,' he said.

'No they aren't. They are our ladders. You are sabotaging us.'

A farmer, observing how the white farmers around him were being forbidden to plant crops by the black mobs, thought he would accept his fate and simply leave. But the mob leader came and told him to plant his crop: tobacco, the chief currency earner. 'What's the point, you'll only take it.' 'No, you plant, you'll be safe.' He planted, the crop was a good one and when it was reaped, baled and ready, the mob leader told him that now he must get off the farm. 'I am taking your farm and your tobacco.'

This tale could be repeated in a hundred variants.

Some white farmers are in Mozambique: they had to begin again without capital, implements, machinery. They will survive: they are skilled and hardworking. Some are in Zambia, invited by the black government: white farmers in Zambia produce nearly all the food. They are in New Zealand, Australia, Canada . . . and the people in Zimbabwe are starving.

A month ago came this tale. The black occupiers of a white farm, a ranch, drove dozens of beasts into a dam and drowned them. They would not let the farmer feed and water his beasts: drought, great heat, and so they died. Africans love cattle, their 'mombes': cattle are currency, riches, links with the past, a promise for the future. Hard to believe that any African could harm one of these precious beasts. What has happened?

It is very easy to corrupt a country, a people.

And now a small, more hopeful story. On a pig farm the animals were dying because since the white farmers had been thrown off no one had fed or watered them. And drunken blacks had hacked pieces of meat off the pigs and left them to die. A white woman vet stood there, weeping, helpless, forbidden to help the pigs. But one of the new settlers, unseen by the mob, came to her and said, 'We are townspeople, we have these animals now and don't know how to look after them. Please help us.' They had taken a couple of the dying pigs and put them in a shed. And the white woman went with him and began teaching him and his wife how to look after the pigs.

East meets West: *The Elephant in the Dark*

Idries Shah was invited by the University of Geneva to lecture on 'Salvation as a total surrender to God: an attempt at dialogue between Christians and Muslims', and became visiting professor there in 1972–3: this book originated then. The title, *The Elephant in the Dark*, from the fable of the elephant experienced differently by people according to their subjectivities, refers to the long interaction between Christianity and Islam, even during the thousand years we were at war or hostile: sometimes in secret and kept out of the knowledge of rulers and courts; sometimes with the aid of the said rulers; sometimes – and much more than we know – open and thriving, but since fallen into oblivion, or concealed because such amity was a threat to the machinery of national hostilities.

This is a time when historical blockages are being dissolved by scholarship; our trouble is we don't know the half of it, and our minds are still 'set' in ways now not only obsolete, but useless, or harmful. Shah's method, as always, is to show where scholars from East to West have unearthed materials: this has been his aim since his first book on mysticism, *The Sufis*, put together information already available, but not yet noticed for what it was. His way, too, is to illustrate large and complex

247

themes by that one exemplary anecdote or quotation: you will seek in vain for lengthy exegesis, or dry intellectualism. This is why his work always comes as a salutary reminder as to what is possible in scholarly writing: it is admirable above all for its economy, its elegant pithiness. When you have finished with even a little book, like this one, you find yourself in possession of the necessary basic information.

Information is what he says we lack above all: Christians more than Muslims – our set of mind has always been to regard *them* as 'Ignorant, astray and in need of saving'. Ignorance of Christian thought and mores is not lacking in Islam; but respect for Christianity is built into the foundations of Islam in the Koran – thus, for instance: 'Say: "We believe in God, and that which hath been sent down to us, and that which hath been sent down to Abraham and Ishmael and Isaac and Jacob and the tribes; and that which hath been given to Moses and to Jesus, and that which was given to the Prophets from their Lord. No difference do we make between any of them: and to God are we resigned.' Therefore, among Muslims – and there are 400 million of them distributed from the Atlantic shores of Morocco in the West to China, the Philippines and Indonesia in the East – you will find respect for Christianity and for Jesus, who is regarded as a pillar of their religion and called Al Sayyed – the Prince, or 'the Lord'.

This book aims at redressing balances; and to say what we have in common, on what we can build.

On our interlocking history, for a start. It began before Muhammad, with friendship between Christians and believers in the tradition of Abraham. It was cemented in the time of Muhammad: a Christian recognised the 12-year-old boy as a future Prophet, and enjoined his people to take care of him; and it was a Christian who confirmed the validity of his visions. Later, Muhammad laid down the foundations of respect for

Christianity by precept and example: in short, there was a difference between what he taught and what his successors made of
it. The essence of what religious people should have in common
is given in an anecdote of a friendship, in Libya, between a
Franciscan Italian, of modest origin, who was a scholar, and
the mayor who was a prince, a fervent Muslim and illiterate.
Where they were at one was 'in their indifference to illness,
their complete disregard of material considerations, their deep
understanding of human suffering and misery, and their charity
which was unsmirched by egotism and knew no bounds. Both of
them submitted to a higher will with the blind faith of children.'
'Submission to God' is the elephant – but it is explained here
that this is not a question of an emotional commitment. 'The
teaching, by both Christians and Muslims, over the centuries,
that it is not enough to seek God, but that He must be sought
in a certain way, and that if this is not understood it can be no
search at all, since "the search" can nurture greed . . .'

Further, there is by no means only one approach: Shah's
previous books on Sufism (an Islamic form of mysticism) have
illustrated that an approach to mysticism can be secular, even
materialistic – to use that word in its philosophical sense. This
book illustrates the religious road to that place where all the
ways lead – surrender, submission. Shah returns again and again
to the concept from a hundred angles. Submission 'has for the
Muslims a social and administrative equivalence. Since the
Koran enjoys certain forms of behaviour, of conduct of state
and the cultivation of moral virtues . . .' Or as Saadi put it: 'The
Way is not otherwise than in the service of the people. It is not in
rosaries and prayer rugs and robes . . .' 'Truthfulness, honesty,
dedication to ideals . . .' Shah uses illustrations taken from
tradition; for instance, Al Ghazali's tale of the Seven Valleys,
accepted by both Muslims and Christians as a map or a guide
of the Journey to God. He provides an exposition of the basic

Arab root 'slm' and its associated word-groupings, – Islam, Muslim, Salem, Salaam, and so on, to explain: 'It is impossible to exaggerate the significance of this constellation of terms and meanings; for the Arab-speaker they constitute a constant reminder of the diverse aspects of their religion and its meanings, and a permanent facility for confirming these concepts without having to rely only upon interpretation by later ideologists.' This is a hint about where one is to look for explanations of the basic unity of Islam, which is not fragmented compared to other religions.

This book seems to be essential at a time when the Islamic world is enjoying the economic renaissance which profoundly affects us all; also the two religions which have shaped our respective cultures are engaged in deliberate and self-conscious attempts to overcome barriers which humanity can no longer afford.

'What novel or novels prompted your own political awakening?'

Is this symposium a symptom of the perennial itch to control literature: 'Ivory Tower vs. Commitment'?

My generation knows where a demand for 'political' novels may lead, but since it seems history is no longer taught, people may have forgotten that for decades in the Soviet Union and its satellites stereotyped, boring – dead – novels were written and published, a dreadful warning – and literature there has not recovered yet.

Few novels written to a formula have any life. That is because real novels are written from the solar plexus.

Animal Farm, the best and most influential political novel of our time was written out of bitter personal experience. (It is read up and down Africa now: are we surprised?)

Readers often confuse a novel that describes politics with one that pushes a message. Both are called committed. *My Ripple from the Storm* is a case in point.

I Know Why the Caged Bird Sings was written from burning experience. So was *Cry the Beloved Country*. They did not need debates about the virtues of political writing.

The Making of an Activist and *Black Pain* (invented titles) are written from the same part of the brain that makes a pamphlet die on the nest.

As for what novels prompted my own political awakening: as a child I read Dickens and had only to look around me (the old Southern Rhodesia) to see what he described. But do we call him political? His 'message' was that injustice is wrong. Our time has the honour of narrowing what were broad and generous and complex definitions; 'political writing' meant, for decades, communist writing. We have still to recover from that habit of mind: Political Correctness is its heir.

The most significant book to come out of Africa

Forgive me for carping but why should *one* book be the most significant to come out of Africa? Is it likely with such a vast continent and with such a history, there should be one book more significant than another? These things change with time and its emphases. Nothing in our time has approached the influence of Ibn Khaldun's writings on north Africa, or Ibn Battutah's (fourteenth century). Isak Dinesen's *Out of Africa* has had and will continue to have an influence because of its literary quality. As for politics there is one immediate and obvious book – *Cry the Beloved Country*, by Alan Paton. This was like a bugle when it first appeared and still has great emotional power. Because of this, a smaller quieter book by him, *Too Late the Phalarope*, has been ignored, though a better novel about the evident and concealed psychological drives in apartheid South Africa – or in any racist culture – has not been written. In its time Olive Schreiner's *The Story of an African Farm* had readers all over the world. Tsitsi Dangarembga's *Nervous Conditions* speaks to black women about their situation in a way no other book has. Nawar El Saadawi's *God Dies by the Nile* is a great novel by any standards. There has been this explosion of fine writing out of Africa in the last 50 years.

The Sufis

This review attempts to answer, within the scope of Idries Shah's books, questions asked by people sincerely puzzled by the recent reintroduction of the Sufic tradition by Shah, and the ways it is manifesting itself.

A light is shining. Around this light are set, at various angles and distances, screens that have different patterns pierced into them. The light is being sifted into these patterns over walls, floor, ceilings. People in the room may decide to study the patterns, claiming that this one or that is superior. The light stands for a truth which is central to mankind, the screens for national or historical cultural patterns. These local patterns may be studied, even supported, with profit, provided it is remembered that the light is the source of the patterns, it is the light which is mankind's goal. The word 'light' has been used in every mystic tradition as a symbol for God, the Absolute, the Beloved, the King, the Simurgh, Truth, Life of the World – a hundred other terms. Many of these have for us an association with the past. Yet the modern astronomer who, without ever a thought of mysticism, might distrust everything about it, but who thinks in terms of the breeding, the wasting, the deaths, the rebirth of galaxies and universes – which use of his mind is leading him to the Reality behind manifestation – is nearing that area which he might say he suspects. He would not call this practice of his mind 'Sufism' which may – at certain times, for some people – say, in the words of the thirteenth-century sage Shabistari: 'He who upon creation meditates doth well.' He is in an antechamber of the mind which Ibn al-Arabi eight centuries ago described as 'She' – a Sufic technical term.

> She has confused all the learned of Islam,
> Everyone who has studied the Psalms,
> Every Jewish rabbi
> Every Christian priest.

Or:

> When description tried to explain her, she overcame it,
> Whenever such an attempt is made, description is put to flight
> Because it is trying to circumscribe.
> If someone seeking her lowers his aspirations (i.e., to feel in
>   terms of ordinary love).
> There are always others who will not do so.

Or, in Rumi's words – it can be a help to contrast some of the many ways the same idea can be put:

> Intelligence is the shadow of objective Truth.
> How can the shadow vie with the sunshine?

Or, Rumi again:

One went to the door of the Beloved and knocked. A voice asked: 'Who is there?' He answered: 'It is I.' The voice said: 'There is no room here for me and thee.' The door was shut. After a year of solitude and deprivation this man returned to the door of the Beloved. He knocked. A voice from within asked: 'Who is there?' The man said: 'It is Thou'. The door was opened to him.

(These extracts from *The Way of the Sufi*, translations Idries Shah)

It was easier in the ancient world, perhaps, when culture was more unified than it ever has been since, to grasp a concept of something hidden, but ever-present, central but many-featured. They could travel from place to place paying their respects to Astarte – Ishtar – Aphrodite – Nana, and others, or to Thoth – Idris – Enoch – Hermes – Mercury, knowing these were manifestations, the names, of principles and powers, the same for all places, all times. Probably this kind of recognition of deeper unifying realities has not been equalled again until our time; it is found again, or something like it, in the minds of those scientists and thinkers out on the frontiers of today's thought, people who need no common language to understand symbols or concepts accepted by all of them as representing how far mankind has got along a certain path.

The difficulty many people experience seems to me partly because of the compartmentalism of the way most of us have been trained to think, which begins in the nursery school and its divisions into play, work, sleep-time, eat-time, rhythm-time, noise-time, quiet-time, is confirmed in succeeding schools and their 'subjects' of arithmetic, reading and so on, to end in the university student's specialisations and his mind like a box full of labelled drawers. This is of course our misfortune and not our crime, but the beginning of transcending it is to recognise it. The other principle we absorbed with our nursery milk is that everyone is entitled to everything on demand (in theory if not in practice). People of earlier 'more primitive' cultures were wiser, more humble. They knew they needed intermediaries to approach the All High; or, if they aspired themselves, submitted themselves in patience to a preparation.

The inner Reality – God, or what you will, has always had its technicians, who understood each other's tongues, terms and methods even when in different mystic traditions, who gave their knowledge to those ready for it, and who were prepared to learn – in the Sufi phrase, asked to 'learn how to learn' – which is the first and essential step.

These technicians were not always what was expected. There is the tale of the important men who thought they were the representatives in their own country of a certain great Sage, and who, travelling to visit him, were irritated by the rough noisy behaviour of their illiterate muleteers. On arrival at the Sage's beautiful, cultivated, elegant precincts, they saw him salute the muleteers, and understood they had been deluded: it was the muleteers, whom they had despised, not themselves, who were the real representatives. (This tale is in the Hasidic as well as the Sufi tradition. A version is in *The Tales of the Dervishes*, a collection of teaching stories used by Masters from the seventh century till today: they have the pulsing yeasty rough quality that identifies source material, before it gets smoothed down and prettied up: we know some of them in versions for entertainment.)

The same point is made in a tale from Saadi: 'A man met another who was handsome, intelligent and elegant. He asked him who he was. The other said: "I am the Devil." "But you cannot be," said the first man, "for the Devil is evil and ugly." "My friend," said Satan, "you have been listening to my detractors."' (*Bostan*, Shah's version, *Reflections*.)

To hold in one's mind that a central transforming force is always at work in the world – the force of evolution itself – enables one to see that a person may be learning while not knowing he is doing so. 'Nobody can stop the process of learning, real questioning, even if only because our ancestors started on this course many thousands of years ago. They set us on this course and we cannot escape from it' (*Reflections*). The contention is that unless a man is enlightened, has been transformed into the high condition possible to him, he does not know his state, or stage, or what it is 'the old nurse' – the processes of ordinary life – is teaching him. He knows that he is unhappy and always yearning for something other than what he is – that is all. There is also the tradition of the unknown good men. 'There are several forms of invisible saints corresponding with the general human need for a certain representation of psychic or psychological activity in the whole community' (*The Sufis*). 'Among them there are four thousand who are concealed and do not know one another and are not aware of the excellence of their state, but in all circumstances are hidden from themselves and from mankind. Traditions have come down to this effect and the saying of the saints proclaim the truth thereof, and myself – God, be praised – have had ocular experience of this matter.' (*Hujwiri*.)

To be 'on the path without knowing it' is, then, man's condition; but that is a different thing from deliberately inviting transcendental states of mind out of context of one's own state of development. To grasp that mystic states are not the aim of study, but a means to an end, is usually hard for someone already tinctured by other sects or cults to do; it is likely that these 'ecstasies' – a technical term for the large variety of altered mental states – are the bait which has led one to mysticism. In most disciplines these states are laid before the pupil as the goal. The Sufi Way differs from all others in saying categorically that to regard 'ecstasy' as the be-all and end-all is ignorance of what is possible for men, or greed, or the desire to enjoy sensations for their own sake. Or, as Shah puts it: thrills, spills and chills. A rash, clumsy, or insistent approach to 'the Other' can indeed induce extraordinary – but distorted – states of mind, as can drugs, but to indulge in them, as in drugs, can prevent the student from ever stabilising his consciousness on the plateaus that are possible to him. 'Man has an essence, initially tiny, shining, precious.' Its development in a certain well-tried way is, Sufis claim, their speciality. Many of the experimenters with drugs, or with 'ecstasies', ruin the delicate machineries of their minds, waste their real potential; many of the poor people in our mental hospitals are there because, through bad luck or the ignorance of our medical profession, they have invaded a realm which an unprepared person can only do at risk. (This is where the saying originates that the mad are under the direct protection of God; of the idea that the mad are closer to God than the sane.) Sufism, then, emphasises continually the dangers of greed, of experimenting without guidance; that to want something for oneself before one has reached the stage of being able to see oneself as part of something greater, and which must grow as a whole, is self-defeating. Man is not alone; is not a glorious individual – or not in the way he thinks. His 'personality', what he ordinarily knows of himself, is an assembly of shadows, of conditioned reflexes; his real individuality is hidden and will emerge slowly during the process of learning, like a stone in the tumbling machine which will show, after a rough passage, its real intrinsic qualities. He must stop saying: 'Give it to me now! I want it now!'

Nasrudin walked into the city of Konia for the first time. He was at once struck by the number of patisseries. His appetite sharpened, he went into one of these shops, and started to devour a pie. Certain that he would get nothing out of this ragged apparition, the owner rushed at him and cuffed him. 'What kind of a town is this?' asked the Mulla, 'a place where they hit a man as soon as he has started eating.'

(*The Exploits of the Incomparable Mullah-Nasrudin*)

Or, put differently:

Nasrudin was mending a roof one day when a man called him down into the street. When he went down he asked the man what he wanted. 'Money.' 'Why did you not say so when you called to me?' 'I was ashamed to beg.' 'Come up to the roof.' When he reached the roof Nasrudin started to lay the tiles again. The man coughed, and Nasrudin, without looking up, said: 'I have no money for you.' 'But you could have told me that without bringing me up here.' 'Then how would you have been able to recompense me for bringing me down?'

(*The Sufis*)

Of all the literary forms used by the Sufis – parables, anecdotes, conversational exchanges, recitals, stories – the 'joke' merchant Nasrudin is the most remarkable.

Mulla Nasrudin is the classical figure devised by the dervishes partly for the purpose of halting for a moment situations in which certain states of mind are made clear. The Nasrudin stories, known throughout the Middle East, constitute one of the strangest achievements in the history of metaphysics. Superficially, most of the Nasrudin stories may be used as jokes. They are told and retold endlessly in the teahouses and caravanserais, in the homes, and on the radio waves, of Asia. But it is inherent in the Nasrudin story that it may be understood at any one of many depths. There is the joke, the moral – and a little extra which brings the consciousness of the potential mystic a little further on the way to realization.

(*The Sufis*)

This book, quite the most remarkable I have read in my life, for its range and its implications – my first encounter with it was like a depth-charge – is an essential for anyone interested, even casually, in Sufism.) Nasrudin was designed to cross frontiers, to defy national prejudices. Today he is found in a film made in the Soviet Union, quoted by Christians, diluted in jokes everywhere, claimed by the secular Turkey which suppressed the dervish orders which gave him birth. 'Nasrudin exists at so many depths he cannot be killed' (*The Sufis*). *The Legend of Nasrudin*, dating from at least the thirteenth century, is studied with the jokes, and is printed in *Thinkers of the East* – a collection of Sufic material which is more accessible than most. An account by a student of a recent stay in a Naqshbandi circle in Pakistan where the study was based on a cycle of the tales is available (*New Research on Current System*). From this it emerges that the difference between a more formalised study and even a quite casual reading of the jokes is one of degree, not kind. A Nasrudin 'joke' may at first seem unfunny, or pointless, but will after study change and begin to reveal itself: you have uncovered the first level of meaning, and will soon observe your thought patterns shift as you watch them; you will have made the first crack in the wall of assumptions, the conditioned thinking (designated 'The Old Villain') which imprisons each and every one of us, the worst of which is to think that the visible world is all there is, that a man's or a mouse's view of life is the true one.

'Every day,' says Nasrudin to his wife, 'I am more and more amazed at the efficient way in which this world is organized – generally for the benefit of mankind.' 'What exactly do you mean?' 'Well, take camels for instance. Why do you suppose they have no wings?' 'I have no idea!' 'Well, then, just imagine, if camels had wings they might nest on the roofs of houses and destroy our peace by romping about above and spitting their cud down on us.'

(*The Sufis*)

This kind of thing is not solemn enough for some people until they have adjusted their ideas away from thinking that 'the quest' is what they think it is, and until they can recognise the yeast working generally, around them, in the different levels of life – until they have begun to experience change: the proof of the pudding is in the eating!

Again and again, in every possible way, Nasrudin hammers away at the barrier preconceptions put up against under-standing.

A would-be disciple, after many vicissitudes, arrives at the hut on the mountainside where the Mulla is. Knowing that every single action of an illuminated Sufi is meaningful, the newcomer asks Nasrudin why he is blowing on his hands. 'To warm them, of course.' A short while afterwards Nasrudin blows on his soup. 'Why are you doing that, Master?' 'To cool it, of course.' The disciple leaves Nasrudin; he is unable to trust the man who uses the same process to arrive at different results.

(*The Sufis*)

Initially there is often intense puzzlement, suspicion, all kinds of variation on this theme:

'I want an answer to these and these questions.'

'But the questions are answered in one, or sometimes several of the pieces or stories in the books. And the books comprise the study: they have been carefully assembled to provide the "bridge" from ordinary thinking to Sufic thinking.'

'I have only read two of the books, and I haven't found the answers there.'

Or, this one:

'I want the answers to these questions.'

'The answers are in the books.'

'I have read the books and haven't found the answers.'

'How have you read the books?'

'As I always read books: I bought them last week and found them so titillating that I have already read them all.'

'But part of the study is to learn to read in a different way, to put aside the way you have been taught to read, what is now called "linear thinking", and to allow this material to permeate you. You can use it for fun, or for curiosity or for titillation if you like – but that isn't what is being offered.'

People approach Sufis demanding to be given what they are already used to, in the ways they are used to:

A monk left the Sage Bahaudin Naqshband saying: 'Shun that man, for he will only occupy himself with trivia. I have travelled from China to drink his wisdom and he offers me a children's tale.' Bahaudin, commenting on this, said: 'There are a thousand books of classics, all written to illustrate a dozen truths. There are a dozen tales which contain between them all those truths. If it were not for the demand of many for the appearance of quantity rather than relevance, the first letter of the first word of a single children's story would suffice to instruct man. It is because the learner is of such poor quality that the teacher has to repeat, enlarge, and make bulky things which the student would not otherwise be able to see at all.'

(*The Dermis Probe*)

(From this book and from *The Wisdom of the Idiots* it is possible to catch something of the flavour of a Sufic school in action.)

The need for a teacher to adapt what he is giving to local conditions, local sets of mind, means that these questions may be asked: 'Wasn't it the case that while the versions of Sufism were local, the claims made were dogmatic and put forward as universal? Were the teachers in question really relativists who acknowledged their teachings need not apply elsewhere, or were they relativists who concealed this in order to be more convincing? Do we see them as relativists only in retrospect while they may not have thought of themselves in this way? This seems important if we think the question of "bad faith" is important.'

A teacher can do no more than state what he is doing. Idries Shah, like the exemplars of the past, has said in a hundred ways, in his books, letters and lectures, and for the ten years he has so far been at it, that 'a school is a temporary thing, which will be dismantled as soon as its work is done. That this "school" is carefully designed for the needs of "the time, the place, the people." That this temporary framework is what we call a "vehicle" and that after it is dismantled, many people who were hostile or indifferent to the live school, when it was operating, because it refused to conform to what they wanted it to be – it could not do this, because of its nature – will then take possession of it, freeze it, make something permanent of it. This has happened to every "school", every replenishing of the vital stream in the past. That it is bound to happen is something taken into account and allowed for: a thousand sects and cults now existing, not to mention some political and social groupings, are the "husks" of former Sufic schools which are now institutionalised, and dead.' It is surely not in bad faith to say: 'I am in possession of this material; it is my job to offer it to you; this is the way I have to offer it to you. The "vehicle", this time, is partly the book. And I say over and over again in every way I can that words are not Sufism, but explain and prepare the approaches to it; that Wisdom is not in books, only how to find it. But man's present state is that of one who uses words, books, to acquire information; behind information, in a different range altogether, is Wisdom: therefore I build the approaches to the "study" through words. There have been teachers who taught through silence – through their presence in a place; or through gestures, music, dances, hieroglyphs, designs, and in a hundred other ways, each designed for the time and the place. But what I am doing is this, which I describe to you as I do it. If you want something dished up in another way – look elsewhere and not to me. The people who want what the live Sufic tradition is offering will take it in the form in which it is given, and will be prepared to discard the form at the right time. The imitators and the scholastics will not.'

Sufism does not attack religions, which are seen as 'the screens' the light falls through. Formal religion is a stage a person may go through as are atheism or agnosticism; the hot denials of the passionate atheist are seen as a religious emotion, no different from the affirmations of the emotional religionist: 'God' is in both. The rationalism of the currently acceptable intellectual creed is seen as a dogma born of ignorance.

> 'All religion, as theologians – and their opponents – understand the word, is something other than what it is assumed to be. Religion is a vehicle. Its expressions, rituals, moral and other teachings, are designed to cause certain elevating effects, at a certain time, upon certain communities. Because of the difficulty of maintaining the science of man, religion was instituted as a means of approaching truth. The means always became, for the shallow, the end, and the vehicle became the idol. Only the man of wisdom, not the man of faith or intellect, can cause the vehicle to move again.
>
> (*The Way of the Sufi*)

This cornucopia of a book scatters a vast range of information about Sufism, from the Idries Shah seminar at Sussex University, which is useful for describing Sufism within our conventions of scholarship; to comments on group recitals and their use; letters and lectures from a wide variety of cultures and times; excerpts from classical Sufis – Khayyam, Saadi, Rumi, Attar, and so on.)

265

There is a tale of how Moses rebuked a man for offering to comb God's hair, and wash His robe, and kiss His head: God rebuked Moss saying: 'Thou hast driven away a worshipper from the nearest to Me that he could approach. There is a gradation in all men: each will perceive what he can perceive and at the stage at which he can perceive it.' (*The Way of the Sufi*)

One religion is not better than another: each is an expression of local needs. Islam has housed many classic Sufis who are comparatively well known. The 'Sufis' – they would not be under that name, of course – of earlier times, are not known to our scholarship – considered as defective – or not known as teachers in the same tradition: Pythagoras is one. The West's ignorance about Islam, because of the centuries of war between it and Christianity, adds to prejudice about Islamic Sufism. (*The Caravan of Dreams* has information about Islam, Islamic cultures, which is a useful corrective to this ignorance, which to many of us it has not occurred is pretty disgraceful.) Easier because of long familiarity to see Plato as a teacher deliberately taking logical thinking to extremes to demonstrate its absurdity than to recognise the same thing in some exchange between Malamati dervishes who caricatured the behaviour of their pupils to show it up – a technique still very much in use by Sufi teachers now.

Beyond religion, most of whose practices are the ethics of the society in which it operates codified, is a range where experience becomes more complex than the rigidities of good/bad, black/white.

A theologian was ill. He had heard that Nasrudin was a mystic; and in his semi-delirium convinced himself that there might be something in all this, after all. So he sent for the Mulla. 'Prescribe a prayer which can ease me into the other world, Mulla,' he said, 'for you have the reputation of being in communication with another dimension.' 'Delighted,' said Nasrudin, 'Here you are: "God help me – Devil help me!" Forgetting his infirmity the divine sat bolt upright, scandalised. 'Mulla, you must be insane!' 'Not at all, my dear fellow. A man in your position cannot afford to take chances. When he sees two alternatives, he should try to provide for either of them working out.'

(*The Pleasantries of the Incredible Mulla Nasrudin*)

A question like: 'But what about a personal God, and the importance of this to so many people?' falls away. St Theresa of Avila experienced 'His Majesty'. St Theresa the Little Flower talked of 'My little Jesus'. A crazy person may say 'I am God' – but so did Hallaj, one of the greatest Sufis of all time, who was judicially murdered because he said, in a mystic state: 'I am the Truth.' A Spanish peasant girl sees a vision of the Virgin. Sorcerers raise the Devil, horns and all – Spanish St Theresa saw the Devil until she had got past that stage. Adam and Noah, Abraham and Moses talked with God, in a way which sounds like son with loving father. In India there is a hierarchy of deities which are experienced in the stages of the Hindu disciples. An African witchdoctor experiences God according to the realities of his part of the continent. The modern astronomer has his moments of vision when the skies his mind inhabits become a mirror for something beyond. The light can do no other than fall in the patterns of the screens – the mind of the experiencing person, which has been formed, been set, by his culture, his experience, his prejudices.

Again and again one is returned to this point: one can do no more than start from where one is. And it is not an unuseful exercise to use this thought in an effort to find out where that is.

Or, as Shah puts it: 'If you are uninterested in what I say, there's an end to it. If you like what I say, please try to understand which previous influences have made you like it. If you like some of the things I say and dislike others, you could try to understand why. If you dislike all I say, why not try to find out what has formed your attitude?' (*Reflections*).

The Ice Palace:
Frozen secrets stranded in a waterfall

The superlatives are all worn out; we have used them too often while trying to make some good book visible among others clamouring for attention. 'Unique!' 'Unforgettable!' 'Extraordinary!' But these words are used of any old rubbish. Peter Owen says *The Ice Palace* (*Isslottet*) by Tarjei Vesaas is the best novel he has ever published, and that is saying a lot.

Although the author was born in 1897, his books are far from old-fashioned and traditional: he experimented with new forms, was described as a modernist.

This novel won the prestigious Nordic Council Award in 1963. Tarjei Vesaas has become a classic. Coachloads of people go on pilgrimages to his old home.

It is the atmosphere, the style, that make this novel. It begins, 'A young white forehead boring into the darkness. An eleven-year-old girl. Siss. It was really only afternoon, but already dark. A hard frost in late autumn. Stars, but no moon, and no snow to give a glimmer of light...' But we are behind that young forehead, inside a child's world of events and encounters, ordinary enough to adults, but full of mysterious and half-understood intimations.

One little girl, the orphan Unn, has a secret, something terrible – we never know what it is – which she promises to tell her new friend Siss; but instead, the very day after the promise, she is impelled to explore the caves of a frozen waterfall, further and deeper into the shining heart of the ice.

> The new room was a miracle, it seemed to her. The light shone strong and green through the walls and the ceiling, raising her spirits after their drenching in tears.
>   'Of course! Suddenly she understood, now she could see it clearly: it had been herself crying so hard in there. She did not know why, but it had been herself, plunged in her own tears.

There she dies. The whole community searches for her, and some even clamber over the surface of the frozen fall, but it is only her friend Siss who catches a glimpse of her, like an apparition inside the ice palace, looking out through the ice wall.

In the spring the frozen river melts, and all is swept away in the floods, the secret too. Meanwhile, Siss is trying to make sense of what happened. We see with her, feel with her, understand why she may not tell what she knows. The irony is that she has nothing to tell, only that there is a secret. If she did break what she saw as an implicit promise to the dead girl, the adults would only say, But is that all? Yet the 'all' is terrible, it must have been, and the little girl knew it was.

This tale is like a legend. Easy to hear as you read voices singing the lines of the ballad it could so easily be. Part of the reason for this the author did not intend, for time has taken a hand, adding a dimension of far away and long ago. Tarjei Vesaas spent his whole life in the country, and the tale is set in a community of a kind that could not exist in our brutal and ugly time. Sometimes when you read or hear about a community in the past, before it was cracked apart by aeroplanes and trains and cars and tourists and radios and television, it seems like an organism, each person with a function, a role, each playing a part. These people in the rural district are a whole, everyone knowing at all times about the others and what they are doing and feeling.

The sense of mutual responsibility is so strong it is like another character in the story, as if, at any time you liked, you could appeal to some invisible council of collective decency. There are few things in literature more touching, more admirable, than the way this community of adults and children cares for Siss, a little girl frozen with shock and with grief. They understand that she needs to identify with Unn, to stand on the edge of the school playground, just as Unn did – that child who came from far away in Norway, because her mother died, to live with an aunt she hardly knows. But Unn had stood there because she was strong, to show everyone that she was, while Siss is like a pillar of ice. Slowly the child thaws, and because of the delicate, perfectly timed kindness of teachers and friends, she returns to life.

'Up on land there are slashes and scars on the river banks, upturned stones, uprooted trees and supple twigs that have been stripped of their bark. The blocks of ice tumble away pell-mell towards the lower lake and are spread out across it before anyone has woken up or seen anything. There the shattered ice will float, its edges sticking up on the surface of the water, float and melt and cease to be.'

How simple this novel is. How subtle. How strong. How unlike any other. It is unique. It is unforgettable. It is extraordinary.

She neither saw nor heard the waterfall, it was lower down. Here there was merely a whisper of water as it travelled downwards and up at the outlet it was quite still and noiseless.

This was the outlet of the great lake: a placid sliding of water from under the edge of the ice, so smooth that it was scarcely possible to see it. But a veil of vapour rose up from it in the cold. She was not conscious that she was standing looking at it; it was like being in a good dream. A good dream could be made out of so simple a thing. She felt no pangs of conscience because she was out on a walk without permission, and it would perhaps be difficult to find excuses for it. The placid water flowing away from the ice filled her with quiet joy.

She would probably lose her hold and fall down into a hollow where the shadows were, this time too, but it was a good moment and the other was chased away again by the sight that streamed towards her: the great river coming noiseless and clear from under the ice, flowing through her and lifting her up and saying something to her which was just what she needed.

They were so still, she and the water . . .

Problems, Myths and Stories

We take stories and storytelling for granted. The great reservoir of myths, legends, parables, tales, that we dip into for entertainment, use for films and plays, refer to so as to elucidate a point or draw a parallel – it is always there and we hardly think about it. Tales are as old as humanity, like a long shadow thrown by our history. How old? We don't know. Whenever we reach a point where it seems impossible to go back further, then we can be sure that soon the dark of our ignorance will yield to research and, behold, it is evident that the long shadow showed itself much earlier than we had thought. I like to think that the Neanderthals developed from grunts and barks to 'Once upon a time . . .' I asked an anthropologist who said, 'Impossible, they did not have the mental capacity.' I objected, 'But let us suppose this Neanderthal returns from the hunt and says, "I visited our grandfather's grave and I saw him talking with the white bear". That is a story.' He said, 'The first part of that sentence is possible, the second part is not: they did not have imagination.' Two hundred thousand years those Neanderthals lasted: in that time grunts could have become, 'I saw my dead grandmother talking to an owl', or so it seems to me. But we have a need to denigrate the past and its people, to

273

put ourselves at the height of achievement, human and animal.

We have not until recently been asking ourselves, 'What is the function of storytelling? What are stories for?' And that is extraordinary in itself. We tell stories all the time. Everybody does, recording our experience, perhaps even shaping it. When a woman returns from a supermarket and says, 'Guess what, I saw Dick in the cheese department, but he wasn't with Betty, he was with some new woman', that is the beginning – and the middle – of a story, though we do not know the end yet. We tell each other stories all day, and we daydream and fantasise, and when we fall asleep we tell stories again, for dreams are stories, not only wildly surreal, but as matter-of-fact and consistent as a B-movie; they can be horrific, or funny, or entertaining and even instructive, telling you things your conscious mind has not yet caught up with. And there is a hint, perhaps, of what stories may be about – or some of them – suggesting that they not only order experience, which for some reason we need to do, but accept inputs from other regions of the mind.

Quite recently, let's say in the last ten or fifteen years, the use of stories as education has been generally acknowledged, even in the academic world: to have said twenty years ago that stories had this function would have been greeted with derision or indifference. Stories were entertainment, and that was the end of the matter. As soon as the idea surfaced, the facts stared us in the face and soon traditional tales were claimed by feminists, seen as messages from oppressed people, politicos of all kinds.

Recently I read an anecdote about an Inuit society, I suppose in Northern Canada, since the book was by a Canadian author. A little boy has gone into the forest where he has killed a rat, for fun. The elders of the tribe take this seriously, because if animals are treated frivolously and without respect, then they won't come and keep their side of the bargain, which is to allow themselves to be killed for food and for their skins. And so it was: the animals kept away and the tribe began to starve. The child was told to go again into the forest and apologise, north, west, south, east, to the animals for the rat. And the animals returned. This tale was used – for all I know still is – to instruct small children. From it we may gather that not all Inuits have always been creatures of ice and snow, but lived in kinder habitats sometimes.

The Nigerian author, Mariamne Bá, unfortunately no longer living, wrote a book, *Too Long a Letter*, a middle-aged woman telling a friend about the terrible thing that has happened to her. Her husband has fallen in love with a girl the same age as his daughter, and married her, and she, the author, is without a husband, but not without a home, since the extended family has resources denied to the tight little family we are used to. But in the course of this 'letter' she tells quite casually, how a young girl is sent to her grandmother to further her education as we once sent middle-class girls to be 'finished'; and this education consisted of tales, which instructed her in her own proper behaviour, the history of her clan and tribe: customs, manners, mores. That was education, and in some parts of the world still is. Tales are seen as a repository of information, used to instruct the young: along with entertainment comes the message.

British tales are few when compared with those of the Germans, the French, other countries. We have nothing like the Brothers Grimm and our 'fairy' tales are mostly imports from France – their origin is hinted at by the fact that 'fate' tales is a better translation. Is this great lack in our culture because we were so often conquered, and every time the stock of tales became less? The Romans – what did they destroy? We had four centuries of them. The Angles, the Saxons, the Danes, the Norsemen, the Normans. Conquerors often destroy their victims' cultures as a matter of policy. In Southern Rhodesia, where I grew up, the British actively discouraged Shona and Ndelebe cultures, on the grounds that they were backward, and what we were bringing was civilisation. One may easily imagine the Romans doing the same. I have a Shona friend whose grandmother was storyteller for her clan, but he knew not one story when I begged him to write them down. 'The Jesuits beat all that out of me,' said he. Literally – beat. He was flogged, all the children were, for any hint of 'backwardness'. A couple of years ago I was in Zimbabwe at an occasion where people were dancing their contributions to the festivities, but I said I would tell a story, which was Idries Shah's *The Man, the Snake and the Stone*. (It was the right length.) I was impressed by how they responded, as if they were sitting round a fire listening to a tale-teller, an active audience, very different from our passivity: groans, excitement at the right places, clapping, clucking their tongues. And then a woman said, 'What a pity we have forgotten so many of our stories.' But Idries Shah's *World Tales* offered to libraries there (and a library may be a shelf under a tree) has long queues waiting for it. 'Yes, we have a story like that one – my mother, grandmother, great-grandmother told us stories, I remember now . . .' And so stories may be lost, or half forgotten and may come back again, perhaps changed, adapted.

We have imagined tales travelling from culture to culture, or as it were spontaneously generating like an emanation of the spirit of a people: now we see them as deliberately introduced – which does not contradict either of the other two theories. Idries Shah has told us that tales are continuously being fed into cultures everywhere, by masters of the art, the Sufis, experts on human psychology, tales described as being of different kinds and having different functions. Some have immediate charm and magic – for instance, Cinderella which is so to speak one of the Ur-tales, with literally hundreds of variants. We may wonder about its potency, but that is as far as we go. The teaching stories have dimensions not available to ordinary enquiry, and of these I am not qualified to speak. I want to talk about the reception and use of this material on a lower level, that of the ordinary reader, or pupil, or student, and about literature in general, which we must look at now as possessing areas inter-penetrated by high influences. It is easy to see, for instance, how Nasrudin jokes become acclimatised everywhere from Central Asian tea houses to pubs and bars. There are tales that have left their origins and become transmogrified into novels and short stories. *Appointment in Samara* is one: people destined to die on a certain day will do so, even if they travel to avoid their fate. *The Treasure of the Sierra Madre* is another, about the curse of gold and greed.

There are aspects of tales that we take for granted, but which we could examine to our profit. One source of tales is the Bible, which once everyone knew, but now only a few people. Until recently – let's say until the Second World War – people went to church on Sundays and heard there some of the most glorious prose ever written in English, in the King James Bible. Every Sunday and often in between too. This as it were unofficial or parallel education was classless: princes and paupers, labourers and farmers and lords and ladies, sat in those pews and heard language which fed into the prose of writers, some of them fine writers, others not, for you may hear the rhythms of the Bible running in poor writers' language as well as in good ones.

Doth not Wisdom cry? And understanding put forth her voice?
She standeth at the top of high places,
by the way in the places of the paths,
she crieth at the gates, at the entry of the city . . .

Or:

Man that is born of woman is of few days and full of trouble.
He cometh forth like a flower and is cut down,
he fleeth also as a shadow and continueth not . . .

Or:

Vanity of vanities, saith the Preacher, vanity of vanities, all is
vanity.

Or:

What profit hath a man of all his labour which he taketh under
the sun?
One generation passeth away, and another generation cometh:
but the earth abideth forever.

The point is, this was an influence that affected everyone who
went to church. That is to say, the majority of the population.
A literary education, and in storytelling, for in the Bible there
is everything from the bloodthirsty and the brutal to the tender-
ness, for instance, of Ruth. This immersion in fine language
lasted for generations, from when the Bible was translated from
Latin, so the common people could understand it and it was
no longer the preserve of priests. That voice has fallen silent.
When we talk of 'dumbing down' – and this goes on now
everywhere, and has become a major complaint of our time –
it is astonishing to me that no one mentions that not so long
ago we heard or read the Bible, and do not now. My poor
father was dragged to church as a child twice on Sundays and
to Sunday school as well, and said Sunday was for him and his
friends a black hole in every week, but he said too, often, that

he owed his love of good writing, and of literature, to that education, the Bible.

It was an education, too, in many-sidedness, subtlety. I wonder if the simplemindedness of much new writing, the narrowness of judgement, stereotypical goodies and baddies, is due to the loss of that broader experience. 'Dumbing down', the complaint goes, means that people cannot understand long words, or read long books; they complain about 'difficult' books, which their grandparents read with ease, but surely this must be at least partly because their experience has not included that other influence? When a child went to church, and had to sit through hours of being bored, he or she had to take in the long words and try to understand them, and difficult ideas and often powerful and often bloody stories and the ambiguities of the parables. No one lowered the level of the discourse, chose simpler words, or made easy difficult ideas, for the children's sake. No concessions were made. The church-going experience said that life was deadly serious, they were expected to understand the words and ideas above their heads, to make efforts. The unspoken message was that life was important, they were important, and everything was expected of them.

Now contrast their weekly experience, the strongest cultural one in their lives, with the children's programmes on television, which are jokey, giggly, familiar, everything is a laugh, and the unspoken message is that nothing much will be expected from these children, nothing difficult demanded, nothing is important.

The clock cannot be turned back, and church-going has gone as a general experience, but storytelling and reading has not, and used well could supply what once the Bible did.

There have been other books as powerful as the Bible. Let us take one, *Kalila and Dimna*, translated by Ramsay Wood. The origins of this book go back into the mists of myth. Here is one version. When Alexander the Great left India, he had put into place rulers chosen by him. One of them was a bad man and an unsatisfactory king. Then a sage, Bidpai, said to his wife that he was going to the palace to reprimand and warn the king. While she wept and wailed, he did go to the palace, demanded an audience, and for his temerity was flung into the bottle dungeon, in other words the sewers. That night the king was watching stars on the roof of the palace and it occurred to him that he was after all a very small item in the cosmic ledgers. At that moment there appeared to him that Stranger Dressed in Green who figures in so many Sufi tales. He said, 'Because you have for once in your life had a thought not concerned with your magnificence and importance, I am going to give you some advice. If you go hunting tomorrow in such and such a direction, you will find treasure.' Next day off went the king with his court, and when he saw a ragged figure by the roadside, he reined in and said, 'Ho, fellow, I am looking for treasure that has been promised.' 'If you are King Dabschelin,' was the reply, 'the treasure is waiting for you in that cave over there.'

In the cave the king found mounds of precious stones and gold, but after some minutes of jubilation he said, 'Wait! I already have treasure houses full of such things, why do I need more?' Then he saw a book, which he opened, but could not make sense of it, so he took it back to the palace to puzzle over until he remembered the sage he had had thrown into the dungeons. He had the man taken out and washed and brought before him. 'Can you explain this book to me?' he demanded, and Bidpai said he could and at once began instruction. And that is how the history sometimes begins of this book which is a vast collection of animal tales and fables, some of which can be found in the canon of Buddha tales, when Buddha was a deer, a monkey, a lion; while some are to be seen on rock carvings in North India. How old they are we don't know. So here again, when we probe into origins, history unfolds earlier … earlier … One of the book's sources was a treatise by a certain Kautilya, on the art of government, dated at 300 B.C., but he wrote as the last of many authors on government and administration, and there is no way now of seeing why this – to us – so ancient a book was seen by him as a mere latecomer in a series. Here we may be reminded of Ecclesiastes's 'Of the making of books there is no end', – but after all, of those innumerable and – to him – wearying books we have very few left.

This book is at times called *Bidpai*, after the sage, sometimes *Kalila and Dimna*, and has had hundreds of years of energetic life. It has been described as 'having been more widely translated than the Bible'. In this country the first translation was in the sixteenth century by Sir Thomas North, who translated Plutarch into a work which was the source of Shakespeare's knowledge of the Roman world. North's Plutarch was popular reading, and so was his version of *Bidpai*. There followed dozens of versions of the book, twenty of them in the hundred years before 1888, after which there were none. So, once anyone with a claim to literary education had read *Bidpai*, but now few people have even heard of it.

The Persians heard of this wonderful book, used in India to educate rulers, and sent ambassadors who had to steal it, so closely guarded was it. It became a precious book to them, too. It was translated into many languages and tales from it spread everywhere, becoming absorbed and assimilated. When I was in Mexico, at the university, a professor said that tales from the book, and the idea of the book itself, were part of Spanish popular culture to the point that peasants telling and retelling the stories believe them to be Spanish.

The frame story concerns a ruler who is bored with his life and who, told that a white bull has been discovered lost and wandering, orders that it should be brought to him. The bull becomes a friend and adviser, but two jackals, Kalila and Dimna, were jealous of the noble beast's influence on the king, and had it murdered. One may easily imagine how peasants and common people everywhere identified with this, as easily as the princes who were given the book as a manual of advice. Machiavelli's *The Prince* is supposed to be a descendant. One great Persian book, *The Lights of Canopus*, of Sufi provenance, was derived from it, centuries after its origins. What an influence that book has had, and not only on folk culture and on literature: from it were inspired illustrations in Moghul art – they can be seen in the British Museum.

It is not possible to imagine European culture without *The Tales of Bidpai*, nor English literature without the Bible.

There are influences that echo down to us from before either. Once humanity used 'oracles', where voices emanating from sacred sources answered questions, but in our time we tend to see them as a variation of our agony aunts. People travelled long distances to consult oracles, and we still want to be told what to do and how to think by problem-solvers and gurus. 'Oracles' are by no means all in the past. In Zimbabwe, for instance, there are shrines and holy places where the shamans – wise women and men – still offer advice in the names of the ancestors, or other-worldly guides. These can be skilled politicians, and perhaps this may throw light back onto the oracle phenomenon, which even now may create awe and that type of curiosity which betrays a desire, or at least a readiness, to believe.

Recently a large crowd collected in Matabeleland, at the memorial to one Alan Wilson, to whose name is always attached the words 'Last Stand'. Alan Wilson's Last Stand was an exemplary tale told to white children. He and his company stood their ground against attacking Matabele warriors, and were killed.

The memorial has always been a totem for the whites, a way of defining themselves, and execrated by the blacks as a symbol of white conquest. But, behold, the shamans announced that their wisdom would be delivered at this memorial. People in the crowd, both black and white, protested at the choice of this place. And this is what the Wise Ones said – or at least, how it was reported to me:

> 'And why should we not speak in this place? Oh, shortsighted ones, blinded by your immediate interests. You never see anything in perspective and from a higher viewpoint. Alan Wilson was a brave warrior killed fighting for what he believed in and he was killed honourably by brave warriors. Alan is as much an ancestor of Zimbabwe as the brave men who killed him. We honour him. When will you learn to see things as we do, who see far into the future, and understand how to judge events, refusing easy revenge and retaliation?'

In that context, this was dynamite. All of Matabeleland was simmering with rage and the desire for revenge because of Mugabe's massacres of the Ndebele. Mugabe was – and is – fomenting hatred against the whites. Yet here was a mouthpiece of the Ancestors putting the weight of traditional wisdom against everything that was being popularly felt and said. This was no misty Oracle, clothing advice in riddles which time would unfold. And this event, and others like it, make us wonder if the ancient oracles intervened similarly in politics and policy.

There is something else about this event, relevant to our theme. It is the tone of what was said, which surely has to remind us of the sagas, that seem so far from us today. They were told – or sung – for centuries, in the halls of the powerful, in hovels, in marketplaces, in forests beside fires that frightened bears and wolves. The sagas defined those people's idea of themselves, reinforced codes of behaviour, of honour. Long ago – but they still have a powerful effect. You may hear, in Iceland, modern people passionately arguing about characters in a saga. There is a wilful woman in the saga called *Burned Njal*, Hallgerdur, who has been brought back into relevance by the women's movement. Men tend to hate her, women to admire. But the point is, the tale is alive and potent.

But that was the oral tradition: when we in our time talk of stories, tales, we often forget that for most of human history – thousands of years – tales were told or sung. Reading came much later, is comparatively recent, and changed not only the ways of receiving tales, but the actual machinery of our minds. The print revolution lost us our memories – or partly. Before, people kept information in their heads. One may even now meet an old man or woman, illiterate, who reminds us what we once were – what everyone was like. They remember everything, what was said by whom, when and why: dates, places, addresses, history. They don't need to refer to reference books. This faculty disappeared with print. It was an effect, I think, that was not foreseen, and surely this should make us at least wonder what unforeseen changes may result from the current technological revolution: television, radio, the Internet, computers. How will our mentation be affected? Will the changes be to our advantage?

The novel is what we think of first, these days, as the most representative kind of literature. Very recent is the novel, even if we take Cervantes as the starting place, even more so if we start with the English eighteenth century. It has been said that the novel is the art form peculiarly of our time, that we take it altogether too much for granted, that it is a storehouse of information about the world we live in, different cultures, peoples, ways of thinking.

The novel has always been embattled. Ever since I came to

England in 1949, I have been reading that the novel is dead. It is a favourite complaint of critics. Meanwhile the novel seems to be doing very well everywhere you look. The novel has been – is – seen by dictators as dangerous. And it is: Solzhenitsyn's *The Gulag Archipelago*, it is often said, was the major influence in bringing down the Soviet Empire. Moralisers and preachers saw the novel as frivolous and perverting. Jane Austen returned a classic defence to accusations of triviality in *Northanger Abbey*:

> ... there seems almost a general wish of decrying the capacity and undervaluing the labour of the novelist, and of slighting the performances which have only genius, wit and taste to recommend them. 'I am no novel reader ... I seldom look into novels ... Do not imagine that *I* often read novels ... It is very well for a novel ...' Such is the common cant. 'And what are you reading, Miss – ?' 'Oh, it is only a novel!' replies the young lady while she lays down her book with affected indifference or momentary shame. 'It is only Cecilia, or Camilla, or Belinda'; or, in short, only some work in which the greatest powers of the mind are displayed, in which the most thorough knowledge of human nature, the happiest delineation of its varieties, the liveliest effusions of wit and humour are conveyed to the world in the best chosen language.

The novel has always provided characters and situations that people argue about, influencing them to emulate (not always happily) or avoid. We may remember Goethe's *Werther*, which caused young men to throw themselves off cliffs and under horses all over Europe. Lovelace was a pattern of male profligacy and influenced the literature of the time, particularly Russian – we owe Raskolnikov to Lovelace. Becky Sharp identified a certain type of young woman, new in Society and in literature.

So, to look into literature for models, for comment on good and bad behaviour, for instruction, is nothing new: we have always done it. From the animal fables that are as old as we are able to imagine, and the parables of the Bible; from sagas and epics, from the songs of troubadours and trouvères, and all the way to our most characteristic form, the novel, we have used stories and storytelling.

In the East, the figure of Nasrudin, known also as Joha and the Hoja, provides a cultural template from Albania to Afghanistan. Nasrudin/Joha/Hoja tales have been around a long time in the West, but Idries Shah in the 1960s, when making literary material available from Sufi sources, reintroduced Nasrudin tales in new and fresh forms. He told us that the materials he was contributing to our culture were a mirror in which we could see ourselves; he was defining and illustrating an attitude that was already ours. There is a Nasrudin tale of the man who picked up a mirror from the ground, grimaced at what he saw in it, reasoned that it must be something unpleasant to have been thrown away – and dropped it. But whatever we do see in it, the impact of Shah's work is surely a speeding up of that process which we refer to – in shorthand – as 'growing up'. We all know that a novel, a story, read when we are twenty, looks very different when we are fifty, or seventy. But a Sufi tale may change from year to year, or even month to month, hinting that we are in the middle of a process of sharp acceleration. That quality seems to me the most remarkable, the most easily seen, when studying Shah's work. It changes.

What an experience it is, reading perhaps for the twentieth time a Nasrudin tale, which at first seemed flat, pointless, certainly not a joke – and then suddenly, there it is, the meaning. Or one of them? And what has happened? It is not the story that has changed, we have. Or, we are for the first time reading in a heightened, perceptive state; because there is another aspect of the tales, the material. We have been told that our mental states continually fluctuate, and that we are hardly aware of it, or are aware only of its cruder manifestations. We say, 'I'm dull today', or 'I can't concentrate', contrasting what we feel with what we were yesterday and what we hope we will be tomorrow, or in an hour's time. You may read a passage that one day is vibrant, alive, electric, but a week later you read it and it is flat and you can't find in it what you did before. But to see fluctuations in our mental state, you don't need Shah's material, it can happen with ordinary books. For instance, I once read Isabella Bird's *A Lady's Life in the Rocky Mountains* and it was so alive to me, so present, that I was that intrepid lady riding down a mountain path in a blizzard with only a cardigan to keep her warm, and with cold legs because she'd taken off her stockings to make into rags for her horse's hooves to stop them slipping on an icy path that had a cliff on one side and a precipice on the other. I was the woman lying at night in a shed with the temperature degrees below zero, looking at the stars through a hole in the roof through which snow was falling to cover the floor and her . . . and re-reading the book a month later, I found the magic gone. This kind of experience may make you question the reliability of your own mind even before the experience of Sufi material; make you even more eager to examine it in this new light.

I certainly do not want to suggest that Shah's work should be used as people have used books for centuries, looking for auguries and advice by opening them at random. 'I didn't know what to do, so I opened my Bible and read, "Fear not, for thou shalt not be ashamed", and so I decided to sell my corn.' That kind of thing. But if you have absorbed Shah's work, then tales come into your mind when you find yourself in similar situations and enable you to examine where you stand, what choices you have.

It is impossible to read much of Idries Shah and not to find your mind widened. Not possible to ask, when a calamity happens, 'Why me?' (the car accident, the plane crash) if you have absorbed the Nasrudin tale that is summed up thus: *He fell, but my neck is broken*. There is a tale that always makes me laugh, while reminding me of a certain solipsistic tendency we all have. Nasrudin wakes his wife to tell her he has had an inspiring thought, namely that everything in the world is organised for the benefit of mankind. 'Just think, if camels had wings, they would go romping about on our roofs and spitting down their cud, and what a nuisance that would be.'

And there are unexpected resonances, such as when finding in your mind a tale that apparently has nothing to do with the dilemma you are in (so that you suspect the machinery is malfunctioning). But then as you go along the relevance becomes only too clear. And this is similar to the sometimes surprising messages of dreams.

The reactions of other people to jokes and tales can be unexpected and very useful: Nasrudin was riding along on his donkey when it shied because frogs in a pond ahead began loudly croaking. He was saved from a fall into the water. He threw handfuls of money into the pond. When asked why, he replied that he was rewarding the frogs.

This tale inspired in a friend paroxysms of rage. Not polite surprise, incredulity, but literally shouts of rage. He could not tolerate that frogs were being given what they could not use. You've guessed it: this man is the meanest I've known, devious and dishonest.

Wine is often mentioned, usually as an analogy for a certain state of mind. A young man who had just read a book by Shah protested that it was all about drinking. I joked that he was an example of the tale about the man who complained to an encyclopaedia compiler that it was all about money, when in fact there were only a few references to money. 'Obsessed with drink,' said this youth, who was an alcoholic. None of us by now may be unaware – so much is written and said – that strong reactions to something can conceal (or reveal) secret strong attractions, opposition, addiction.

There is a Nasrudin tale about the man with two wives, one pretty and one not, and when asked which he would save if both were drowning, he asked the ugly one, 'Can you swim, my dear?' I have heard a feminist reject all of Shah, root and branch, because of this 'sexist' tale.

When someone objects that it was 'unfair' when an instructor cuffed a youth about to set off to fetch some water, on the grounds that it would not be much use hitting him after he had spilled the water, then it is not difficult to see that this person has problems with authority.

A man I know decided not to do business with someone, because of a Nasrudin tale. Nasrudin regularly crossed a certain frontier to trade. The Customs knew he was smuggling but could never catch him. Years later, when he and they had retired, they asked him what it was he had been smuggling. 'Donkeys,' he said. The potential partner saw this tale as advice on ways to cheat Customs. 'I like this guy Shah,' said he, 'he understands business.'

Again and again through Shah's work are reminders that our culture has lost certain attitudes to higher thought and experience, which are part of other cultures. For instance, when told a story, in some parts of the East, the hearer will ask, 'What can I learn from this?' I find these hints intriguing, to say the least. Did we have this attitude once, but have lost it? May one imagine a child, let's say in old Afghanistan, as a matter of course being asked to think about a tale, when he or she has done with the fascination of it, the humour? What other capacities have we lost that we don't know about? Or perhaps never had? Or only certain people had them? There are hints and intimations everywhere.

To regard literature as a serious matter, for people who took themselves seriously, was common, I would say, until about the end of the Fifties. I think the hedonism, the drugs ('If you can remember it, you weren't there' – said as a boast) of the Sixties was responsible for a general lowering of standards, a barbarising.

There used to be a phenomenon, The Educated Person, who assumed reading was part of education. They would know the classics of their own countries, currently approved modern books, perhaps the better known classics of other European countries, and all this on a solid basis of Greek and Latin. (This was of course a Euro-centred education.) Possibly a couple of classics from the East were added, the Vedas, the *Mahabharata*, and, until a century ago, *Kalila and Dimna*, or *Bidpai*. And this was not only for upper-class people, because you can find in novels of the past how poor people aspiring to better things valued books.

People then could read the best that had been written, but since that time literature has exploded everywhere, geographically, so that if you visit a country and say, 'Give me a list of your good books', then it will certainly fill pages. Countries that had few authors, or none, now have many. The novel travels well . . . it has always been its own creator, because only the author has been able to say what his or her novel should be. An art form that began in this country with *Tom Jones* – picaresque tales; *Tristram Shandy*, that surreal squib of a book; or novels written in letter-form like *Clarissa*, cannot accept strictures about what it ought to be. It is this flexibility that has enabled it to adapt to any culture. For instance, in Zimbabwe there are good novels written by people whose grandmothers were storytellers, whose heritage was oral. The expansion has not only been geographic, for the novel has proliferated into a hundred new forms. Science and space fiction, women's writing, black writing, the 'magic realism' of South America, factoids (where reporting and imagination merge, sometimes remarkably), novels using the dialects of the computer – I could go on, but Goethe now could not read all the good novels that are being written, and nor could any reader during the last thirty years. This is a new thing. The 'Cultivated Person' has had to relinquish any attempt at 'keeping up', and is probably specialising. You may meet science-fiction addicts who disdain 'mainline literature' and conventional readers who wouldn't dream of reading science or space fiction. Alas, new snobberies seem to be born with every human breath.

To deal with this vast new challenge all kinds of defences have been invented, one being that very old one of the barbarian who, faced with a culture she or he does not understand, says that it is no good anyway – The Dead White Male is to this point. Another says that there is no such thing as good and bad writers, all are the same – but we need not waste time on the extremities of (mostly) academic folly.

At the same time as this great spread and proliferation of literature, there is a completely new thing, a generation of young people, who may have spent fifteen, twenty years studying, have carried off prizes and attracted acclaim, but who have read nothing, know nothing outside their school or university curriculums, and are not only ignorant but incurious. To spend an hour with such a person challenges any idea you might have had about education. If you say, 'Do you realise you are the first generation who did not take it for granted that reading is part of education?' then you may easily find yourself shouted at, and called an 'elitist'. You cannot have a conversation, because they can only talk about themselves, their friends, gossip about the currently famous, shopping, food. They live in tight little self-enclosed worlds. It is true that some, reaching their twenties and finding themselves so disadvantaged, compared with their contemporaries who have read, start trying to catch up. Not easy when you haven't got the habit of it, perhaps only read slowly from lack of practice, and are coping with the pressures of being an adult – which now have to include drugs as well as sex and work.

A great deal of effort is going into trying to get children to acquire the reading habit: exhortations, lectures, easy access to books – never has a generation had it made so easy for them to read.

Yet far too often you are forced to realise that when you belong to a reading generation, there is a whole web or map of references, information, knowledge that you have taken for granted; you realise that reading has been a parallel education, filling and extending what education you in fact did have. With contemporaries you talk from inside this web, or net, or reference, but with more and more of the young, you choose your words, try not to use long ones, so as not to hear 'I don't know that word, what does it mean?' And you know that a careless reference to, let's say, Goethe, will bring blank looks. 'What's that?' Patagonia, The Cultural Revolution, the Mongols – 'What's that?' The Renaissance, the Russian Revolution of 1917, Dante ... 'What's that? What was that?'

After 9.11

Busily promoting my book *African Laughter* I flitted about (as authors do) on the East Coast, doing phone-ins and interviews, and had to conclude that Americans see Africa as something like Long Island, with a single government, situated vaguely south (The Indian Ocean? What's that?). In New York I had the heaviest, most ignorant audience of my life, very discouraging, but the day after in Washington 300 of the brightest, best-informed people I can remember. To talk about 'America' as if it were a homogeneous unity isn't useful, but I hazard the following generalisations.

America, it seems to me has as little resistance to an idea or a mass emotion as isolated communities have to measles and whooping cough. From outside, it is as if you are watching one violent storm after another sweep across a landscape of extremes. Their Cold War was colder than anywhere else in the West, with the intemperate execution of the Rosenbergs, and grotesqueries of the McCarthy trials. In the seventies, Black Power, militant feminism, the Weathermen – all flourished. On one of my visits, people could talk of nothing else. Two years later they probably still flourished, but no one mentioned them. 'You know us,' said a friend. 'We have short memories.'

Everything is taken to extremes. We all know this, but the fact is seldom taken into account when we try to understand what is going on. The famous Political Correctness, which began as a sensible examination of language for hidden bias, became hysterical and soon afflicted whole areas of education. Universities have been ruined by it. I was visiting a university town not far from New York when two male academics took me out into the garden, for fear of being overheard, and said they hated what they had to teach, but they had families, and would not get tenure if they didn't toe the line. A few years earlier, in Los Angeles, I found that my novel *The Good Terrorist* was being 'taught'. The teaching consisted of the students scrutinising it for political incorrectness. This was thought to be a good approach to literature. Unfortunately, strong and inflexible ideas attract the stupid. Britain shows milder symptoms of the same disease, so it is instructive to see where such hysteria may lead if not checked.

The reaction to the events of 11 September – terrible as they were – seems excessive to outsiders, and we have to say this to our American friends, although they have become so touchy, and ready to break off relations with accusations of hard-heartedness. The United States is in the grip of a patriotic fever which reminds me of the Second World War. They seem to themselves as unique, alone, misunderstood, beleaguered, and they see any criticism as treachery.

The judgement 'they had it coming', so angrily resented, is perhaps misunderstood. What people felt was that Americans had at last learned that they are like everyone else, vulnerable to the snakes of Envy and Revenge, to bombs exploding on a street corner (as in Belfast), or in a hotel housing a government (as in Brighton). They say themselves that they have been expelled from their Eden. How strange they should ever have thought they had a right to one.

The Past is Myself, Christabel Bielenberg

A welcome reissue of a book that in the sixteen years since its publication has lost nothing of its value. An Englishwoman married a German lawyer in 1934, and worried, but not unduly so, by Hitler, then went to live in Germany, among liberals who could not believe it was happening. Then they had to, and quietly formed links which led to 20 July 1944, and the failed plot to kill Hitler. The author's experience was not of immediate horror and challenges to conscience, the black and white pictures created by the appalled incomprehension of those who did not live through it, but something more like a polluted fog that slowly thickened. In it occurred brutal incidents, like the Jewish doctor who warned her that in using him for her children she invited reprisals, and who then disappeared. Adam von Trott appears again as in other memoirs, a tragic figure distrusted in his country and in ours, vainly trying to attract the attention of the Allies to make us recognise and work with 'the other Germany' who, these conspirators believed, could bring down Hitler. Certainly 'the other Germany' is described here. The Black Forest villagers who sheltered her were so little affected by wartime propaganda that a shot-down American airman was treated like an honoured guest. Reading this we have to remember that Hitler killed twelve million people, of whom six million were Jews, the others mostly brave Germans. Wars – all history – become fixed in patterns that seem to have been inevitable. Who can say now what might have happened if we – Churchill – had believed von Trott and his friends and made an appeal to the other Germany? Which, says the author, ceased to exist when we began the mass bombing of German cities. The feeling was: What difference whether we are anti-Hitler or not, we are being savagely and barbarously bombed anyway. 'But who started the war then?' – must be the indignant response of a British reader. 'Who set off the bombs?' But it seems citizens do not identify with their governments, not when things are going badly. Or even when they are going well. Who dropped those bombs on Nagasaki and Hiroshima? Certainly not you and I.

Christabel Bielenberg continued her quietly resourceful resistance to the end. It was because of her that her husband did not die with the other conspirators.

The Story of Hai

Is it being said too often how much we in the West have suffered because of the long wars between Islam and Christianity, leaving us biased and with gaps in our information? I think not. It is easy enough to remark, but hard to take in, the long-term implications of the fact that while all those great civilisations blossomed everywhere else, little Europe was backward and ignorant. Or rather, we admit our time of darkness, but not the brilliance of the other civilisations, Islamic and other. Balkh and Baghdad, Cordoba and Granada and Toledo, the cities of North Africa and of India and of China – if some of the crumbs from their tables came our way, if they sent us, occasionally, a missionary, we were indeed fortunate. Infinitely provincial, and barbarous they thought us then; some think us provincial now. But there are all kinds of new bridges being built where there have been none for centuries; and connections are being revealed in the most unexpected places. One is this book. It looks as if our Robinson Crusoe was inspired by it as much as by Alexander Selkirk the real-life castaway. An English translation of *The Story of Hai bin Yaqzan* was published for the first time direct from the Arabic in 1708; there had been previous translations based on a Latin version. In 1719 Defoe brought out his *Life and Strange Adventures of Robinson Crusoc.*

Known to us as Abubacer, Ibn Tufail, otherwise Abu Bakr bin Abd al-Malik bin Muhammad bin Tufail al-Qaisi, was born about AD 1100 near Granada. Physician, philosopher, mathematician and poet, he was adviser and physician at the courts of Granada and of Prince Abu Sa'd Usuf in Morocco. He wrote extensively on many subjects, but virtually only *The Story of Hai bin Yaqzan* survives. The best-kept Arabic text is now in the Bodleian.

Ibn Tufail offers us alternate beginnings to his tale. Some sources claim, says he, that Hai was one of those formed without parents, generated from mud that has some rather extraordinary qualities; but he, the author, prefers the version that there was a beautiful princess who, giving birth in equivocal circumstances, cast the baby, like Moses, into the water, sealed into a little coffin. God, hearing her prayers, saw to it that a strong current bore the baby to a near island. It was the night of the highest tide of the year, and the waves took the coffin into a wood. The tide receded. A doe who had lost her fawn to an eagle heard the cries of the infant and, standing on her hind legs, she broke open the coffin, already loosened by the waves, with her front hooves. She suckled and cared for Hai. Brought up among animals, yet Hai knew he was not one. He contrasted his naked body with theirs, so decently covered with fur, and he made himself coverings from a dead eagle's feathers. He saw the animals had capacities he lacked: they ran faster, had sharp horns and teeth and talons. Yet he was as strong as they by using his wits. The just published *Marcos, Wild Child of the Sierra Morena*, by Gabirel Javier Manila, is about a Spanish child who lived by himself in the mountains, and he described the same process. Marcos, while living with and befriended by animals, taught himself to understand his own humanity by matching his capacities with theirs. He was educated by the animal not the human world, but he learned by observation and reflection that while he shared the animal world, at the same time he transcended it.

So, too, Hai in this story which is an analogy or metaphor, describing the development of the human mind.

Hai's animal mother, the doe, grew old and feeble, and he cared for her, but she died. The sorrowful boy, then aged seven, tried to revive the corpse and, failing, wondered where the life that had gone away had resided. In a remarkable passage Hai dissects the animal, examining its organs one by one, meditating on the bodily processes and commenting, among other things, on the circulation of the blood. This passage reminded me of when, reading for probably the 999th time something that occurs in every textbook, it seems, we ever publish: 'Between the Greeks and Copernicus the whole world stagnated in darkness' – I chanced on a description of how Mamoun, the son of the Caliph Haroun El Raschid, experimented with his courtiers in his palace gardens with shadows and sticks of various lengths, to determine how the earth turned.

Hai, too, 'observed the motion of the moon and the planets very closely, and discovered that they had many minor orbits, all however contained in one great orbit which moved them from east to west in a day and a night . . .'

Hai discovers fire, and how to use it for light and for heat and for cooking his food. He meditates on the different animal species, seeing what separates them and what they have in common, and he concludes that there is an animal spirit, as there is a plant spirit, and that these are related, and that he is related to both, but is separate. He reflects on inanimate things that do not sense or feel or grow, like earth, water, air and flame; and deduces from their properties certain laws, which he then applies to himself. Thus, one after another, he accomplishes stages in the knowledge of himself and his environment; reasoning and deducing, he discovers the laws of the physical universe, and comes to an intellectual conviction of the existence of a Creator. But he did all this through the powers of reason, through the intellect, by thinking; not by means of the direct perception of the Seer – a difference which is encapsulated in the old story of Avicenna (Ibn Sina), the savant and philosopher, and Abu Said, the mystic:

When the philosopher and the Sufi met, Avicenna said:

'What I know, he sees.'

Abu Said remarked: 'What I see, he knows.'

Then Hai came to the limits of what could be discovered by reason, and went beyond it. But: 'Explaining this state which he reached is impossible. Any attempt is like someone trying to taste a colour and requiring that black, say, is to be sweet or sour . . . hearken, then, with the hearing of your heart, and stare with the vision of your mind at what I point out to you. Perhaps you will find in it guidance that will lead you to the proper path.'

We have to reflect on the fact that the Eastern cast of mind took this germ of a story, of how the infant knew himself to be alone in a world where he had to find a foster-mother to survive, and slowly discovered that everything around him had lessons for him; he could understand through the use of the faculties that man has, first his position in the natural world, and then his relationship with his Creator. The same tale, handled by the robustly down-to-earth, dominating and inventive Western mind, became a fascinatingly detailed story of how a castaway overcame physical problems. Step by step the house is built, tools are made, animals tamed, food grown – and Crusoe dreams of human companionship, watches for a sail.

But: 'Hai had roamed the length and breadth of the island and found no trace of another human being, a circumstance which gratified him and satisfied his requirement of privacy and solitude.'

Another human did come, by chance; not a Man Friday, but Asal, a contemplative like himself. Asal's story was this: his island home had brought to it 'a religion devised so as to project upon the world of the senses examples which would parallel events in the higher world, and be as shadows of real events'. But the people had turned his religion into an affair of externals. There were these two lively and intelligent boys, Asal and Salaman. Asal, hearing the hidden message in this religion, had grown beyond it, but his friend Salaman clung to the obvious and literal meanings, and became the jealous custodian of the outwardness of religion.

Hai begged Asal to let him travel to this other, benighted island, and tell the people of the wonderful truths he had discovered, for 'he felt a great pity for mankind'. Asal told him it was useless, for the people 'were distracted from their remembrance of God by their trading and selling and did not fear a day when their hearts and eyes will be transformed'. Nevertheless, the two travelled together to Asal's island, where Hai found it was as Asal had said. Salaman had the people enslaved.

And so Hai and Asal returned to Hai's island, to resume their search for God.

'This is . . . what there is of the tale of Hai bin Yaqzan and Asal and Salaman. It has included material which is to be found neither in books nor in ordinary conversation . . .'

Hard to convey the flavour of this wonderful story, which manages to be lyrical and full of sober thought at the same time. More poem, perhaps, than prose. It is certainly hard to put down once you start reading.

Sufi philosophy and poetry

One of the aims of Octagon Press is to offer books, both newly minted and traditional, in the Sufic tradition. An increasing number of people interested in a field previously considered 'specialist' have available to them a good selection of the classics in one form or another. Difficulties have never been minimised, the chief one being that there have been translations without insight into what gave these works their essential value: some scholars did not have knowledge of Sufi thought and specifically Sufic literary devices. But it is possible to get at least an idea of a strong and flavoursome original even with a translator lacking this knowledge, if he has been aware of the contending possibilities of a word or a phrase. As Edward Eastwick says in his preface to *The Rose Garden*: 'If the Eastern saying be true that "Each word of Saadi has seventy-two meanings" there is room for a septuagint of translators.' This translation of *The Rose Garden*, made in the middle of the nineteenth century, was obviously a labour of love, and the just word for it is, I think, reliable. It is impressive to see Eastwick wrestling with himself and the authors of other translations for that exact shade of meaning. *The Rose Garden* has eight sections: 'On the Manners of Kings'. 'On the Qualities of Dervishes', 'On the Excellence of Contentment'. 'On the Advantages of Taciturnity', 'On Love and Youth', 'On Decrepitude and Old Age', 'On the Effects of Education', 'On the Duties of Society'. These are not essays or disquisitions; each is a little landscape of tales, maxims, aphorisms, reminiscences, verse and poetry in different manners – an art form which seems to me singularly attractive. How is it that we have been pedagogued into accepting such exclusivity in the categories of our literature? Poetry is poetry, prose is prose, and never the twain shall meet . . . But perhaps we are not so compartmented after all. I think of Thoreau's *A Week on the Concord*, that amiable mingling of reflection, nature observation, remembrance, and apposite quotes of prose and verse – and is it possible that our habit of putting quotes into novels or biography from other people's verse and prose, as chapter or section headings, is an expression of the same need? – for the effect, if not the intention, is to break down barriers, to create a liberating sense of comprehensiveness.

Saadi lived in the thirteenth century. He was a poor man, a 'wanderer on the face of the earth'. He was instructed by the Masters Gilani and Suhrawardi. Refusing riches and favours when these were offered, he deflected them to others. 'He lived to the age of 120 years . . . and spent thirty years in various countries acquiring learning; and thirty years more in travelling and making himself practically acquainted with things; and thirty years more in the environs of Shiraz, in a spot which for beauty equals the Garden of Paradise, and where men of learning and eminence resorted to him and where he employed himself in devotion' – says a fifteenth-century biographer. He wrote the Persian classics *The Orchard* and *The Rose Garden* in the space of two or three years. 'In the case of *The Rose Garden*, Saadi has accomplished the feat . . . of writing a book which is so simple in vocabulary and structure that it is used as a first textbook for students of Persian, and appears to contain only moralistic aphorisms and stories: while at the same time it is recognized by the most eminent Sufis as concealing the whole range of the deepest Sufi knowledge which can be committed to writing' (Idries Shah, *The Way of the Sufi*).

Elegant compression is Saadi's literary quality. To quote from a work whose aim is to illustrate by juxtaposition is, I suppose, risky:

> They who the faults of others bring to you,
> Be sure they'll bear to others your faults too.

And this:

> All Adam's race are members of one frame,
> Since all, at first, from the same essence came.
> When by hard fortune one limb is oppressed,
> The other members lose their wonted rest:
> If thou feel'st not for other's misery,
> A son of Adam is no name for thee . . .

Oriental Mysticism illustrates the devious routes some Eastern works have taken to reach us. The original, in Turkish (called *The Remotest Aim*), was translated into Persian, and then – as Professor Palmer frankly admits – was 'arranged' by him 'to give a clearer and more succinct account of the system than would have been afforded by a mere translation'. And there you have it. But the book is not without interest, and indeed invaluable, because it does so aptly illustrate this problem of the academic approach: although mechanical and lifeless, *Oriental Mysticism* has been regarded until now as essential reading for students. But it does have a useful glossary of technical and allegorical expressions in use among Sufi poets.

An edition of *The Walled Garden of Truth* represents new

work being done to give these ancient classics contemporary life. David Pendlebury, talking of Major Stephenson's, a previous translation, puts it:

> I became rapidly convinced that buried deep in this formidable tome there lay a message of great directness and power, but that in its present form there was precious little chance of that message ever reaching precisely those people who might derive most benefit from it . . . Frankly, it does not seem designed to be read, but rather to sit there on the shelf, yet another chilly monument to academic endeavour.

That edition was a sixth of the original material, and Pendlebury reckons his selection to be about that in relation to Stephenson's – so this does not pretend to be more than a sample, a taste. He has chosen what has made an impact on him personally, with no attempt to systematise; careful to exclude what needs familiarity with Muslim ways of thought. The result is something fresh and lively, as if old Sanai (he lived in the twelfth century) were speaking personally to you – always the sign of a good translation.

> Man and his reason are just the latest ripening
> plants in his garden.
> Whatever you assert about his nature,
> you are bound to be out of your depth,
> like a blind man trying to describe
> the appearance of his own mother.
> While reason is still tracking down the secret
> you end your quest on the open field of love.

The Afterword discusses a variety of topics: the problems of honest translation in this field, Sanai and his relation to other poets working in the same tradition, our possible attitudes to such material, the rhyming patterns of Persian verse. This is an wholly admirable essay – for its simple explanations of complex problems, for the large amount of information given in a small space. Not least is a little exposition of 'the secret language' traditionally employed by Sufi poets. This is based on the concept that sounds are in themselves representatives of greater truths or realities. (I am afraid it is impossible not to debase the idea in such summary writing as this.) The concept is the key to the 'adjab' system in use throughout Eastern literature – the numerical equivalents of letters – and to one of the meanings of the saying: The secret protects itself. Because this was not understood was a reason for the failure of many until now accepted translations. But once understood, even superficially, the idea helps to unlock technical terms like Love, Cheek, Pearl, Fool, He, Cupbearer – and so on, indefinitely. Thus it is that every word will have its unfolding meanings, not from a base of individual fantasy or a freak of choice, but from the sounds which compose it. Sometimes respectable in Islam, and with great influence, Sufis have at other times or in different places been persecuted: this sound system, in use for many centuries, has been employed in what we would describe as a 'political' sense, enabling messages, recognition signals, ideas, to pass from place to place, even from culture to culture – back and forth, for instance, during the Crusades, between people nominally at war but considering themselves one in reality – concealed in what seemed like (and was on one level) a poetic code, a convention, a conceit.

As Sanai puts it here:

> . . . for until a man steps out from impurity
> how can the Quran step out from the page?
> The letter of the Quran is in itself

no panacea for the soul:
Goats don't grow fat on the goatherd's call.

So the statement is that the deeper meanings in this kind of literature await one's application; but that in the meantime the surface of the page is clear to everybody, and useful on any level one is able to grasp hold of it – and very enjoyable, too.

The Way

Among the Dervishes is the record of a remarkable journey, the modern version of an old quest tale. For one thing, Omar Michael Burke set off without knowing where he was going or how he would go. He had a small legacy, some time, much curiosity, and the attitude of mind necessary to meet real dervishes. His journey took shape as he went. He was directed from country to country, person to person, by the dervishes themselves, in a manner that only at the end did he understand had exemplified the dervish belief that you don't find out by being told about a thing, but only by experiencing it. 'Because they have to give you a fair hearing. This hearing is listening to words, seeing things, feelings things, doing things. The people have been trained to believe that anything that can be *done* is either inborn, like a talent, or can be learned by the stringing together of a number of words. This is one of the grossest impositions which have ever been perpetrated . . .' He travelled on foot, by camel caravan, by lorry and by plane, at one point and in order to cross a certain frontier, without papers and disguised as a mulla, never knowing if next he would be the guest of the richest man in the world, or of a smuggler, but always inside 'the world within a world' which is the Sufi network inside orthodox Islam. His journey, then, was not one accessible to the academic scholar, or the idly curious, and this book is invaluable and in various ways. Several different kinds of specialists should read it, for a start. It is also funny, in its dry way: Burke has a wry eye for the contrasts between his sets of mind and those of his hosts. Variations on this conversation kept happening: 'As a Westerner I am trained to use my critical intelligence. It is my birthright.' 'Very laudable. But since it doesn't seem to have got you very far, how about suspending it for a time and trying to learn in a different way?' And variations, too, of an encounter between Idries Shah (known in dervish circles as the Studious King), who was in Damascus at the same time as the author, and a group of Western esotericists, who sound as if they must have been theosophists. Shah had been asked to address them, and they settled down for what they were expecting, a lecture on what Shah describes as 'spills, thrills and chills' – otherwise things that go bump in the night; whereas what he had to offer was something quite different.

Burke's journey began by his being accepted as a student in a monastery like a medieval rocky fortress hidden in north India, but was soon sent away from it to penetrate Mecca – like Burckhardt and Richard Burton before him – without the benefits of Islam, for although christened Omar by his mother 'in a moment of poetic delight', he was not one of the faithful. Being dark-eyed and dark-haired, speaking Urdu, Persian and some Arabic, he let these advantages suffice, since he was the guest of people who don't ask questions about a man's origins, and took no lessons in how to seem an orthodox Muslim. The friend of a friend in Port Sudan, a Pathan, arranged for him to be ferried across the Red Sea by men who transport pilgrims too poor to pay the usual fares. He was set down outside Jeddah in sand dunes where he spent the night half-buried, for safety and for warmth, and in the morning found another friend in

Jeddah's souk, and by him and *his* friends was taken to Mecca in a way that bypassed the Wahabi policemen. Done this way and with this sort of aid it sounds easy; ordinarily a non-Muslim cannot do it: the combination of the matter-of-fact and the impossible gives this episode a true Arabian Nights flavour.

After Mecca, by camel to Nefta, an oasis in Tunisia called Jewel of the Sahara. Much picturesqueness of all sorts: brigands, cameleers that sound as obliged to give their money's worth as New York taxi-drivers; mirages, palmtrees and so forth, but also camel soreness, from which he was cured by being pummelled all over for ten minutes like 'fat merchants and soft women unused to the ways of the desert, oh warrior!' But his goal was a dervish settlement where, with the sheik's permission, he applied Western techniques to establish that the 'trance' achieved by a certain kind of dervish 'dance', or exercise, was not a hypnotic state as ordinarily known. None of his finds, he decided, were scientifically conclusive; but I think this chapter would be of value to researchers. From Nefta to Istanbul, and contact with dervish orders supposed to be extinct – they were suppressed by Ataturk. But people whose mode of being has nothing to do with politics or familiar organisation survive: what he found there was astonishing, but by then he was shedding fast the preconceptions taught him by the West.

Dervishhood is not a goal, as one takes formal vows in a monastery, or becomes a professor of cybernetics. It is a stage in a process, that of learning to be a Sufi. One hopes to be worthy of being accepted as a dervish. Then one is a dervish for a time. After that there are other stages. Dervishes are on different levels of development. Nor is there only one kind of dervish. Many techniques of learning are used and at the same time. There is nothing static, nothing rigid. The dervish 'Ways' are everywhere in the Muslim world – but in other places as well and, as Burke found emphasised again and again during his travels, are being naturalised in the West for the first time in centuries as part of a long-term and deliberate evolution. The 'Ways' are in continuous communication with each other. Pupils may go from one to the next learning part of what they have to from one teacher, and then from another. Some orders are geographically based, are well known. Others have no physical base, are invisible to an outsider. Some are centred on practical work. There are many deteriorated Ways which have become repetitious, have 'lost their juice'. An account of a visit to such a group, of Chistis, in India where the author – although knowing very little at that stage – seemed to them like some sort of higher being, sounds like a fresh illustration of 'In the country of the blind the one-eyed man is king'.

One dervish Burke met was like the Western idea of them, as colourful as you like, a white-sheeted gaunt figure, with shaved cranium and a prayer rug looped over one shoulder, he was a Callendar, and the Way has something in common with the Indian fakirs. But most were modern people, living modern lives, earning their living in unexotic ways.

Light is thrown – unfortunately much too briefly, in all sorts of unexpected places. A man who had been a Soviet worker in Bokhara for twenty-five years talked about Sufism in the USSR, how it is spreading, the psychology of communists as seen by Sufis.

The Master of the Afghan Mint, now dead, then over ninety, spoke of Gurdjieff, who ran off with certain 'secrets' before he knew how to operate them.

The Sufi attitude towards 'second sight' and similar phenomena:

These are normal, not abnormal developments. They are of no value in themselves, partly proved by the fact that the experiences seldom have practical value. For every happening of this kind that is a warning or can be turned to practical use, there are a hundred which are not of any use. Why is this? Materialists

311

would say that it merely proves that the power is fitful, partial, something of little account. What they do not know is that these are signs. They are encouragements, they show that the recipient has a real chance of developing his 'gifts'. They are signs that the time has come for self-work. Most people cannot use them because they do not know that this is the *alif* (letter A) and that the *be* follows, until there is a *iaa* (last letter of the alphabet).

In Kuwait the Emir was shocked by Western attitudes to charity. A charity, explained Burke, is an institution that collects money and gives it away under the supervision of the authorities. And in most Western countries giving away money without keeping records would be considered illegal. To which the Sheik replied by recalling

> ...your saint Nicholas. You celebrate his day at the same time as you celebrate that of the Blessed Jesus ... the Christians remember him best because he gave secret charity. You see, if you give charity and know that the person to whom you give knows, you risk his feeling obligated to you. It is bad enough, surely, to be in the position of giving at all, and realising that you may be giving because it makes you feel happy. You are being rewarded for your action, instead of helping others without reward. I call public giving or even giving which is recorded anywhere a shameful and degenerate thing.

In Egypt, in 'an enormous room completely lined on three walls with books, most of them in Oriental languages, the fourth wall all glass and looking out on a fountain set in a rose-garden', the host told Burke the true history of the Assassins, a name chosen because it resembled the real name, Asasiyin – those of the Source, 'and because it was very close to those whom you in the West called the Essenes of Palestine. Hasan, son of Sabah, the so-called Old Man of the Mountain, was playing a double game. By creating an aura of terror he was able to wield power and preserve the community at a time when it was threatened, in Persia and Syria, from all sides. No actual assassinations were ever carried out.' Says Burke: 'If you told that to most people, they would think you were an Ismaili trying to "improve the image" of your forbears.'

> You can believe what you like. The real fact is that this system, call it what you will, was most concerned about saving the most important knowledge available to mankind. This method was a master-stroke.

In the Western area of Afghanistan whose centre is Herat, live the followers of Isa, son of Maryam – Jesus, son of Mary, who can 'recite the succession of teachers through nearly sixty generations back to Jesus'. They hold that Jesus escaped from the Cross, was hidden by friends, and helped to India where he had travelled in his youth. There he settled, to end his days in Kashmir as a revered Teacher ... no prudent reviewer could do less than warn that parts of this book may be found abrasive. I tried this history of Jesus out on a person whose point of pride is an unrelenting rationality, atheism, as it were, squared: the result, surprising to me, was anger.

Dervish attitudes to the West are often not complimentary, rather like an adult towards a particularly crude adolescent who fortunately is due to grow up soon. We are materialistic, that is our prime fault, but this word does not mean, usually, what it does when we use it; it is not the shades of our philosophical opinions that are considered important, or even interesting. No, we are acquisitive, grasping, greedy, wasteful. We despoil and lay waste and our 'freedom' is nothing of the sort. 'You are free to destroy ...'

Burke ended in Kafiristan, where few travellers go, and there met the Baba MacNeill, a Scotsman who, after the First World War during which he had met an Indian 'preaching a form of Sufism' that he at length found unsatisfactory, went East to look for the sources. But these days you don't have to go East, the author concludes his book, quoting the dervish saying: 'I have my Way which suffices me, in accordance with my place in the world and the part of the world where I find myself.' For, as in the best tales and legends, he had travelled only to find himself on his own doorstep.

It was a sheik in Alexandria who had advised: 'My son and brother, too many Westerners become orientalised. This sometimes because they seek spirituality in the East and therefore everything in the East is for them or can teach them something. Do not be like them.' And, asked: 'What in the West can we cultivate to make our own tradition stronger?', he had given unexpected examples.

The first was team-spirit. This enabled man to understand what it was to work with others in harmony. The second was not democracy, but a preparation for it. This enabled one to value democracy which itself was a prelude to understanding of the real equality of man. The third was respecting other people. This enabled one to respect oneself. But you cannot respect yourself unless you respect others. This is a great secret . . . I was to be very sure that I realised all these three valuable secrets were points of development which were already deeply rooted in my own culture. It was for me to help them grow, to defend them, to work on them. Unless you have the three things in your heart, you are a hypocrite if you say that you are looking for a teacher.

A week in Heidelberg

Once, not long ago, let's say between the two big wars, the name Heidelberg meant the murderous formality of duels and coveted facial scars, meant cold northern Prussian manners. I did not expect this delicious little town lying between its hills on the river Neckar. Interesting that it was the rituals of duelling everyone knew about, but not the deliciousness. The town is undamaged, at least by recent war; General Eisenhower was at the university here, and that is why the town was not bombed in the Second World War; the war planes only showered down propaganda leaflets. The lesson here, must, you would think, be an imperative for every nation aspiring to peace.

The hotel I was in was Perkeo, called after a semi-mythological dwarf or jester whose name, it is claimed, comes from his habit of saying '*Why not?*', when offered yet another drink, so often that the barrel large enough for his thirst is the size of a large room. Presumably he was not a German dwarf, or at least used the habits of polyglot courts.

The hotel is for tourists and is amiable, and not efficient to the point where you get irritated by it, and, besides, Germany's reputation for efficiency may awe its foreign visitors into an anxious examination of their own lax ways. One day painters were at work on the hall of the hotel and the stairs, with difficulty being polite to us guests so inconsiderately going in and out, disrupting their professionalism, but they left an unpainted patch on the corridor wall the size of a medium plate and no one noticed. This made me feel better about how I so often have to despair; *why* is it everyone else finds it so easy to be tidy? Each room is an example of well-planned compression, useful rather than charming, but when I went to the window I saw not only the opposite wall and roofs but a sill slightly higher than mine, and to one side, and there on a nest that edged part of the sill with clay – each beakful flown up from the river and carefully plastered on – a pigeon was sitting. But soon it got off the nest and stood near it, a slim bird, not a matron, so this was probably her first season as an adult. Then off she flew, and the ledge was empty, and you could see the nest was not a new one, it was breaking here and there and had a smoothed-out look because of the rain falling on it; a sitting bird must often be behind a drip drip drip of water. This was last year's nest and possibly even a fixture, and the sill is regarded by the pigeons as their property.

There are old streaks of droppings down the wall, and the window behind the sill looks as if it has not been opened for some time, and yet there was a light in the room, and curtains.

Heidelberg is full of birds. You can hear them all day and on my visit, half the night too, since it was May, mostly the sharp clarity of the blackbird's song, but there was a great deal of general gossping and twittering of an observational kind from birds hard to identify. How should there not be birds when every little side street seems to end in a garden or a park or a square and there are trees everywhere, and for no more effort than a brief flight, on either side are the hills and woods where you expect to meet, at any turn of the path, Goethe's characters, or Goethe himself, an affable fellow, and a friend of birds. His

statue is in a park on the hill, but it is not the great and formalised Goethe Heidelberg evokes. Never have I been to a place
where I felt so much and at once, 'But I know these houses,
and above all the walks and hills'. And it was because of Goethe,
who wrote about this landscape.

If there are so many blackbirds, I thought, then how about
enticing them to my sill? I put out pieces of apple and almost
at once there he was, a male blackbird, and I stood as still as
I could just behind the net curtain and watched a blackbird
from closer than I ever have, a bold, black, glossy bird, with a
bright yellow beak and eyes outlined in orange. He knew I
was there, or something was making him nervous, and he kept
jabbing his beak hard into the apple flesh, then stopping to look
at the white screen close to him, and then there was another
series of quick downward jabs ... to shrink yourself down in
imagination and see that gleaming weapon just above you, what
a horror, the worm's eye view – but then he seized the apple
fragment in his claws and was off to the fork of a tree where
I watched him demolish the apple. The female came next, a
modest, shy brown bird, and she pecked hastily, with many
glances around, and then she too grabbed the apple and bore
it to safety. For the eight days I was there I put out bits of apple
and as soon as I did the birds came, and at least the female was
the same, because some bird larger than she had pecked out a
lump of feathers from the top of her head. Could this have been
because of disagreements over my sill with its bonanza of fresh
apple pieces?

The dark young pigeon had not been sitting on eggs, she had
either been resting on the nest, or practising to be a grown-up
egg-layer and sitter. I never saw her on the nest again, but on
the first evening, going to bed, I saw her drowsing in one corner
of the sill, away from the nest, and several times in the night I
got up to have a look, and there she was, eyes shut, unmoving.

At the very first light she was off, for by 5 a.m. the sill was empty. The second night the pigeon did not come and I was quite absurdly disappointed, but there was a sweet intimacy in it, the bird sleeping there through the night so close to me. But pigeons are not solitary characters, and why was she not with her flock? The third night, she came back. The fourth, she was not there when I went to bed, but was when I woke at two. Now, surely that was strange? She must have been with her fellows when they all decided to give up the day and go to sleep, but then – well, what? Had she been pushed off the ledge or bough they were on and then flew here by herself, where at least her back was protected? Was this an oddball pigeon, a solitary, an eccentric, or perhaps one merely tolerated by her fellows?

On the roof of my house in London are often pigeons, far too many of them, and this year there are two young pigeons, last year's hatching, slightly smaller than the others, shapely and glossy and fresh, like this young bird in Heidelberg, and they are bullied and jostled out of the way when there is food, and are always on the very edge of things, squeezing into an opening among the feeding birds to grab a beakful, and then quickly off, or perching on the roof at the edge of a line of birds and often dislodged by the others. They have a hard time of it, the young birds, and so it will go on until they too are solid citizens and can use their weight to oust the young ones.

One afternoon the pigeon was there on the sill and seemed to be suffering badly from mites, for she was poking her beak hard into her feathers, here, there, as if targeting an itch, and then she scratched all around her eyes. I wondered if the old nest was harbouring mites, and that was why she had got off it so quickly, but if so, why was she able to sleep comfortably through the night so close to the nest? Perhaps mites sleep too, was my next probably absurd thought. At any rate, for all the time I was in town, the pigeon spent most nights on the sill, and I looked out for her.

Heidelberg has a ruined castle on an overlooking hill, and that is what the tourists come for, because it was once the most important castle in that part of Germany, with a history whose names still reverberate, and some of its visitors' names too, for all the romantic poets came there and wrote poems about the place, Goethe being only one. It is very large, not so much a castle, as an association of castles and fortresses, built at different times, by different kings, and falling into ruin because of wars and storms. Gardens surround them, and they ring with bird song, for it is truly a paradise for birds. Being May it was nesting time and surely there must have been hundreds of nesting pairs, for everywhere you could see them, blackbirds being the most evident, going in and out of the curtains of ivy that cover old walls. Ivy, old ivy, with thick stems, draping high stone walls, is the best possible place for nests. For one thing, no cat could get up. High on the crumbling towers and battlements and in holes in the walls where stones and bricks have been dislodged, there are nests, and even some food for the birds at rooftop level, for plants and grasses grow up there, and a small sapling's roots are digging down into the masonry, and if the structure holds there will be a tree.

Not only all around, but above this mass of the castle, are terraces of gardens, and on one peaceful grassy place where fountains gently burble, the guidebook says a terrible battle was fought. Then, the Thirty Years War didn't do well for this place, and the gardens fell into neglect, and hundreds of years later were restored 'in the English manner', but previously were in the French manner, which means that every plant was in its place and severely dealt with if it stepped out of line.

Birds, birds, birds ... We walked along a path between old trees and a blackbird shot past, its beak full, and suddenly you had to see the whole place, the castle with its turrets and towers and roofs, the sheets of ivy hundreds of feet deep and wide, the trees, the hills, the fountain, the river Neckar, as a bird must. 'And who are all those creatures wandering about, what are they doing in our place?' – so you may imagine the birds, irritated perhaps, but tolerant, and concluding, 'But they don't really get in our way'.

I was in Heidelberg for the rehearsals and then the first night of the opera Philip Glass and I did, *The Marriages Between Zones Three, Four and Five* and I could write a piece all about sitting in the stalls every day watching and listening how it came together, but even walking to the theatre, or strolling around it, the State Theatre of Heidelberg, a delightful little theatre, you hear birds, the songs of birds, and when I hear in my mind the delectable music of the opera, it is counterpointed by birdsong and particularly the brilliant inventions of the blackbirds.

There is another thing. When you walk from hotel to theatre, along old streets from which the city fathers and mothers of Heidelberg have decided to banish for ever any modern unpleasantness, you smell – can that be? – yes, it is vanilla. The streets of Heidelberg are scented with vanilla from the cafés and cakeshops. There is a McDonald's but it has been put into an old house and you have to look twice to see the sign.

Dancing with Cuba, Alma Guillermoprieto

Few dancers write memoirs, and so the world of dance remains an elegant mystery to many of us, despite lovelorn films like *Red Shoes* or reverential ones like the Margot Fonteyn series. A recent review of Robert Altman's *The Company*, in the *New York Review of Books*, insists on the anti-romantic view of dancers, who are not to be seen as moths dying ecstatically in the flame of their art, but more like nine-to-five office workers, plodding through their duties. No blood-soaked ballet shoes, *please*, no tortured insteps. But this will not do, for those of us who remember Ginger Rogers picking herself up and dusting herself off, with shoes full of blood, or, for that matter, The Little Mermaid, dancing for love on feet like knives. This author, a dancer, comes down on the side of sacrifice. Her despatches from the barre are full of painful disciplines, all so that we may continue to gawk at those apparitions like dragon-flies, or, as she puts it, '... pure limpid dance, so free of sentimentality that it seemed to be performed by a flock of subtle iridescent birds.'

Before she went to Cuba, Alma Guillermoprieto danced in New York, poor, often hungry, and this Vie Bohème has seldom been made to sound so delicately romantic, illuminated by the tender comradeship of those who have nothing to share but their generosity of spirit. They sat together all evening in the Russian Tearooms over a single cocktail; they told each other of discoveries like 'an enormous platter, for ninety-nine cents, of noodles cooked with all kinds of vegetables and chicken! It is unbelievable!' But in Cuba she was a comrade indeed, because Westerners in Cuba could only be there for ideological reasons. She was unpolitical, did not read newspapers, understood nothing of what went on. Hindsights and insights come at the end of the book, but meanwhile we toss with her on an ocean of incomprehension. She was expected, for instance, to teach dance without the use of the essential mirrors, because communists must repudiate the vanities of capitalism. Who is speaking? Who uses this kind of talk? Everyone, but this gem is from her boss, one of the inflexible dogmatic females that afflicted communism from Warsaw to Vladivostok. Ideology was indeed the reason for deprivations, but this one was at a remove. Vanity had nothing to do with it. Fidel Castro insisted on a Palace for the Arts and Dance, the way later dictators felt they had to have national airlines, for prestige, but he had no feeling or respect for the arts, and so they were underfunded. No money for mirrors, or for music.

This is a tale, then, of artists, poets, dancers, architects, bewildered, always in conflict, trying to keep alive standards which they knew were essential, but which were suspect, not to say dangerous. A familiar tale now, we have heard it over and over again, but it was new to them.

Alma was guiltily resistant to exhortations like, 'The Revolutionary is consumed by this uninterrupted action which has no other end but death, unless the construction of socialism on a global scale is achieved.' (Che Guevara.) She was suspicious that the atrocious suffering of the sugar workers, as bad as that under their former owners, was justified thus: '. . . slaves' work that a free man can assume only on the basis of the most profound revolutionary consciousness.' (Fidel Castro.) Mind you, this insistence on suffering did continue a theme from the New York days. Martha Graham, in a rage, pinched an errant dancer and said that pain was necessary for dance. 'I think,' says our author, 'that at that stage in her life she wanted to contribute to our training by guaranteeing we would suffer.'

A sapient friend told her that she was someone with an outstanding talent for suffering, but this was not what she meant when she wrote to a friend that 'I'm beginning to understand that I've been greatly deformed by capitalism.'

Her stock of common sense that revolted against the communist rhetoric, did not prevent her from falling in love with communism, like so many, and partly because she was being introduced to real poverty, real suffering, the hardships of the countryside, and of the workers. Partly though because this inclination towards sacrifice, pain, death, has such deep roots in our natures that we have not begun to understand them, I think. She fell in love with Fidel too, not to mention 'a real guerilla revolutionary' who subscribed to Che's dictum that in order to have a meaningful life and contribute to the wellbeing of the human race, it is necessary to die, and fast.

In country after socialist and communist country, people fell in love with their Leaders – and this has dark roots too.

Easy now to mock at the submission to the Revolution that so many artists accepted, hearts aflame, heads full of doubt and dislike. She most sincerely hated the false glamour of Revolution, and as sincerely believed in it. This young woman, not yet twenty-one, devotedly teaching with inadequate materials and improperly trained pupils, goaded by ignorant bureaucrats, supported only by the loving friendship of equally fragile people, fell into depression and breakdown.

Two tales illustrate the gap between the image of Revolution and its reality. Oscar Lewis, the American Anthropologist, author of *The Children of Sanchez*, was invited by Castro to Cuba, because his work, said Fidel, was more revolutionary than a thousand speeches. Fêted and honoured, Lewis asked only that the people he interviewed would not be punished if they expressed doubting views on Castro and Cuba. Fidel promised. Then, the Chief of Police, Fidel's pal, Pineiro, intervened. 'It wasn't entirely clear to me why the Chief of Police should be so interested in Lewis's project,' confesses Alma. Next came the persecution and the imprisonments. Hard to imagine a more painful awakening than when the People's Revolution turned its hatred on him. Lewis very soon died, and surely it was from a broken heart.

Then there was the scandal of the junior school, children of peasants, whose quarters were discovered smeared with shit and angry graffiti. Alma's superiors agreed it was not enough to give children lessons and exhortations: they need love. And they were missing their families. These same insightful adults, in their roles as revolutionary leaders, could not admit this, or act on it. They lectured the kids thus: 'The party rescued you from poverty, gave you a future, you ungrateful antisocial brats, you should be ashamed.' This kind of tale has been told often enough, in the later days of Revolution, but then it was a bitter shock. Meanwhile our poor author was ill, wandering in the forests of depression, without a guide. Chat about Freud and the unconscious might have been just the thing in New York, but not in Cuba. But she was certainly socially responsible, unable to commit suicide because she could not find a mode of suicide that would not upset or distress other people.

To her relief she was sacked by the jealous boss to whom she was preferred by her pupils.

And so back to New York, safety, plenty, and understanding of her state of mind. Invited back to Cuba to restructure the

School of Dance, she refused. Instead she became a journalist, and, later, a writer. Here she is, this honest, insightful, informed witness to our turbulent days.

This book will make a good number of aged people like myself wince, and laugh at youthful folly, but laughing out of the other side of our mouths we do sometimes suffer strange feelings of loss. Everywhere are the poor, the unfed, the insulted, the injured: it was nice, for a time, to think there could be an end to all this.

Dancing with Cuba is a useful source of information, and these intrigued by Fidel will find plenty here to ponder. The man who makes four-hour speeches and finds people to listen to them must have something more than is granted to most orators.

Cuba hasn't done well. There is not much to admire in the way of social achievements. The people are a different thing.

Those musicians of the Buena Vista Social Club, for instance, ignored for years, recently discovered, wonderful television programmes made about them – who could forget their humanity, and their humour? They have charmed the world.

Better think of them than the complex of buildings of the Escuelas Nacionales de Arte, now thought to be a masterpiece, falling down and threatened by the jungle. Fidel can't be bothered.

Of herself the author says: 'No one ever asked me then, and I don't know if I myself understood that I had a life that was not only extraordinary but *real* – the kind of life that doesn't happen by accident, but is put together slowly and with effort.'

For a Book Trust pamphlet

Into a very large bookshop the other day came two girls of about fifteen, both as excited as if off to a party, but when they saw all those books, shelves upon shelves of them, their faces became apprehensive and they stood very close together, staring around. They were about to turn tail, but I went up to them and asked if they needed help. They were looking for a book, they said. Which book? Well . . . they didn't know. Their teacher had told them they must read books and not watch so much television. They had had no idea there were so many books. No, there were no books in either of their homes, their parents did not read books. I stood with them and saw through their eyes a space the size of a warehouse filled with thousands of books, each one an unknown, a challenge, a mystery. So I went with them to this section and that, explaining how the store was laid out, how the divisions represented novels, biography (stories about other people), autobiography (stories by people about themselves), animals, travel, science, and so on. They went out with half a dozen books, and I hope that later they did return to a bookshop.

I think that people whose profession is books, or who have been brought up in a household where books are taken for granted, can have no idea of the confusion, the dismay, the discouragement, that must afflict young people advised to read, when they have no parent or older friend to advise them.

I left that bookstore wishing there were a book of simple – perhaps even oversimplified – suggestions for reading, to help young people. Or, for that matter, older ones, who may suddenly realise that their experience has deprived them of that great pleasure, reading, the adventure of literature, of the pursuit of knowledge, which can begin for the lucky ones when they are very young indeed, and go on through a lifetime, with happy discoveries all the way, when you may take a book down off a shelf – perhaps by chance – and find you have stumbled on a new world whose existence you had never even suspected. Here is that book. The suggestions made by contributors are all because of personal enthusiasm or admiration or love for a book, and that is the most important thing of all: love of literature, of books, of ideas, is communicated by the enthusiasm of a teacher. When one meets some person, young or old, who says, I was so lucky, I had this teacher who influenced me – this is always because the teacher was in love with literature, with science, with an idea, and this lucky pupil absorbed the love through osmosis. A cold way of teaching, analysis, exegesis, does not create readers who experience reading or the pursuit of ideas as a continuing passion.

This book is the equivalent of the enthusiastic teacher whose pupils are fortunate, and who bless them through their lives. It is a book so obviously essential, so necessary, that the question must be, why didn't it come into being before?

And now a personal note. It happened that I left school when I was fourteen, and thereafter educated myself with reading. It took a long time – years – for it to occur to me that after all I was only one in a long tradition of women who for one reason or another (in the old days it was because girls did not go to

327

school, their brothers got the education) educated themselves in their parents' libraries, or with books they begged, borrowed, or stole. Virginia Woolf was one. But there were books in the house where I grew up, where I had parents who saw to it that I had the best that had been written – certainly not only from the English tradition – and where there was an atmosphere that took for granted that books are necessary for the good life. I was fortunate. I had advice. But I know that there are young people everywhere, particularly in what we call the Third World, and even in the fortunate rich part of the world, who dream of an education and cannot have one, who long for books and cannot get them, and who have no one to advise them. I can only too easily put myself into the position of some person – not necessarily a child – who has missed out on an education and dreams of having books to remedy the deficiency and enable him or her to become, after all, an educated person. It is my hope that this most useful book will find its way into the hands of such people. And, too, into the hands of parents, for there is a generation of parents who are trying to help their children but – themselves uneducated – do not know how.

There are also young people who, having taken A-level literature, have found that familiarity with the four set books – that is all that is needed in some places now to claim an education in literature – has given them a thirst for more.

To end with, a tiny tale. In Africa, in an area far from a town, in a bush school, which did not expect to educate its pupils for more than half a dozen years, a boy of ten was found with a stolen book under his bed. It was a tome of advanced physics, of which he could not have understood one word. 'Why did you steal this book?' 'But I want a book. I have no books. I wanted my own book,' said he. 'But why did you steal this difficult book?' 'I want to be a doctor,' he said, most passionately weeping, and clutching the book to him.

The Three Royal Monkeys, Walter de la Mare

Some books read in childhood put such a spell on you that for ever after you remember something like those sunset clouds illuminated pink and gold. *The Three Royal Monkeys* is the story of three brothers whose father, the brother of Assasimmon, Prince of the Valleys of Tishnar, exiled himself, with his sons, to wander the world and learn what he could. On his death and their mother's, the three make their way home to Tishnar's valleys, through dangers and enticements such as the beautiful Water Midden. They carry with them a talisman, the Wonderstone, that glows sweetly or angrily, and which they must on no account lose. It is Nod the youngest, the heir to the magic, who must carry it, but he is careless and easily led astray ... There are echoes here of myths and legends and older tales in the genre, but this reworking of an old theme is I think unique for the charm of its writing. De la Mare was, after all, a fine poet.

The book is out of print. I found a copy in a secondhand shop and read it to find out if it really was the wonder I thought it. Yes it was and is and sits in my memory side by side with *The Secret Garden, The Jungle Book, Alice in Wonderland.*

'Their torches faintly crackled, their smoke rising in four straight pillars towards the stars. And, listening, they heard, as if from all around them in the air, clear yet strangely small voices singing, with a thin and pining sound like glass. It floated near, this tiny multitudinous music . . .' I wish I were ten years old again, sitting under a tree at the edge of the bush, reading this tale for the first time, and enticed 'beyond and beyond, forest and river, forest, swamp and river, the mountains of Arakkaboa – leagues and leagues away'.

Catlore, Desmond Morris

This new book is because the first, *Catwatching*, was such a success, provoking storms of questions from all over the world. Some of them are dealt with here. There is, too, more cat history, but I think facts are often just stated and left at that (here and in other cat books) when surely they demand further investigation. For instance, why did the Egyptians worship cats? They weren't noticeably more stupid than we are. They had a Dog God and a Cat God, but it was the cats who had the special place, as if they were believed to have special qualities. Some esoteric traditions regard cats highly, one for instance saying that nature 'played a trick on cats, giving them "consciousness" but not "intelligence"'. It would be nice to know what this actually meant. Whatever was the quality that made Egyptians worship cats was probably the same one that associated them with magic and witchcraft in Europe. Could this only have been their remote and enigmatic air? That cats have something about them not found in dogs, pleasant as they are, is why – some cats lovers believe – we continue to be fascinated by cat behaviour. But not all behaviour of all cats, who can be clever, stupid, brave, cowardly, mean, magnanimous, honourable, sneaky, interesting or boring – just like people. And here we are on the borders of the same mystery humans confront us with: what is personality, why are people (and cats) born different, what are these differences? It seems to me that science is not equipped to deal with this – not yet, I hasten to add; while at best novelists can't do much more than describe and hint. It is one thing to make a list of a remarkable cat's remarkable qualities, but another to explain why you will remember him as you do some people, who are so much more than the sum of their parts.

I do think Desmond Morris doesn't make allowances for the way cat 'signals' may mean more than they do in 'nature' – whatever that may mean after thousands of years of cat–human interaction. For instance, a cat closes its eyes when it is being praised: because it doesn't like being stared at, he says; but in one cat I had it was coquetry, a game developed over years. (Yes, she was a vain and frivolous cat.)

There are a whole range of questions raised by other animals, as seen by cats. When you see a large dog amiably permitting kittens to play all over it, or a dog and a cat wrapped together, asleep, or a cat taking refuge on a dog's back when chased by another dog, then how should the questions be put, let alone answered. What does a cat make of its owner feeding birds, its natural prey? When two cats take their places every evening on a bag of peat a yard away from where the hedgehogs are due to come for their milk, and sit there watching, absorbed, for half an hour, an hour, while the animals drink and scutter about – why do they do it? They are as detached, as intent as – scientists! One of them turns his head, knowing I am there too, watching from behind the window: he looks at me, could not be asking more clearly, 'Why are you feeding these creatures? They don't even live with us!' But we do not share a language, not really, only with difficulty, doing our best across the species barriers: there is no way I can explain the hedgehogs to him.

The Englishman's Handbook

Idries Shah lived and worked here for many years, writing books about the Sufi tradition, of which he was the exemplar for our time. He wrote about travel, magic and shamanism, the reconciliation of religions, made fresh translations of Sufi classics and poetry, and of the Nasrudin corpus of jokes, and was well known as a savant here, in Central Asia, and generally in the Muslim world. He also wrote about the British, which he was peculiarly qualified to do, being an Afghan with a Scottish mother, and having that useful double vision, one eye the outsider's, the other a native's. For years he collected examples of our eccentricities, as two earlier books, *The Natives are Restless* and *In Darkest England* illustrate. He amuses himself with definitions, starting this book – published posthumously – with 'Who, or what, exactly, is a foreigner?' Tricky stuff. When he complained to the local police that next door's music was driving him mad, he was told, 'But they are ethnic and entitled to it.' 'But I am ethnic too,' said Shah. 'Don't I have any rights?' 'Not ethnic enough, mate,' pronounced the policeman.

A Briton abroad, described as a foreigner, said he couldn't be, he was English.

Shah pretends to believe that we create confusion to annoy

foreigners so that they depart, never to return, a more devious method than A. N. Wilson's direct, 'What England needs is fewer people. More trees. And a ruinously strong pound to discourage all potential or transatlantic foreigners.'

A deliberate crankiness is encouraged. Anthony Burgess in an interview said that the only good food in the world is in Manchester. 'The French think their food is good but of course it isn't.'

We admire gentle lunacy. 'A recent Navy broadsheet revealed that there are 17 captains at sea supported by 42 admirals. Forty-five if one includes the apothecaries.'

Confronted with this kind of thing Shah postulates an English Group Mind, partly because he has a readership abroad among people anxious to understand our peculiarities, and they expect a General Theory or Thesis of the kind that is anathema to us. Our hidden agenda is not to be specific, but to cultivate an evasiveness which we associate with orientals. It is we, he claims, who think like wily orientals.

'We' are the English, but he suggests we might have an oriental inheritance. Bizarre? Recently, in our press, I have noticed random references to our possible Asiatic beginnings, which spur agreeable speculation. In Nuristan live a white-skinned blue-eyed people, said to be descendants of Alexander's troops, but recently in north-west China were found graves older than Alexander's army, and in them tall, fair-haired people, a discovery which chagrined the Chinese and surprised the archaeologists. Hundreds of years ago a Central Asiatic tribe dislodged by some climatic or social change began a long trek westwards. A slow trek. Ptolemy described it living near today's Magdeburg, and Tacitus as settled east of the Elbe. Before we Angles arrived in England our home was Schleswig Holstein, which for a long time we called Anglia Vetus, Old England. Anyway, here we are, spiced with Roman, Saxon, French,

Viking, Norman and of course black genes, but retaining, Shah claims, the characteristics of that old tribe which was democratic, easily electing and deposing chiefs, and footloose by temperament. A people may retain its nature for centuries. In Neil Ascheson's *The Black Sea* is described one who, having left Greece hundreds of years earlier to live near the Black Sea, returned to demand, 'Let us in.' 'Why should we?' 'But we are Greek.' And they still were.

'I ought to know a tribe when I see one,' says Shah. 'I was brought up among them.'

We behave like a tribe, absorbing outsiders, but indifferent to the fate of foreigners, as exemplified by the Englishwoman who, told about a mine disaster that killed 500 Chinese, 200 Koreans, 100 Russians and one English engineer, said 'Poor fellow', and hoped he hadn't suffered.

This is such a funny book. To find oneself laughing aloud as the winter dark closes in, and the Middle East boils and bubbles – now that really is something.

A. E. Coppard

These short stories are as fine as any we have. In friends' houses, on the shelves where the books stay which will be kept always, you find Coppard. Talking to people, not necessarily literary, who have read their own way into literature, and who use books for nourishment and not debate, Coppard's tales are found to be treasures. He wrote a good many, some now in collections hard to come by. They are not widely known or quoted. Yet that they can have a general appeal was proved when recently they were adapted for television: like Lawrence, Coppard tells a good story.

He was an exquisite craftsman, and wrote well-made tales. But their shape was that of the growth of people or events, so that watching one unfold, you have to cry 'What else? Of course!' as you do in life. Coppard's work owes everything to this quality of knowing how things must be, how they have to work out. He understands growth. Nowhere are cataclysms or marvels, not so much as the whiff of a foreign port or an exotic person. If there's a sailor, then he has come back from somewhere and will be off again.

There is a steadily flowing stream in English writing that is quiet, low in key. To this belong E. M. Forster's tales, some of

Kipling, and of H. E. Bates, many of D. H. Lawrence; here too belong the poems of W. H. Davies and most of Walter de la Mare. They are English, full of nature and the countryside, straying very little into towns and streets. Thinking of Hardy, also a country writer, helps to see a difference. Sorrow and rebellion rage in Hardy; nothing of the kind in Coppard, who doesn't believe in tragedy. He was one of the people who helped me to understand that very English man, my father, whose relationship to the countryside he was brought up in was like Coppard's. It is a sparrow's-eye view, sharp, wry, surviving, and not one that can quarrel with the savage economies of the field or the hedgerow.

I was lucky enough to meet Mr Coppard. It happened that we were once two weeks together on a delegation to the Soviet Union, which was a minuscule effort, common then, towards peace between nations. There were six of us, under conditions which made us get to know each other pretty well, one being that we were all working so hard sightseeing, and talking about what we saw, and violently disagreeing, that we slept very little. What came out strong in him was his inability to play the role 'writer'. He didn't like making speeches, he didn't like formal occasions, or conferences or big statements about literature. He did like talking half the night to an old pre-revolutionary waiter about Tolstoy, or examining the plants that grew beside the field in a collective farm. He liked flirting in a gentle humorous way with the beautiful girl doctor at the children's holiday camp. At a formal dinner he was talking to the young poet who spent much time tramping around the country by himself: Coppard knew England through walking over it.

He was a small man, light in build. At that time he was 72, but looked 60, and with a boyish face. Characteristically he would stand to one side of a scene, in observation of it, or quietly stroll around it, his face rather lifted, as it were leading with his chin, his nose alert for humbug, or for the pretensions of the rich or the powerful – about which he was not passionate but mildly derisive. The thing was, he did not have it in him to be solemn. His favourite writer was Sterne, his book *Tristram Shandy*, he was amused by philosophers and had his poets by heart.

How did this original creature evolve? He was born in 1878 in Folkestone in Kent, 'the son of George the tailor and Emily Alma the housemaid' – Alma, he was sure, from the battle of that name.

'Seventy-five years have passed since I occurred . . .' he almost begins his autobiography, *It's Me O Lord!* – a couple of paragraphs come first, pointing out the impossibility of expecting him to tell the truth or not to puff his own work. He did not get more than halfway through his account of himself because he could not resist following every attractive byway into anecdote.

His childhood was hard, but there is not a tincture of self-pity in his memories of it.

In her widowhood my mother became something of a martinet; she had no time to be kind, my father's death having sunk us at once into destitution. At times she was subject to fits of wild maniacal laughter, at others to torrents of tears. In between she was always fighting against the persistent outwearing of every piece of clothing or boot we possessed, as well as the inevitable neglect we, her four youngsters, and the domesticity suffered from her twelve-hour daily absence at a laundry where she had had to start out as a plain ironer from eight o'clock to eight o'clock at twenty-seven pence a day, and where she achieved the heaven of her ambition when she was later promoted to first class at two and six per day.

My father was a radical, all tailors were radicals then, free-thinkers to a man and scoffers at hellfire and so were all cobblers.

I recall him as a nice young man of medium height and lean stature, with a chestnut beard, large reddish nose and thick disordered dark hair – indeed he was always rather untidy, for a tailor, anyway. He wore the cutaway bobtail coat proper to the time, and a billycock hat, but tailor though he was he never had more than one at a time. He never seemed to walk with any objective, but just strolled along as though in meditation, with one hand in his trousers pocket and the other folded behind his back. He loved flowers, birds, the open air and to go a-roving over the hills for mushrooms, blackberries, nuts, cowslips, whatever was reasonable and free, but being doomed, as he knew, by tuberculosis, he became careless and something of a drinker and so we were always shockingly poor.

Coppard was nine when his father died. His schooling then ended, because some doctor said his liver would not stand it – on which event Coppard writes: 'This interdiction was accepted almost happily and consolingly by my mother, I never went back, my schooldays were ended. That's the kind of mother to have, the kind I had, credulous, superstitious, beautiful, comic, heroic, a rare woman whom I never seem to have loved much or honoured enough.'

Coppard then became a vendor of paraffin, shouting Oil, Oil, from street to street.

He was already educating himself, loving Chaucer, Shakespeare, Milton, Wordsworth, Keats, Browning and Whitman, getting only 'a thimbleful of joy' from Byron and Shelley, hating Dryden and disliking Donne.

In the pursuit of culture and understanding of literature I had no tutor or mentor or fellow-seeker after such righteousness. I continued to follow my instinct. What else could I have done? There were no night schools or evening classes for my purpose,

I had to find my own way and my instinct seldom misled me. Certainly I was never bored, I have never in my life experienced that so common malaise. Nobody could order me to study some book because it was renowned or esteemed; I was not set to prepare any papers for scholarly or examination reasons on subjects that were of no interest to me; I obeyed no alien direction, my own was good enough always.'

He was mostly an errand boy, running for auctioneers, cheesemongers, soapsellers, carriers. He was a messenger boy for Reuter's. 'From the age of sixteen to twenty-six my life now appears to me to be a sort of kaleidoscope of running, reading, falling in love and trying to write verse.' The verse was not very good, though some got printed, but soon he came to short stories: he never wanted to write novels.

And now his life began to open up from drudgery. He went to Oxford, having like Jude a passion for the essence of the place, and he was happy there, and made friends, and married. He was a socialist, secretary to the International Labour Party, spent much time walking, and then, though he loved his friends and their company, longed for solitude.

By then he had sold stories to all the literary magazines, and had a small reputation. How to manage without a salary? he wondered, deciding not to keep books, or to run around for other people ever again. He had 50 pounds. He found a minute cottage in the middle of a field near Oxford, and there he went to live and to write, throwing himself entirely on the rewards of literature, while his mother-in-law and his wife demanded: 'God above, has he gone daft?'

On the contrary, it was exactly what he should have done.

I soon got used to my new status as a writer – having published a book I thereupon became somebody! Life at Shepherds Pit continued the same, just as delightful in the exquisite tranquillity there. I could almost believe now that the seasons never did change their character then, that summer was always there and I always in the open with the birds and the trees and the postman, the thrift of the land and the freedom.

He was the most lovable of people, and it is evident in every word he wrote.

A *Festschrift*, Idries Shah

It has become a truism among orientalists, since the Victorian and later rediscovery of the contribution of the Saracens to civilisation, that during the late Middle Ages the West was far behind the achievements of the new culture of the Middle East. We hear of the public libraries and street lighting of Moorish Cordoba, the academics of Fez, the science of Baghdad and Samarkand, and how the scholars of the West flocked to these and many other centres to possess themselves of the knowledge which the caliphs concentrated and developed from the rubble of the previous centres of learning in these areas. And then, so the story goes, the tide turned. The East fell into lethargy, and the West snatched up the banner of progress. One could fill a book with the generous plaudits for the role played by Islam in the cause of learning, culled from our own scholars. But Islam remains a mystery, and the (often rhetorical) questions are still being asked, by the academics of the East and West alike: How and why did the East lose its power to transmit its ideas to us? Was there anything left to pass on?

Sufi Studies: East and West, a collection of scholarly papers by literary men and scientists, by experts on religion and orientalism, by people from the top echelons of learning in both worlds, answers both of these questions in a way which has probably not been done before. The book, published in celebration of the 700th anniversary of the death of Jalaluddin Rumi, one of the Eastern poet-philosophers best known in our culture, takes as its theme the vast amount of work done in less than twenty years in bringing Eastern thought in a usable form to the West, by Sayed Idries Shah.

The East 'lost its power' to communicate partly because its thinkers did not study us and the priorities which motivate us. They failed to put their thought in a form which paralleled our concerns. At the same time the long period of Western self-satisfaction – only now coming to an end – meant that people on this side were not motivated to seek for valuable insights among a collection of peoples in the Middle East who seemed unable to defend themselves against our growing economic and military might.

When an occasional oriental did in fact bestir himself to analyse the successes of the West and applied the resulting lessons to a teaching aimed at awakening the East, the results were more than dramatic. One such was Sayed Jamaluddin Afghani (1838/9–97) who is the founder of the struggle of Islam for freedom from colonial hegemony, regarded as one of the greatest figures produced by the East. It is noteworthy that his kinsman, Sayed Idries Shah, is often likened to him by several of the contributors of this *Festschrift*.

Today, in the United States alone, there are over three hundred university and college courses in psychology and sociology and other branches of the humanities, which use materials based on the work extracted by Idries Shah from Islamic tradition. This is not because people today turn more readily to the East to solve their problems: that is a preoccupation of those who follow gurus. It is because Shah has asked and answered the fundamental question: 'How is the thought of the East to be

projected to the West so as to answer some of their own questions, and not to try to impose upon its people only what we
might want to tell them?' It is the difference between proselytism
and education. This robust and informative symposium, astonishingly readable, is the evidence of his success in this ingenious
and skilful undertaking.

Arabs and Jews, Hindus, Christians and Muslims, a Chinese,
an African, a Turk and a Hungarian: as befits an international
assemblage of scholars, we find them all writing their accounts
of some part of Shah's work. The section of 24 potted biographies of the authors is a useful introduction to the kind of
people concerned in this newly mined treasure and the skills
which they bring to their task. It is almost a briefing on the
inter-disciplinary capacities of contemporary scholars. Their
approaches are almost all distinctive: ranging from the expected
to the entirely new. Professor Chen concentrates on Shah's
teaching-stories and sees them from the literary, Chinese and
Christian viewpoints. Professor Hamarneh, based in Poland,
analyses Shah's impact in historico-social terms. What is particularly striking here is how Shah's twenty books are seen as
vital and essential by eminent people who are themselves rooted
in what have been seen as entirely different, sometimes even
mutually hostile, ideologies.

Judge Makram Ebeid, the influential Coptic-Christian layman
of Egypt, and Dr Bankey Behari, a notable Hindu monk, examine his work and concur in finding in it dimensions which
humanity sorely needs for the improvement of the human lot.
The same sort of reaction has been seen for some years in the
West. Shah may not be dearly loved by irascible scholars whom
he has outpaced, or by cultists who run after stage orientals.
But he is authoritatively held to be the first Islamic worker
since Al-Ghazali (AD 1058–1111) to hold his own with Western
thinkers, both in the literary and scientific fields.

The score of workers whose efforts are collected here have undoubtedly done their homework. This must have involved them in reading something like a million words of Shah's books, and familiarising themselves with papers and articles which in the past decade have accumulated in reprint form from Arabic, Persian, Urdu, English, Spanish, Turkish and French. There has been very little overlapping in the text, in spite of the wide dispersal of the contributors: consummately well orchestrated, the papers are edited by one of the greatest living authorities on the East, and this quality shines through, as with all Professor Rushbrook Williams's work.

Each writer has selected some specific and important highlight in Shah's books, which he has sought to present to be intelligible to specialists and also to the general reader. Professor M. Y. Haschmi, the philosopher and scientist, of Aleppo, notes how Shah has demonstrated the internal coherence of the ideas with which he has worked, in a manner which has not been done before. This has had the effect of removing the Western objection that there are so many forms of Islamic experiential philosophy that they must be mutually contradictory and hence only of local value. The redoubtable Iranians, Professor Arasteh and Aga Ahmad Saidi point out the uncanny ability to transpose Eastern ideas into English, and how, in a lucid and apposite form, Shah's 'ancient Oriental' concepts are on a par with the most advanced ones of the West. The Indian thinker, Dr Hidaya-tullah, emphasises how this can be done only when the very essence of the Eastern approach has been assessed and applied to the new area: 'He did this by disclosing the perennial and pre-existing truths that are timeless in their reach and universal in their appeal.'

Another clue to the question about why more cultural inter-change does not take place is to be deduced from Professor I. H. Qureshi's chapter. You may have the materials, and you may have the desire, but have you got the ability to do the job? The sources and literature of Islamic and Sufic thought cannot, he avers, be plumbed even by deep scholars until a key is provided. And by this he does not only mean Western scholars. Qureshi is one of the world's specialists in this field, and he ought to know.

Mir Basri's paper introduces quite one of the most important elements in the study. He emphasises the instrumental nature of so much of the new ways of thinking introduced and illustrated by Idries Shah to the West. It is worth noting that the effect, both in form and content, of the materials has been so powerful that it has received very comprehensive recognition. Basri is echoed by Professor R. Ornstein (*The Psychology of Consciousness*, London 1972, 224–5):

> A new synthesis is in progress in modern psychology . . . such a new formulation is currently being presented by Idries Shah . . . modern technological work is coupled to the special form of literature which he has recently reintroduced to this culture.

This extract clearly shows how a distinguished contemporary psychologist can easily apprehend that the value of the books is not in any system which they might purport to provide or explain; nor, indeed, to any ideology or automatic activity. The application, as well as the content, exists in reading and understanding the books themselves. This concept is obviously not so unfamiliar to a scientist as it will generally be to someone in the arts, despite many protestations to the contrary.

The literary editor of one mass-circulation daily has already assured his readers that Shah's books work away at the mind whether one wants them to do so or not; and his opposite number in a religious journal begs his readers to beg, borrow or steal the Shah books and to read them. The interest of this book, together with the fifty-nine redoubtable wellwishers in the scholarly field named in it, makes it an unusually valuable one.

The Nine Emotional Lives of Cats

The cat books I like least generalise: All cats are proud ...
selfish ... manipulative ... independent ... adorable ... I like
better 'My cat Fluff enjoys ...' 'Next door's cat ...' The anec-
dotal; and what's wrong with that? We deal in anecdotes all
the time, getting information about people, and cats. And they
tell about the variations in cat behaviour, for cats are as different
from each other as people. I look back at a long tale of cats,
and see individuals.

Those who have read this author's *When Elephants Weep*
and *Dogs Never Lie About Love* know that he achieves his
empathy with animals by what has to be described as total
immersion. Wanting to learn about cats he put a random assortment into what is as near to cat heaven as you can get. New
Zealand: a rain forest, interesting walks, a beach, a cat-friendly
house and cat-liking people. The freedom gave their natures
scope, and we may contrast a beast's behaviour at the beginning
of the experiment with how it develops.

Jeffrey Masson is reacting against an academic statement that
cats are not emotional. The nine chapters are 'Narcissism',
'Love', 'Contentment', 'Attachment', 'Jealousy', 'Fear', 'Anger',
'Curiosity' and 'Playfulness'. He is not sentimental: one cat,

taken from a refuge, was emotionally damaged by early mis-handling and never recovered. One may cavil at the length of his experiment: a year. It may take four years, more, or never for an ill-treated cat to learn trust.

Reading about these animals' happiness it is hard to think of cats locked out of their homes all day and half the night without food or water 'because cats like their freedom': cats locked out all night 'because cats are night creatures': cats left locked up all day by people at work; cats lonely, neglected, sad. The cats in this tale are in a different world from your average London mog or any suburban cat: cats in luck, cats de luxe.

Jeffrey Masson learns a good deal, but says that while we may infer from what we observe and from the species' evolutionary history, a lot remains in question. Interpreting what they do by our yardsticks, we must miss not only subtle messages but, perhaps, the obvious. To call cats 'mysterious' has not always been to their benefit, but every cat owner has moments of frustration: just *what* is this creature thinking? What does it mean by that movement, that miaow, that purr? Here is the companion of your days and nights but what does he really make of you, of us? And when she gazes off into nothing with those calm eyes, what is she looking at? Gazing into memories, the author suggests, or perhaps daydreams. If cats dream – they do – then why not fantasies?

This enjoyable book is useful for its insights, is full of guidance, but its virtue is, simply, pleasure. What fun these cats have in their paradise. They go for long walks with their human friend, chasing him and each other, play games with him, leaping out from bushes or hiding, often behaving more like dogs. I shan't forget those cats sitting along the beach beyond the water's reach waiting for him and his wife Leila and their little boy to finish swimming and return safely from the strange element; or the cat who learned to lie on the sand and allow the waves to just lap her; or the cat who at last trusts enough to accept an invitation to jump on to the kayak and go for a trip. The luxurious contentment of these cats: that is what he conveys so well.

I do not always agree with him. He says there is no record of a male cat consistently tending kittens. But I've watched a tom who fathered kittens on a – I think – feeble-minded cat, and he taught them everything, how to eat and drink, use litter boxes, then the garden, climb trees, play, while she lay and watched.

He does not record anything like this: my cat Butchkin, otherwise El Magnifico, came up to where I was reading in bed at the top of the house and yowled, and went to the door, came back and yowled, until I followed him down and found a forgotten gas flame beginning to flare on the cooker.

Some cats are like this. Some are not.

Mukiwa: A White Boy in Africa

There have been many gung-ho accounts by white soldiers and by black soldiers of the civil war in Southern Rhodesia. One is by a white soldier who suffered a conversion, so that all wickedness is ascribed to the whites, all virtue to the blacks. Interesting psychologically, but of no use as history. This book's achievement is its balance, because of the author's character, and, too, his special experience as a child.

Peter Godwin's mother was a doctor, unusual for her time in that she took the trouble to understand local Shona custom and medicine. The boy went with her on her rounds. His father ran a big wattle estate, and its successes and setbacks were part of his growing up: Godwin tells of a horrific bush fire when hundreds of workers tried to defend thousands of acres of sisal, while fireballs leaped ahead of them from sector to sector, and animals and snakes fled by. In spite of the book beginning with the first murder of a white person in the war, this childhood is that idyll familiar to us from parts of the world where white children ran wild with black servants as companions: an education of the heart, it could be called.

Shona tales and Shona lore, wild animals, bush adventures – this Eden was interrupted by the cold unhappiness of boarding school. The jaunty tone of the early chapters does not prepare us for what follows, not even his time at St George's, the Jesuit school that was inter-racial before black government. The boy found himself fagging for a black prefect. 'Here I was, a white boy skivvying for a black in a country embarking on a civil war to prevent black rule. I must be the only white servant of a black man in the whole damn country. And I felt oddly special.' Godwin was accused of being a kaffir-lover, but soon was part of the army created to fight for white supremacy. He was a good soldier, and a better one because of his knowledge of the country's people. He was always balanced in that place where incompatibilities try to resolve themselves. He does not labour this point, but it is the theme of the book.

The war in Rhodesia was no simple conflict between whites and blacks. Many blacks fought with the whites. The different black armies fought each other in between fighting the whites. Godwin worked with a Bushman (*Khoi*) tracker, one of those legendary figures able to deduce the movements of an enemy by a broken fragment of cobweb, the alarm calls of birds, the thickness of dust blown into a hoofprint. The allegiances of the villagers were not always with the freedom fighters, who stole their food, bullied them, and often raped their women, but goodwill towards the whites was consistently destroyed by the casual brutality of wartime. The tone of the writing darkens into a contained rage because of what Godwin is seeing done, of what he is doing himself, for the war is brutalising him, just like everyone else. 'Slowly all other life faded. The potent images of war crowded out the memories of life before this, of my very identity. I had become a soldier, a technician of war.' Meanwhile, he was trying to get to Cambridge, where a place was being kept for him. And he did get there, but was sucked back to his homeland, because of the shortage of white soldiers.

There is a remarkable scene in which Peter Godwin guards

Ian Smith who is visiting the arenas of war, and he stands dreaming of killing this man who will not let the unwinnable war end. Two men, alone in a room.

> So this was the man – good ol' Smithy – followed blindly by white Rhodesians even though he had no bloody idea where to lead us . . . an aide arrived with the Close Security inspector. I realised I was standing with one hand on my holster and the other tightly clutching the rolled-up newspaper which I was slapping against my leg. The inspector looked at me oddly. 'Are you all right?' he enquired. 'Yes, sir. Why?' 'You look, well, angry.' 'No, sir I'm fine,' I said, and I turned down the steps and walked away over the flagstoned path and back to the war.

The war over, Godwin returned from Cambridge to become a lawyer. He defended seven Ndebele commanders accused of plotting a coup. The judge acquitted them, but they were at once rearrested under the Emergency Laws inherited from Ian Smith, to spend four years in prison. Peter Godwin decided he did not want to be involved in this kind of law. There were rumours of atrocities in Matabeleland, by the infamous Fifth Brigade, who, according to locals, had nothing to learn from the Gestapo in methods of torture and murder. The risks Godwin took caused the government to describe him as James Bond, while designating him an enemy of the State. In Mozambique, where he was investigating the war, he was captured, but because he knows Chndau, a variation of Shona, spoken in parts of Mozambique, and because the commander as a child had been treated by Peter's mother, and Peter himself, the two men became friends.

This book could usefully be put into the hands of someone wanting a fair account of the war and its aftermath. It is a sad book, because of the truth that emerges as you read: if the whites had had a more intelligent leadership, there need never have been a war. As in South Africa, they might have found a different way. The Mashona are not a vengeful people. There was goodwill for the whites, despite everything, and not least because of the conduct of the Liberation armies. Well into the war there was the oddest event. Villagers made up a slogan which they chalked up: 'We don't care if you hate us.' Challenged, they simply repeated: 'Hate us and see. We won't mind.'

Another incident encapsulates the cackhandedness of the whites. In an area nursed by Peter Godwin to neutrality, a mine on a road outside a village blew up a lorry, with him in it. Reinforcements were flown in. Despite their assertions that they knew nothing of the mine, the villagers had to be punished. Meanwhile, an old woman had seen that Peter was hurt, and brought him a cup of water. A young girl brought him tea. A minute later, they were being prodded into a truck like animals to be taken to a detention camp.

Tricky waters, these – the atrocities, these camps, called concentration camps by the villagers. They have been encouraged to sink into oblivion because of the need to heal the wounds of war, but you hear of them when you are crawling around among the grassroots. Smith has recently described Mugabe's government as terrorists. Why? Because, he says, of their atrocities. It is said Smith did not know about the atrocities committed by his troops. Is it possible? And what does that say about the man? Or is it that the cruelties on his side didn't count, because he was in the right, but the black armies' atrocities were bad because they were in the wrong?

Clarissa

For years only faithful admirers spoke of this book, which had fallen as thoroughly out of sight as ever a book did. Then it was republished in 1985 and soon reached millions via an insipid television series. In the climate of now Clarissa herself had to get the attention, but when the novel first dazzled all of Europe, it was because of Lovelace, who gave a new word to a dozen languages. Clarissa was seen as a tiresome girl, of interest because of the deviousness of her hypocrisy, for her secret desire for a violent end was matched only by Lovelace's desire for his, in a duel. Samuel Richardson's novel was admired for its psychological depth, for nothing like it had been seen before, certainly not *Pamela*, its predecessor. Lovelace was a subtle, not a brutal, seducer, and was admired and excoriated for his lies, his cynicism, his ingenious philosophising, his sophistries, and his knowledge of young women. It was Russian literature which not only first and most generously saluted *Clarissa* but was most quickly influenced. This is easily seen in *Crime and Punishment*, particularly in Raskolnikov, born out of Lovelace's head. When Raskolnikov exclaims that Napoleon was admired for murdering millions while he might not kill even one useless old woman, he is echoing Lovelace, who said that kings may make wars and kill soldiers and helpless civilians, but he would be called a criminal for killing even one person. Hardly likely that this was the first time in history this thought occurred to humankind, but perhaps in *Clarissa* it first reached the common reader. It was Lovelace's protest that expressed some imperative for his time, brought it into the light. And it had prolific progeny. Its brutal logics became the communist, You cannot make an omelette without breaking eggs, and, later, the justifications for murder by self-righteous terrorists. Laclos certainly knew the book: the Marquise de Merteuil lent a copy to the Vicomte de Valmont, who kept it in a locked drawer by his bed. And when Julien Sorel, that most intellectual of passionate lovers, was due to die on the guillotine, the exclamation, 'Never had that head such poetic beauty as at the moment when it was about to fall' was dictated to Stendhal by Lovelace's ghost. Dandyism and crime, sophistry and seduction, heroics and heroism – and philosophical acquittals for even the most sordid brutalities. A prophetic book if there ever was one. If for decades the mere mention of *Clarissa* caused parents to think how they might best lock up their daughters, then even more they wanted to lock up their sons, where their minds could not be poisoned by the wiles of the Clever One, the proud Tempter who, like Nietzsche and long before the idea became commonplace, knew that when God died so would morality, dull old morality, fit only for the simple-minded.

The preface of the Penguin edition hardly mentions the novel's great influence all over Europe, as potent as Goethe's *The Sorrows of Young Werther* a quarter of a century later. Lovelace has been airbrushed out of our story.

Summing up: when Idries Shah died

It is not easy to sum up the life of as multifaceted a man as Idries Shah, who died last winter, and particularly not his literary achievements which covered such a range of subjects and disciplines, amounting to a kind of map of Sufi living, learning and thinking. He was a Sufi exemplar and teacher, that is to say, a mystic, but right from the first of his books where he began to describe the Sufi outlook – *The Sufis* (1964) – he challenged some pretty stereotyped ideas about what a mystic should be. For one thing he was a friend, and often an adviser, of scientists.

The Sufis had a preface by Robert Graves, and attracted attention from some distinguished people, among them Ted Hughes and Geoffrey Grigson. This was remarkable for a book at such an angle to our materialist Western ideas. *The Sufis* is the definitive book for our time: essential to the Sufi way of thinking is that books and teachings are for a time and a stage in culture, and must be superseded. Sufi books are written in response to a demand, say the Sufis, and this one was eagerly anticipated. I was far from the only person who, having heard that a genuine Sufi teacher had arrived, waited for a book that would be called, simply, *The Sufis*. I felt it answered questions I had been mulling over all my life.

357

There quickly followed *Caravan of Dreams*, *Wisdom of the Idiots*, *The Magic Monastery* and *The Dermis Probe* – the reference is to 'The Elephant in the Dark', the little fable about people who feel different parts of an elephant, all believing that what they feel is the whole beast. Each of these, and later books, is a rich mix of tales, ideas, verses, jokes, and at first people's reactions, my own included, illustrated Shah's remark that we should not expect Sufis to teach in an expected manner. With each book there was a slight initial feeling of let-down, even bewilderment, and this was because the words 'Teacher', 'School', 'Teaching', evoke expectations of a person standing in front of a class and saying, 'For the next hour I shall instruct you in so-and-so. Now: a, b, c, d . . .' In a Sufi school you first learn what is being taught and, above all, how. Sufi books are designed to be read differently from our usual habit: quietly, non-argumentatively, willing to absorb what is there, noticing how a question in one part may be answered in another, observing juxtapositions, and intimations of the unexpected, above all not interposing screens of 'received ideas' between the author and one's best self. Perhaps this is what Goethe meant when he said he was a very old man and had only just learned how to read.

From the start it was evident how ignorant we in the West are about the very bases of a practical and living mysticism, and how right Shah was when he told us – repeatedly – that what we needed was information before anything. Thirty years ago cults and gurus abounded: we were invited to go off and find the characteristics of a cult as defined by the sociologists, to be sure not to fall into the trap of despising people who think differently, to be careful not to use the Sufi community as a family or social life, or a means of enjoying exciting psychic experiences – what Shah called 'chills, spills and thrills'. People who wanted a guru or a father figure were urged to go off and find one, because that was not what Shah was interested in.

I am writing as one who studied with Shah as a pupil and the books were part – only part – of the curriculum, but they were read by a variety of people who found them useful. Desmond Morris, for instance, said that a joke or a tale may suddenly explode into meaning, illustrating a situation or a person, perhaps years after reading it. There are people all over the world – I have met them while travelling – who say that Shah's books are the foundation, the 'warp and weft' of their lives, and not least because Shah's explicit warnings prevented them from haring after one of the many phoney 'Sufi' teachers or gurus. Besides, one has only to compare the many-sidedness, the complexity, the depth and variety of Shah's teaching with his imitators. Perhaps its chief characteristic is its precision, the clarity, the sharpness, which is a thousand miles away from the dozy emotions so often associated with 'mysticism'.

Idries Shah was born in 1924 in north India, of an ancient family that holds a special place in the community of the Sufis. This family has always produced remarkable people, influential in their communities – in the world. Idries Shah's father, the Sirdar Iqbal Ali Shah, was a diplomat and worked in cultural organisations designed to bridge the gaps between East and West. He wrote books, still valuable and very entertaining, compilations of tales and adventure, like *The Golden Caravan*, some directly informational, like *The Spirit of the East*. He later lived in this country and taught 'classes'. The Sufis may plant a 'root' in a culture. It looks as if the Sirdar planted a root, and Shah's 'school' encouraged the plant into the light, which he has done openly, strengthening the Sufi current for everyone to see. I have always seen *The Sufis* as an announcement: this is what can be done, and this is what will be done.

It took 800 years to get Sufi thought accepted by orthodox Islam, and since then Muslims have claimed it as their own. A young friend of Shah, a British orientalist, a pupil, was sent by him in answer to a request from a group of Muslim divines in the Middle East, but they had to be persuaded that the Sufis are not a Muslim monopoly by being invited to look again at the Sufi classics they venerated but seemed not to have read. The Sufi reality predated Islam, has always been introduced, secretly or openly, into every culture. 'We work in all places and at all times.' (The word 'Sufism' is not liked by Sufis: they see it as a typical Western abstraction, away from the living reality of the Sufi Way, which is embodied in people.) The actual word 'Sufi' is not necessary for a fresh introduction of Sufi feeling: many an activity or event or series of events has been Sufic, but no one has known it, perhaps not even the people involved. Many books have been for a Sufi purpose, the word never being used. There are times when a transmission of Sufi truth is possible, because cosmic influences are in alignment – '... the appropriate wave of the unseen laps upon the shore of possibility ...' – and times when nothing happens because nothing can. This has the remotest connection with astrology, fortune-telling and horoscopes.

People are always asking, 'But what is Sufism, what are the Sufis, surely it can be put into a few words?' There are some statements, almost aphorisms: for instance that in every human being is an initially tiny, precious, shining thing, capable of development, which can bring her or him to fulfilment. Or, that the Sufi truth is at the core of every religion, its heart, and religions are only the outward vestments of an inner reality. This last is helpful to people like myself, who find it hard to see in religions anything more than systems of indoctrination with perennial tendencies towards the persecution of differently thinking people.

People say, 'But these secrets, why don't people simply say what they are, and be done with it?' In the body of work that Shah has left can be found a whole cosmology, the 'secrets' set out as openly as a recipe for soup or instructions how to plant a garden. Clearly, people's eyes slide over them, because they are not set out in an expected way. A fact startling or even shocking in its implications may be part of an anecdote, a joke, or an apparently casual paragraph. Some 'secrets' are to be discovered by letting something simmer in the mind – contemplation. Materials from traditional religion, for instance, the teachings of Jesus, are brought to life by being put into the context of a school. It has been consistently puzzling to me that people can't see what is set out so clearly, even if not in an a, b, c, d fashion. 'The secret protects itself.' In the early days of Shah's supper sessions, because people became used to what seemed like a pretty casual way of doing things, a man sat down next to me and promptly went to sleep. Asked why, next day, he said, 'Nothing was happening, so I thought I might as well have a nap.' Another complained that people drank so much. I have never seen more than half a dozen bottles of wine put out for perhaps up to thirty people. Astonished, I made enquiries and discovered he was an alcoholic. These two tiny incidents illustrate for me why people continue to ask, 'But what *are* the secrets?'

Jokes, humorous tales, are a large part of Shah's work, whether written or verbal. He could be a very funny man. The 'joke' figure, Mulla Nasrudin, is of great importance in Sufi teaching. The jokes cross frontiers, embed themselves in every culture, sometimes on the level of pub humour. Shah published three volumes, *The Pleasantries of the Incredible Mulla Nasrudin*, *The Exploits of the Incomparable Mulla Nasrudin*, *The Subtleties of the Inimitable Mulla Nasrudin*. There is a chapter devoted to the Mulla in *The Sufis*. Some jokes are immediately funny or informational, others flat. Their property is that the joke which seems merely silly may years later suddenly come to life: it is said this happens as the student – or interested reader – develops understanding. A little book, *Special Illumination*, is about the Sufi use of humour; not an academic treatise, but taking the reader through a sequence of tales, explaining possible meanings.

> If you want special illumination, look upon the human face:
> See clearly in laughter the Essence of Ultimate Truth.
>
> (Jalaluddin Rumi)

Rumi was a great mystical teacher of the thirteenth century, whose *Masnavi* is a mine of Sufi ideas. It still enthrals readers. But Shah warns not to fall in love with the great classics of the past. 'People study Rumi and turn themselves into perfect replicas of fourteenth-century people.' For classics to be of use, we need a Sufi to choose the parts that are still relevant, and put them into our context – to 'unlock' them.

Learning How to Learn (1978) is Sufi thinking put into our terms. 'Psychology and sociology – that's your mind set.' This book is accessible to people who experience other books as difficult or off-putting; though perhaps they may find it helpful to remember that Edward VII, seeing one of the first motor cars come hissing and grinding towards him, said, 'Good God, it's the Devil!' It cannot be described as a soothing read. How about this: 'The human being is so intensely standardised that an outside observer, noting his reactions to various stimuli, need not infer an individual controlling brain in each person, but would rather infer the existence of a separate outside brain and the people as mere manifestations of its will.' *A Perfumed Scorpion* followed: the scorpion is the unregenerate human being. *The Commanding Self*, Shah's latest published book and just out in paperback, is based on letters to him asking for clarification, interviews, question-and-answer sessions, lectures. The commanding self is that mix of primitive and conditioned responses, common to everyone, which initially inhibits and distorts human progress and understanding. 'Do you want to lead an angry, biting life?' A tiny tale: a complacent would-be pupil is asked, can you accept the fact that soon you will not like yourself as much as you do now? And to his pupils, sitting near, the teacher says, 'Those of you who do not think well of yourselves, stand up.' And the whole row of his senior pupils promptly stood up.

Oriental Magic, with a foreword by Dr Louis Marin, Director of the Ecole d'Anthropologie de Paris, describes and compares Jewish, Babylonian, Egyptian, Iranian, Indian and Chinese magic, the practices of the Atharva Veda, and of the Fakirs. Probably it is the historical and cultural information here that modern people will find most interesting.

When Shah was young, he travelled extensively, collecting – among much else – proverbs and folk sayings. These appear throughout his work. Sufis say that in apparently trivial or worn out proverbs and clichés are often depths of wisdom, and it is a mistake to dismiss them. Contemplating them may bring one into contact with the other dimension which it is the Sufis' function to cultivate.

Shah also collected folk tales. *World Tales* is the result. I have yet to meet anyone who is not fascinated by this book, even those who yawn at the idea of folk tales. Each tale has a scholarly – and often startling – note about its provenance. Some have taken root all over the world. When I gave the book to Shona and Ndebele friends they were delighted to find tales that are part of their traditions. 'Fairy' tales were originally called 'fate' tales: they may embody the other dimension if not too debased. Some originated as Sufi teaching stories. Nearly all Shah's books include tales, some of extreme antiquity, some from the Middle East (like the Bible parables) and Central Asia and elsewhere. In *Caravan of Dreams* Shah spoke openly, but briefly, about the Sufi use of tales, and at even greater length in *A Perfumed Scorpion*. Sufis have always taught through stories, and pedants and traditionalists have perennially complained – and sometimes about the greatest of the Sufis – 'But these are merely tales of the kind you tell to children.' The claim is that the action of the genuine Sufi teaching story is 'direct and certain' upon the innermost self of the human being, and this is true whether or not the said human is prepared to acknowledge that he or she has an innermost self. This attitude to literature brings us into an unfamiliar relation with our own literary heritage. The tales, anecdotes, illustrative recitals, jokes are not meant to be attacked by the intellectual apparatus. 'There was once a little boy who pulled apart a fly, and when he had a heap of wings, thorax, head and legs, asked, "But where *is* the fly?"' It does not matter if feminists claim 'fairy' stories as a female tradition, or socialists say they are about the class struggle: it is a free country. But they are using the tales on a technically lower level than was the intention.

A book for which I have a particular weakness is *Tales of the Dervishes*. Some are part of many countries' store of stories, but here they are restored to an original state, sharp, taut, pithy, without storyteller's tricks or the elaboration that may soften and distort. A note to 'The Dervish and the Princes' is informative: 'Many have been misled, because this kind of literature has its own conventions, into believing that Sufi classical writings are not other than technical descriptions of psychological states.' The notes are helpful in understanding some of our own literature. An appendix lists authors ranging from Abu Bakr, 634, a Companion of the Prophet, to Sheikh Daud of Kandahar, 1965 – fourteen centuries, including some of the great names of Eastern classical literature who are known to us: Avicenna, Ansari, Al-Ghazali, Sanai, Attar, Rumi, Jami – all great masters of the Sufi Way.

Thinkers of the East contains directly informational material about the Sufi Way.

The Way of the Sufi contains among much else sections on Al-Ghazali, Attar of Nishapur, Ibn el Arabi – known to the West in the Middle Ages as Doctor Maximus – and Hakim Sanai. It is composed of portions of their work. Four Major Orders, Chishti, Qadiri, Naqshbandi, Suhrawardi, are here: all have had an enormous impact on the Muslim world, and on the West too. There are teaching stories, themes for solitary contemplation, letters and lectures. It is surprising how often this book turns out to be people's favourite: there is a kind of magic about it.

A tiny book of compressed aphorisms is *Reflections*, a very concentrated dose of Sufi thought. For instance: 'I have heard all you have to say about your problems. It is my view that your real problem is that you are a member of the human race. Face that one first.' This is by no means a clever turn-off, but the essence of the situation, hard to accept and then to apply. What happens to our pet beliefs and convictions that what is wrong is that we are women, or men, or black, or old, or poor? 'No, you are a human being. Face that one first.'

Advice couched in a line or two can keep one engaged with it for years. 'Service is the performance of duty without either reluctance or delight. It is this which sharpens your perceptions.' And that brings us to the Sufi attitude to emotion, possibly the most abrasive to the West, which values emotions and ever stronger sensations. Remarks like 'Nearly all so-called religious and mystical experience is in fact no more than emotion' shock many good people. Throughout the whole body of Sufi literature the point is repeated in a thousand ways, not least in the Nasrudin jokes. A sick man sends for the doctor, saying he has a temperature of 107 degrees. The doctor replies, 'You don't need me, you need a fire engine.'

The book which perhaps encapsulates the Sufi Reality is *The Book of the Book*. It contains nine pages of print, but all the rest of the pages are blank. It predicts all possible responses to itself. This tiny, highly-charged tale is like a mirror reflecting much more than is in the area it is apparently meant to reflect. Every time I read it, I see more in it.

Our attitudes to literature are very primitive, says Shah, and they will be seen as such by our successors. Some books are designed to be read in company, others in solitude, others at special times and places. Some have in them encoded information for initiates, or passages deliberately inserted to deflect or mislead sensation seekers. One easily observed practice of Sufi literature can be seen in Shah's work, when he expands and elucidates in one volume a trend of thought that has been left in the air in a previous volume. The actual structure of tales may be designed to affect thinking: an example is Amina Shah's *The Tale of the Four Dervishes*, where four men meet and tell stories that lead to other stories, illustrating the complexity of life, of cause and effect, and at least temporarily deflecting the mind's habitual responses away from the sequential, the a, b, c, d, the either/or modes of thought.

Shah created the Octagon Press so as to keep up with his flow of books – some were published by conventional publishers – and to keep existing classics in print, or those which needed new translations. Among the former is Al-Ghazali's *The Alchemy of Happiness*. My favourite is *The Secret Garden* by Shabistari of the fourteenth century, which was the answer by a sage to a friend asking, 'What is mysticism?' It is in the form of questions and answers. Another book under whose spell I fall each time I read it is *The Journey of the Soul*, in a new translation by Dr Riad Kocache. It is supposed to be the inspiration for *Robinson Crusoe*. *The Revelation of the Secrets of the Birds and Flowers* by Al-Muqaddasi, who died in 1280, is in a new translation by

Irene Hoare and Darya Galy. It is described as 'astonishingly modern' in its psychology. Sanai's *The Walled Garden of Truth* and Jami's great love story *Yusuf and Zulaikha* are newly translated by David Pendlebury. The English, it is fair to say, have always had a feeling for Eastern literature: astonishing how much was translated in the nineteenth century. Octagon republished Gertrude Bell's version of Hafiz, the poet who had such an influence on Western writers – Goethe, for instance. Also Richard Burton's wonderful *The Kasidah*, the book which Isabel Burton said she could not read without shedding floods of tears, though she did not, to say the least, admire his religious beliefs. Shah invited Ramsay Wood to make a new version of part of the great classic *Kalila and Dimna*. It was first translated in England by Sir Thomas North, whose version of Plutarch influenced Shakespeare, and there were many translations after that: twenty in the century before 1888. Then it was forgotten. This great book, which originated in India about two thousand years ago, has been described as being as widely translated as the Bible.

Three of Shah's books illustrate his versatility. Two are about this country, *The Natives are Restless* and *Darkest England*; both are very funny and, if abrasive, useful because of this sharply observant viewpoint. *Kara Kush* is about the Soviet invasion of Afghanistan, in the form of an adventure and love story with accounts of real battles, such as when a whole army of Soviet tanks was brought to a standstill by women and children using sticks, stones, boulders, home-made bombs, catapults and bows and arrows. I am told the book is as good as a treatise on modern weaponry, too. A book for connoisseurs of the unusual and the unexpected.

Octagon has published books that came into being because of Shah's encouragement, and were designed to amplify aspects of his teaching. One is *Journeys with a Sufi Master*, another

People of the Secret: the author, Ernest Scott, was invited to trawl through the centuries to find what evidence there might be for the persistent rumour that there is a hidden directorate influencing human affairs. Two other books in this category are compilations of material from the family's great store, one by his daughter Safia Shah, *Afghan Caravan*, and one by his son Tahir Shah, *The Middle Eastern Bedside Book*. Both are full of delights; there is a great deal that is surprising; and, as with all books from that source, we are reminded of a generosity and largeness of mind in a culture that once, long ago, gave us the concept of chivalry.

Opera

It was in 1983 that I got Philip Glass's letter suggesting we do an opera together, to be based on one of the novels in the Canopus in Argos series. It was unexpected. For me then opera was an unfamiliar world where I sometimes visited. It had all the glamour of distance, unlike theatre, which I had written for and worked in. Everything about writing for opera has been unexpected. *The Making of the Representative for Planet 8* was not the most obvious choice for an opera, and if I had been told when writing that novel it would turn into one, I would have been incredulous. Yet when Philip Glass and I began to meet to discuss the five novels of the Canopus series, this was the one that seemed, then, best for his kind of music. But his music has developed and changed since then. This whole series, the Canopus novels, sometimes described as science fiction, has interested musicians right from the first one, *Shikasta*, and several have wanted to make operas or pieces from them. But I decided to stick with Philip, because we work easily and pleasantly together.

If the question is, why do writers like working on operas, then at least one of the answers must be that most boring of clichés, that writers' lives are solitary, and to be involved in opera is to find oneself in a world that could not be more different from the sober disciplines of novel writing. That is one thing, the pleasures – and perils – of working in a group, but there is something I did not expect when I began. Words are our trade, not merely the sense but the music of words; and in the links between sense and sound are hidden all kinds of mysteries, as poets know. When something you have written becomes interpreted by music, then sounds and thoughts that perhaps you only half-consciously knew were there become real, are brought out by music and the musician. Easy to see this on a physical level. Writing the novel *Representative* I 'heard' the grinding of the ice, the violence of the winds, but the music made variations I had not 'heard'. But when I 'heard' the voices of the travellers in the storm being snatched away to become part of the voices of the storm, I did not know that these voices, as music, would acquire depths I had not thought of. The journey of the Representatives into annihilation, to be reborn as a new whole, had been in my mind's ear as the earthly transmuting to the unearthly, but really hearing it I knew that music enriched it, lifted the idea. An opera involves all the arts. Music, both instrumental and singing, design of all kinds, the magic of colour, the charm of storytelling, words: opening oneself to all this is to find resonances and responses that can be unexpected, may even be the start of a new idea for a novel. My recent novel *Love, Again* came out of my work for opera and in theatre. There is nothing more poignant than watching a play or an opera take shape, blown together for a time and then that's it, the end, and never again will this particular combination of people, talents, sounds, colours, shapes exist, it's gone for good.

When Philip Glass and I decided to do *The Making of the Representative for Planet 8* it took four years from the start of work till the opening night in Houston. Then we decided to make an opera of *The Marriages between Zones Three, Four and Five*, and this time it took eight years, by the time the curtain went up in Heidelberg. I began writing the libretto for *Marriages* during the rehearsals in Houston for *Representative*. *Marriages* is an easy choice for an opera. It has a strong story, whereas *Representative*'s story is the slow freezing up of a formerly happy planet, and how this process as it were crystallises a whole or a soul from the planet's people. Death transcended is not exactly a new theme for an opera, but perhaps this was a new way of doing it.

The story of *The Marriages Between Zones Three, Four and Five* is this. Zone Three is a luxurious prosperous country, using intuitions and all kinds of superior qualities of the mind, but it has gone soft and hedonistic and has forgotten its duty, which is to aspire to better – to Zone Two. The Queen of Zone Three is ordered to marry the King of Zone Four, a crude, rude militaristic country, very poor because its wealth goes on war. This marriage – rather, precisely, the love-making – causes new life to flow in both Zones. A child is born, a boy. The Queen Al*Ith and the King Ben Ata love each other, though at the start they were antagonistic. Al*Ith is ordered away from Zone Four to return to Zone Three, where she is now a stranger. She sues for admission to Zone Two, which is a country as far advanced above Zone Three as Zone Three is above Zone Four. Ben Ata is ordered to marry the Queen of Zone Five, a primitive wild country which has turned to looting and pillage. This marriage, unwanted by both parties, is tolerated by them, feeds new life into Zone Five, and there is a child, a girl.

One attraction of *Marriages* for Philip is that he wanted to write music for a festival. There is a festival in *Marriages*, a women's celebration, and the songs and music are already in the novel. There is also a wedding feast, when Zone Four marries Zone Five, but I had not written the songs for that, in the novel. There is plenty of scope for songs and dances during this wedding. I wrote new lyrics for the opera that are not in the novel, not only for this wedding but in other scenes.

A problem with the libretto was that there is so much plot. We have used the old convention, exchanges of spoken words, to clarify the plot and to move things forward. A good deal has had to be cut. Some of the most interesting parts of the novel simply cannot reduce to fit an opera, but perhaps the music will suggest what has gone.

We have used the switch of gear from words to music sometimes for deliberate dramatic effect, for instance right at the beginning, when Al*Ith is told she must marry the King of despised Zone Four, and her words of protest shriek into song, because of the pressure of emotion. This happens in several places in the opera.

I was surprised when I read *Marriages* again, after several years, to see how much music is part of the story, not just as embellishment, but as part of the structure. For instance, there is a drum that starts, and falls silent, signalling to the lovers when they must come together and when they must part. The actual drum beat sets several of the songs in the novel. The story opens with a chanted children's play song, and this leads to an explanation of the difference between songs in Zones Three and Four, and what they say about the natures of the different countries. There is a song whose words are vital to the plot, and Al*Ith, hearing them, searches in the words of other songs for indications of an older wisdom, lost or half-forgotten. It would be easy to think I wrote *Marriages* with the idea of an eventual opera in my mind, but that was long before I had any idea I would be involved in the world of opera.

One big difference between *The Making of the Representative for Planet 8* and *The Marriages between Zones Three, Four and Five* is that the first opened in four big opera houses, Houston, the ENO in London, Amsterdam, and Kiel in Germany, whereas the second was in Heidelberg's little jewel of an opera house that takes 600 people. Every word can be heard anywhere in the auditorium.

Philip Glass used ideas he did not in previous operas. One is, replacing the strings with a chorus of voices. He made some of the music sound as if just on the edge of tantalisingly strange speech, different for the different Zones. After all, this is a legend, a myth – a fable.

ACKNOWLEDGEMENTS

We are grateful to the original publishers of the items included in this anthology for their permission to do so. Although we have made every effort to contact copyright holders prior to publication, we will be happy to correct any inadvertent errors or omissions; 1: Preface to Norway's Library of World Literature edition of Jane Austen: *Pride and Prejudice* (Gyldendal Norsk Forlag); 2: Preface to D. H. Lawrence: *The Fox*, (Hesperus Press, 2002); 3: Preface to Virginia Woolf: *Carlyle's House and Other Sketches* (Hesperus Press, 2003); 4: 'On Tolstoy', first published as preface to Leo Tolstoy: *The Kreutzer Sonata*, The Modern Library (Random House, 2003); 5: Introduction to Christina Stead: *The Man Who Loved Children*, Everyman's Library (Alfred Knopf, 1995); 6: Preface to *Kalila and Dimna: The Fables of Bidpai* retold by Ramsay Wood (Alfred Knopf, 1980); 7: Speech given on getting the Prince of Asturias Prize, Vigo, Spain, 2002; 8: 'Censorship', first published in Derek Jones: *Censorship: A World Encyclopedia* (Fitzroy Dearborn, 2001); 9: Introduction to Guy Sajer: *The Forgotten Soldier* (Phoenix, 2000); 10: Preface to *Ecclesiastes, or the Preacher: Authorized King James Version*, Pocket Canons, (Canongate, 1998); 11: 'Writing Autobiography', lecture delivered with variations to more to more than one organization and included in an Oxford University Press publication in 1998; 12: Review of *The Amazing Victorian: A Life of George Meredith* by Mervyn Jones first published in the *Sunday Times*, 1999; 13: Preface to Mikhail Bulgakov: *The Fatal Eggs* translated by Hugh Aplin (Hesperus Press, 2003); 14: 'Now You See Her, Now You Don't', written for a *Festchrift* for Muriel Sparks to be published at a later date, to be announced; 15: Preface to Stendhal: *Memoirs of an Egotist* translated by Andrew Brown (Hesperus Press, 2003); 16: Review of *Lost Civilizations of the Stone Age* by Richard Rudgeley, first published in *The Literary Review*, 1998; 17: 'Henry Handel Richardson', review of Richardson's novels first published in *The Spectator*, 1992; 18: Preface to the reissue of *The Golden Notebook* (HarperPerennial, 1994); 19: Review of *The Case of Anna Kavan: a biography* by David Callard first published in *The Independent*, 1993; 20: 'Philip Glass', first published in an English National Opera publication; 21: Review of *Trail of Feathers: In Search of the Birdmen of Peru* by Tahir Shah first published in *The Spectator*, 10 March 2003; 22: 'William Phillips', written on his death, first published in the *Partisan Review*, 2003; 23: 'Books', first published in a special edition of *Index on Censorship: Index on Libraries* to celebrate the new library in Alexandra, Egypt, 1999; 24: Review of *Before my Time* by Niccolò Tucci first published in the 1960s; 25: Preface to Arthur J Deikman: *Them and Us: Cult Thinking and the Terrorist Threat* (Bay Tree Publishing, 1993); 26: Article on a biography, first published in *The Spectator*, 2000; 27: 'About Cats' first published in Patrick Eddington (ed): *Cat Anthology* (Private publication, Salt Lake City, 2000); 28: Review of *The Maimie Papers* edited by Ruth Rosen and Sue Davidson, first published in *The Literary Review*, 1979; 29: Review of *Woman and Labour* by Olive Schreiner, first published in *The Guardian*; 30: 'When I was Young', written for *A Little Book of Advice* produced by Maynard School for girls, Exeter, 2000; 31: Preface to *Writers' and Artists' Yearbook 2003* (A & C Black, 2003); 32: Preface to Simone de Beauvoir: *The Mandarins* translated by Leonard M. Friedman (Flamingo Modern Classics, 1984, 1993); 33: 'My Room', first published in *Granta*, 'London' issue, 1999; 34: 'A Book that changed me', first published in the *Independent on Sunday*, 27 May 1990; 35: Promotional piece written for the Picador release of Nirad C. Chaudhuri: *The Autobiography of an Unknown Indian*, 1999; 36: 'Old', first published in John Burningham: *The Time of Your Life* (Bloomsbury, 2002); 37: Review of *Professor Marten's Departure* by Jaan Kross translated by Anselm Hollo, first published in *The Independent*, 19 February 1994; 38: 'How Things Were', first published in David Morley (ed): *The Gift: New writings for the NHS* (Stride, 2002); 39: Review of *A Nazi Childhood* by Winifried Weiss, first published in 1983; 40: Review of *Knowing How to Know: A Practical Philosophy in the Sufi Tradition* by Idries Shah first published in the *Sunday Telegraph*, 4 October 1998; 41: 'The Tragedy of Zimbabwe', first published under the title 'The Jewel of Africa' (in an edited form to suit American tastes) in the *New York Review of Books*, 10 April 2003; 42: Review of *The Elephant in the Dark* by Idries Shah first published in *New*

Society, 22 August 1974; **43**: 'What novel or novels prompted your own political awakening?', first published in the *LA Times*, 2000; **44**: 'The most significant book to come out of Africa', first published in the *Times Literary Supplement*, 2001; **45**: 'The Sufis', first published in *Books and Bookmen*; **46**: Review of *The Ice Palace* by Tarjei Vesaas translated by Elizabeth Rokkan first published in *The Independent*, 7 April 1993; **47**: 'Problems, Myths and Stories', given as a lecture to the Institute of Cultural Research and then published by them as a monograph (1999); **48**: 'After 9.11', first published in *Granta*, 'USA' edition, 20 December 2001; **49**: Review of *The Past Is Myself* by Christabel Bielenberg first published in 1988; **50**: Review of *The Journey of the Soul: The story of Hai bin Yaqzan* by Abu Bakr Muhhamad bin Tufail translated by Riad Kocache first published in *New Society*, 1982; **51**: 'Sufi Philosophy and Poetry', first published as a review of various Sufi classics in *New Society*, 1975; **52**: Review of *Among the Dervishes* by Omar Burke first published in *Books and Bookmen*, 1974; **53**: 'A Week in Heidelberg', read on Radio 4 as part of its participation in the World Festival of Literature, March 1999; **54**: Review of *Dancing with Cuba: A Memoir of the Revolution* by Alma Guillermoprieto first published in the *New York Observer*, 2004; **55**: Article first published in a Book Trust publication encouraging young people to read, 1988; **56**: Response to being asked about a favourite childhood book: on *The Three Royal Monkeys* by Walter de la Mare, 1998; **57**: Review of *Catlore* by Desmond Morris, first published in *The Spectator*; **58**: Review of *The Englishman's Handbook* by Idries Shah first published in the *Sunday Telegraph*, 1997; **59**: Introduction to A. E. Coppard: *Selected Stories* (Jonathan Cape, 1972); **60**: Review of L. F. Rushbrook Williams (Ed): *Sufi Studies, East and West: A Symposium in honour of Idries Shah's Services to Sufi Studies*, first published in *Books and Bookmen*, 1975; **61**: Review of *The Nine Emotional Loves of Cats* by Jeffrey Masson first published in *The Spectator*, 16 November 2002; **62**: Review of *Mikiwa: A White Boy in Africa* by Peter Godwin first published in *The Observer*, 24 March 1996; **63**: Review of *Clarissa* by Samuel Richardson first published in the *Independent on Sunday*; **64**: 'Summing Up', written when Idries Shah died, first published in the *Daily Telegraph*, 23 November 1996; **65**: Article on opera first published in *BBC Music Magazine*, 12 September 1996.